D0049201

MERCHANTS OF VIRTUE

1 October 2011,

For Mary —

Bravo for your work with Google
and assisting in a shared vision
of sustainable spaces.

With best wishes for your time at
Herman Miller.

Bill Banholm

MERCHANTS OF VIRTUE

Herman Miller and the Making of a Sustainable Company

Bill Birchard

palgrave
macmillan

First published in 2011 by
PALGRAVE MACMILLAN®
in the United States—a division of St. Martin's Press LLC,
175 Fifth Avenue, New York, NY 10010.

Where this book is distributed in the UK, Europe and the rest of the world,
this is by Palgrave Macmillan, a division of Macmillan Publishers Limited,
registered in England, company number 785998, of Houndmills,
Basingstoke, Hampshire RG21 6XS.

Palgrave Macmillan is the global academic imprint of the above companies
and has companies and representatives throughout the world.

Palgrave® and Macmillan® are registered trademarks in the United States,
the United Kingdom, Europe and other countries.

ISBN: 978–0–230–10660–4

Library of Congress Cataloging-in-Publication Data

Birchard, Bill.
    Merchants of virtue : Herman Miller and the making of a sustainable
company / Bill Birchard.
      p. cm.
    ISBN 978–0–230–10660–4 (hardback)
     1. Herman Miller, Inc. 2. Industrial management—Environmental
aspects—United States. 3. Business enterprises—Environmental
aspects—United States. 4. Sustainable development. 5. Social
responsibility of business—United States. 6. Strategic planning—
Environmental aspects—United States. I. Title.

HD30.255.B497 2011
658.4'08—dc22   2011002894

A catalogue record of the book is available from the British Library.

Design by Newgen Imaging Systems (P) Ltd., Chennai, India.

First edition: September 2011

10 9 8 7 6 5 4 3 2 1

Printed in the United States of America.

CONTENTS

ACKNOWLEDGMENTS

I want to first thank the many people at Herman Miller, Inc., for telling me the story of their work and offering many fascinating insights. Over the course of two years, I spoke with too many people to mention, but everyone added an important piece to my understanding of a 20-year campaign to achieve sustainability. I wish I could have included everyone's name as I told the story.

I especially want to thank Brian Walker, the company's chief executive officer (CEO), who authorized in-depth interviews with people around the company, and who also authorized access to Herman Miller's amazingly rich archives. Along with Brian, I want to thank Mark Schurman, an incomparable corporate communications chief. Mark facilitated my research, showed me around Holland and Zeeland, and shared his encyclopedic knowledge of both the company's history and its current operations.

Special thanks also to the roving leaders at Herman Miller who told me their personal stories, even though all of their names do not appear in the book. Among those who spent the most time with me are Willie Beattie, Scott Charon, Bill Dowell, Bill Foley, Jim Gillespie, Bob Johnston, Matt Long, Ray Muscat, Gary Miller, Paul Murray, Ed Nagelkirk, Gabe Wing, and Keith Winn.

Thank you to Herman Miller's former CEOs, who each gave me invaluable perspective and shared many anecdotes: Max De Pree, Dick Ruch, Kerm Campbell, and Mike Volkema. Mike Volkema was especially helpful in providing me with special insights about managing during the rise and fall of the business cycle.

I couldn't have written the book without the help of the rich trove of documents, photos, and videos in the Herman Miller archives in Holland, Michigan. Thanks to Gloria Jacobs and Linda Baron for their cheery company and constant help while I spent days in the archives combing through cartloads of boxes and mountains of paper.

I also couldn't have written the book without building on the work of many other people. Among the writers who have written for or about Herman Miller are Ralph Caplan, John Berry, and Clark Malcolm. Among the authorities on corporate sustainability are pioneers Paul Hawken, Bill McDonough, Amory Lovins, and especially my friend and onetime coauthor Marc Epstein.

The book saw the light of day only because several people trusted in my idea early on. The first was my agent, Helen Rees, who believed in my book when it was just a proposal. The second is Laurie Harting, executive editor at Palgrave Macmillan, who in turn saw the book's promise. The third is my wife, Suzanne, who kept the faith, kept up her support, and kept reading drafts through the long months it took me to figure out what I wanted to say and how best to say it.

Finally, a word of thanks to all those unnamed people who made this book possible. They come both from the ranks of Herman Miller and the team at Palgrave Macmillan. They are roving leaders in their own right, people who make good things happen, day in and day out, with no limelight shining on them, even as they make each new project reach its potential.

PROLOGUE

Paul Murray's boss thought Murray was a hero. In May 1988, Murray took a job on a wood-finishing line in Zeeland, Michigan. He was a paint chemist, a guru in the science of stains, varnishes, and clearcoats. His task was to help Herman Miller, Inc., finish its "flat stock"—desktops, shelves, and other furniture—without paint blisters. Herman Miller had been hauling $150,000 worth of spoiled, blistered stock to the landfill each month.

Murray didn't think of himself as a hero—at least not in all the ways that mattered. True, in his first year, he tuned the coating process so adeptly that he cut the $150,000 loss to just $5,000. But as he sought permits to upgrade the line, state officials calculated that Herman Miller would still emit 100 tons of solvent into the air every year. So much solvent, in fact, that the company would have to install a thermal oxidizer, a special unit for incinerating toxic gases.

Solvents to Murray were like fire—good for some things, abominable for others. Mention the word and he'd tell you about his toddler son, Matt. Between 1979 and 1988, when Murray held jobs as a research chemist at Boise Cascade and at PPG Industries, Matt's skin would periodically erupt in rashes—usually just after Murray got home from work. The boy would then begin to struggle to breathe. A few times, he began to choke—and Murray swept him up in his arms for a dash to the hospital.

Matt suffered from unusual allergies—he nearly died once after touching the skin of a fish. But he never touched the chemicals his father handled. And Murray reasoned that those chemicals, the likes of xylene and toluene, evaporated so fast that they would be gone before he left the lab. Still, he now felt that residues might be the culprit. To be safe, he started showering and changing clothes before coming home from work, and Matt's reactions subsided.

Murray also began to wonder: If I'm doing this to my home environment, what am I doing to the overall environment?

At Herman Miller, a number of years later, Murray began to wonder about the same thing. The $1.6 billion company, best known for high-end, award-winning chairs like the Eames lounge chair and the Aeron desk chair, had long stressed personal values and community responsibility. As far back as the 1950s, company founder D.J. De Pree is said to have remarked that the company "will be a good corporate neighbor by being a good steward of the environment."

But the questions for Murray now were essentially these: Was Herman Miller a good steward in 1988? And was it changing fast enough to remain one in the years ahead? At the time, the company looked good only in comparison to other firms. It still made chairs of wood cut from endangered rain forests. It still sent 41 million pounds of waste to landfills yearly. In 1989, the first year in which U.S. companies reported toxic emissions publicly, it disclosed releases of over 150,000 pounds (for the reporting year 1987). A good chunk of that poundage came from solvents.

It was becoming clear to Murray that a gap had emerged between what companies provided and what society wanted. The gap, in fact, stretched as wide as a chasm.

This book is about the people at Herman Miller who, like Murray, bridge that gap. They end up answering one of the critical questions of our time: Is sustainable business sustainable? Can employees in global companies make great products, take care of the environment, benefit society, and make good money—all at the same time, good times and bad?

The jury was out in the late 1980s. It still is. At only a few companies have people actually succeeded in figuring out ways to bridge the gap. Herman Miller, boasting a 20-year record of awards and kudos for its work, is one of them. Across the company, insiders like Murray rose to the challenge. They showed that companies do not have to endanger the health of ecosystems to produce goods and services for mankind. They can design, build, use, and dispose of things as part of cyclical processes that mimic the cycles of nature. They can build natural and financial wealth at the same time.

Surprisingly, the journey to sustainability at Herman Miller did not take root because a single top manager or the CEO demanded it. At Herman Miller, people like Murray, who worked deep within the organization, desired it. Because the company had a culture of giving its employees the power to make change—an approach it called "participative management"—the change emerged all over. Mid-level leaders, not just the hot-shot bosses, led the campaign to bridge the sustainability gap.

Also surprisingly, the journey at Herman Miller did not take place in a New Age enterprise. It happened in a conservative Midwest manufacturing company. The environmentally minded leaders, though raised during a time of expanded corporate responsibility, were not placard-pumping activists. In keeping with the company's traditions, they were driven by a passion for design, social consciousness, and community responsibility. But they were also sharp-penciled business people. Woven into their beliefs was what D.J. De Pree taught them above all: Producing profits in a business is akin to breathing.

What attracted me to writing this book? Above all, the people at Herman Miller showed something even the activists could not: Sustainability in a large, established business—a company making the "stuff" we all buy—*is* sustainable, if only people go about it the right way. And it can be sustained despite the array of antagonistic forces plaguing every company: indifference and short-termism, a preference for expedient solutions, the constant temptation to sacrifice principles for profit.

It is also sustainable during punishing downturns in business that would bankrupt most companies. In good times and bad, the people at Herman Miller continued to ask new questions, test new ideas, and rethink and restructure the nature of the work to make their business more sustainable.

Another thing that attracted me to writing the book was the breadth of the company's achievements. The diverse cast of leaders didn't address just a few areas critical to sustainability. They addressed many—in research, engineering, finance, manufacturing, marketing, operations—so many, in fact, that the company serves as an all-around model. In many nonfiction books (and I've written them), authors pull vignettes from dozens of sources to show the right way to succeed. They create a composite picture. As helpful as composites are, they can mislead by leaving out blemishes, setbacks, and even the unexpected foundering of an idea in the face of reality.

This book is not a composite. It relates the story of an internal diaspora of green-minded leaders as their journey unfolds over

20 years—with all the setbacks along the way. That authenticity makes the book more compelling. It also brings more life to the journey, illustrating the path forward in an inspirational way.

On the surface, this book repeatedly raises the question: Will the environmental leaders at Herman Miller win? Underneath, it raises a more complex question: How will this band of green-minded leaders do it?

The answer, as in so many stories of people working together, comes down to a principle of management. At Herman Miller, sustainability triumphs because people commit and recommit themselves to the guiding light of company values. Some of these values—responsibility, accountability, candor—reflect familiar work ethics. Others, such as the dedication to problem-solving design, reflect unique beliefs that have been preached since the Great Depression by Herman Miller's founding family, the De Prees. Starting with D.J., continuing with sons Hugh and Max, the De Prees set forth a way of conducting work and managing people that won acclaim for decades—and led to Max's bestselling book *Leadership is an Art*.

So along with being a story about sustainability, this book brings alive the De Pree philosophy. It shows how researchers, designers, engineers, and factory bosses made great things happen by following the north star of values. These people, across the ranks, joined to advance a revolution to create environmental, social, *and* financial sustainability. In back rooms and on factory floors, they achieved new insights, reshaped behaviors, recast policies, and changed the way they worked. They also changed the people around them—and their story can change all of us.

CHAPTER 1

Rosewood

As a soaking mist shrouds Brazil's Atlantic rainforest, loggers topple the massive Brazilian rosewood tree. To get to just one mature rosewood specimen, they gash a road corridor through acres of woods. In their wake, farmers rush in to burn trees and slash along either side of the new jungle byway. Trees give way to agriculture. And the native jungle is lost forever, its burned stumps sprouting like tombstones on a rolling canvas of cattle pasture.

This was the picture in the mid-1980s. The deforestation of tropical forests topped the list of environmentalists' causes the world over. Rainforest Action Network and Friends of the Earth grabbed headlines. They decried the violation of Brazil's natural heritage. They wailed over the loss of species diversity. They sounded the alarm over the costs of losing forests that pumped oxygen into an atmosphere increasingly flooded with carbon dioxide. "The lungs of the earth are burning!" came the cry.

American industry awakened slowly to this alarm. It slept through the early noise of the activists. It hardly opened an eye to the rumblings of U.S. lawmakers, who were writing legislation to save jungle from oblivion. Only in 1988 and 1989 did industry sit up and pay attention. And one of the first of its members to do so was Herman Miller, Inc., the office-furniture maker in tiny Zeeland, Michigan.

Zeeland, a part of Ottawa County in West Michigan, offers an unlikely haven for corporate environmentalists. The Republican Party considers the county a stronghold—the last Democratic candidate to carry it was elected in 1864. West Michigan companies, often founded by Dutch settlers, make clocks, chairs, boilers, plastics, and car mirrors. Along with neighboring Holland and nearby Grand Rapids, the region boasts such a large complex of office-furniture makers—Herman Miller, Steelcase, Haworth, and their suppliers—that it has been dubbed Furniture Valley.

In the late 1980s, this region, on the opposite side of the state from Detroit, became a crucible of corporate environmental activity. Herman Miller, a company formed in 1923, was at the center of it. The founding De Pree family had always favored careful treatment of nature. The surrounding patchwork of farms and gorgeous strips of Lake Michigan beaches called out for it. The De Prees made sure everyone understood that employees had special license to both do their jobs and do well by the environment. From such an understanding, enterprising employees would often emerge who would take on the mantle of environmental activism.

Max De Pree, son of the founder D.J. De Pree, called these people "roving leaders." De Pree, former CEO and still chairman in 1989, talked often of people who take charge no matter what their level in the organization. In his bestselling *Leadership is an Art*, published in 1987, he sized up such leaders this way: "The measure of individuals—and so of corporations—is the extent to which we struggle to complete ourselves, the energy we devote to living up to our potential."

The obvious question for many of these leaders at the end of the 1980s was this: Are we living up to our potential in caring for the environment? Are we helping the company live up to its potential?

The specter of rainforest decimation caught the eye of a couple of roving leaders within Herman Miller. One of them was Bill Foley, the man responsible for evaluating materials the company bought to make its furniture. Another was Bob Johnston, a writer and policymaker responsible for corporate relations. Together, the two men realized that the trees falling in Brazil could shake up their potential to do good at the traditional Midwest manufacturing firm.

Foley, dark-haired and handsome, started at the company in 1979. He began as a factory hand, applying fiberglass with glue to acoustical panels. He opted, while working for Herman Miller, to get a degree in business, and after a couple of promotions, he took the materials-assessment job. Designers came to him when they wanted to specify a new wood for a chair or desk or shelf.

Johnston, a self-starting leader like Foley, thought of himself as a passionate environmentalist. He had previously edited a local newspaper, assigning reporters to write stories on clean water, lakes, and municipal water systems. He joined Herman Miller in 1988, taking a job in marketing writing. When he later took his corporate relations job, people came to him to assess risks to the company's reputation. Johnston often proposed ways to deal with those risks.

One thing common to Foley and Johnston was that they, like the other roving environmentalists at Herman Miller, were 30-something professionals raised during a generation of growing environmental awareness. By the late 1980s, they had witnessed the corporate disasters of the Union Carbide gas poisoning in Bhopal, India; the oil spill of the Exxon *Valdez* off Alaska; and the Chernobyl nuclear disaster in Ukraine. In 1988, they witnessed the commotion over early testimony in Congress about the risks of global warming. They had lived through the passage of every major environmental law: the Clean Water Act; the Clean Air Act; the Endangered Species Act; and the Toxic Substances and Control Act.

And yet when it came to tropical forests, Foley and Johnston were caught unawares. They knew that Herman Miller had a big stake in the ruckus because it made so many products out of wood. The company, which sold $865 million a year in chairs, desks, office panels, shelving, and a host of other furniture items, bought a variety of tropical woods. It used mahogany from Western Africa, "mahogany dark" from Cameroon, teak from Thailand, and rosewood from Brazil.

Rosewood was the object of particular reverence. It adorned the celebrated Eames Lounge chair, a product so loved by designers and high-end furniture buyers that it still sold steadily after 45 years. A cradle of molded rosewood lined with irresistibly soft calfskin cushions, the chair was the company's signature product. Though priced at $2,277, its appeal, luxuriousness, and iconic status—synonymous with Herman Miller—made changing its wood almost unthinkable.

And yet this most coveted material, *Dalbergia nigra,* was coming from a prized rainforest going up in smoke. Everyone in America knew that Brazil's Amazon jungle was in trouble. Besides the daily TV images of charred, smoking forest lands, *National Geographic* magazine had published an article entitled, "Brazil's Imperiled Rain Forest." The issue gripped the public's mind so firmly that in 1988 Sting and the Grateful Dead played benefit concerts to support rain-forest activist groups.

The equatorial countries harboring the revered forests had taken some action to protect their trees. Brazilian president José Sarney ended tax benefits for land developers and banned exports of tropi-cal logs in the fall of 1988. "We must create a nationwide conscious-ness that we are all passengers in the adventure of man on Earth," Sarney said. "The era of unlimited natural resources is over."

At Herman Miller, Johnston was awakened in early 1989 to the grav-ity of the global uproar when a colleague told him about a Michigan State University graduate student who had questioned her at a cam-pus party: With the rainforest being devastated, the student asked, is Herman Miller's use of tropical wood contributing to the problem?

As a former newspaperman, Johnston was surprised that he didn't know anything about the uproar. And yet his company was somehow connected to the devastation. "I was concerned with whether Herman Miller was playing an appropriate role, and had no idea what that role was," he admits. "I felt like I was personally behind the curve."

Johnston, along with Foley, was in good company. Few managers in American companies of the era acted decisively on environmen-tal issues unless a crisis exploded outside their door. That was the case after Bhopal, the Exxon *Valdez,* and countless discoveries of back-lot toxic waste dumps. But Johnston, who had responsibility for dealing with political risks, did not want to wait for a crisis at Herman Miller. He checked pending legislation and found that the 101st Congress had been working overtime on the issue: Lawmakers had just introduced 23 bills related to tropical woods.

It was as if a forest of trees had fallen, and Johnston hadn't heard the timber crashing.

THE NEED TO GET on top of the issue was urgent. The question wasn't just about how to act as a responsible corporation. Herman Miller had acted responsibly for years, starting with founder D.J. De

Pree, who said in 1953, "We will be good stewards of the environment." It was rather a question about what responsible action meant in 1989. The company prided itself on taking leading positions, especially in design. Here, the leader was not out front, but sniffing the wind of change from behind.

The controversy over tropical woods stirred public passions partly because social values were changing: A majority of Americans in the late 1980s felt the environment deserved more attention—even if the companies they worked for didn't act responsibly. A Gallup poll at the time showed that 76 percent of Americans called themselves "environmentalists."

Observers could have asked: Was Herman Miller still up to the job of keeping up with America? Foley and Johnston quickly saw that, when it came to the treatment of tropical wood, the company might be trailing. Adding to their concern, European and U.S. customers had started asking questions about how Herman Miller used tropical wood. European design magazines had even highlighted the issue.

People especially wanted to know about rosewood. Foley did know that the logs arrived at warehouses as bundles of veneer called *flitches*. Each log yielded 500 to 3,000 square feet, the veneer shaved to less than 1/32 of an inch thick. Rosewood was ranked as a wood buyer's treasure. It pleased the eye like an artist's tableau, its colors ranging from chocolate to violet, streaked with dark and light red lines. People fell in love with it. On a chair, it had no peer—every piece of veneer was as unique as an individual's personality.

To figure out what Herman Miller's role should be in managing the acquisition of the wood, Foley began asking questions of the company's tropical hardwood suppliers. He phoned people in Grand Rapids, Michigan; Metuchen, New Jersey; and Hamburg, Germany. "I asked," says Foley, "Can you tell me where this tree came from, the source, where [it was] cut?" Suppliers had few good answers, though, and in any case, Foley wanted more than answers. He wanted paperwork that showed a chain of custody for the wood from the time it left the hands of the logger to when it reached the supplier at the warehouse.

Mahogany sourced in Cameroon came with good paperwork, and research showed the forests there were reasonably well managed. But when it came to Brazilian rosewood, the German supplier didn't know much at all about the veneer's origin. Nor could it tell

Foley how the rosewood was logged. In the same way that jewelers once bought diamonds, the suppliers bought the wood on looks alone. No paperwork requirements existed—let alone environmental standards.

"That's where [the] mystery came in," Foley adds. What route did the wood take from stump to wholesaler? We were putting the pressure on. "We want to know exactly where these logs are coming from."

Foley next looked into the ecology of rainforests. What effect did the tree's extraction have on the natural environment? Rainforest Action Group, Friends of the Earth, Rainforest Alliance, and other groups had people on the ground collecting data. Foley, who had once enjoyed studying sciences like physics and organic chemistry, was looking for such data. Rainforest Alliance maintained that loggers razed 50 acres of rainforest every minute, and that they drove one species to extinction every hour. The groups hardly offered unbiased data. But Foley knew they had the ear of the media, and the power of the bully pulpit.

So he got on the phone to ask: What's really going on in the rainforest? Can we talk?

Foley flew to San Francisco, home base of the Rainforest Action Network, which by then was receiving concert proceeds from the Grateful Dead. At a Thai restaurant where the spicy food burned his mouth, the activists told him stories of logging, burning, and more optimistically, preserving the forests. He quickly realized the group had the same goal as Herman Miller. But their approach came from the other side of the philosophical tracks. From what he could tell, these people hated corporations.

Foley found that the activist groups didn't take a uniform position, and none of them called for an outright ban on rainforest products. They instead called for reforestation and an end to logging in places where trees couldn't rejuvenate themselves. In the end, Foley actually embraced the position of one of the activist groups, that of London's Friends of the Earth (FOE). FOE urged a switch to harvesting tropical hardwoods only if they were grown "sustainably."

Amid his fact-finding journey, Foley funneled all he learned to his boss. In July 1989, she urged company leaders at Herman Miller to change course. The recommended strategy included curtailing the development of veneers from nonsustainable sources, doing more research on the veneers coming from unsustained forests, and developing veneers from alternative tropical woods. His boss's memo to superiors noted: "A total ban on rainforest products could devastate the few countries practicing responsible timber trade and are dependent on that trade as a livelihood."

Foley's boss also informed her superiors: Rosewood looks like the main problem. And Herman Miller buys 500,000 square feet of it a year.

While Foley crisscrossed the continent to gather the scientific data on the issue, Johnston knocked on the doors of lawmakers sponsoring the flurry of bills on tropical hardwoods. In Washington, D.C., a representative from Connecticut, who had sponsored one key piece of legislation, sent him to Keister Evans, an expert who worked for hardwood importers. Evans and Johnston, and later Foley, visited the Capitol repeatedly, seeing lawmakers ranging from John Porter of Illinois to Al Gore of Tennessee.

Together, Foley and Johnston began to piece together a complex picture of the state of rosewood endangerment. Some facts pointed to a clear decision. Others conflicted. Says Johnston, "We didn't want to be on the wrong side of this issue, and we didn't know what the right side was."

Foley and Johnston came to some conclusions, however. They learned that the depredations in the rainforest came, first, from slash-and-burn agriculture; second, from people gathering fuel wood; and third, from bad logging practices. Purchases of tropical hardwood for furniture manufacturing were not, by themselves, wrecking the forests. But they played a role, and in any case, buyers of the wood were under attack from both the media and politicians, no matter the complex nature of the facts. *Time* magazine ran "Torching the Amazon" as its cover story—with a picture of an alley burned through a paradise of tropical plants and animals. The European Parliament, up in arms, was preparing to ban tropical imports to protect Amazon rainforests.

BY MID- TO LATE 1989, Foley felt he probably had enough information to recommend the right thing to do. Still, something was missing. Enamored of the scientific method from his earlier interest in science, he felt he shouldn't have been swayed just by information from non-scientists—from partisans in the hardwood industry and environmental community. To fill this gap, he bought a plane ticket to see Nigel Hepper, an authority at London's Kew Royal Botanic Gardens.

In London, Foley toured the inner sanctum of Kew. Along with a towering menagerie of trees, Kew contained an exhaustive archive. As Foley watched, Hepper pulled out flat specimen drawers full of leaves, flowers, and insects. Hepper, an expert on tropical forests, shared his experiences and research on the depletion of hardwoods. In particular, he explained how the rosewood tree only flourished in a forest alongside many other species. Said Hepper: There is no such thing as a "stand" of rosewood in the Brazilian forest.

What Foley understood was this: Rosewood simply doesn't grow like the oaks in Michigan's forests. The tree can't seed itself and survive except as a loner within a community. And since the natural communities in which it thrived were in decline, rosewood was on the way out. "At that time," says Foley, "it was fairly inconceivable that you could actually go out and do a replanting of rosewood, because of the natural, ecological cycle of how rosewood is regenerated."

And so Foley returned from London with one indisputable fact: In using rosewood, Herman Miller was a party to its decline. What, then, was the right way to treat rosewood?

Banning the use of all tropical wood, as some legislators proposed, didn't seem like the right answer. The better answer seemed to borrow from the concept of sustainability. At the time, the word "sustainability" had just started to slip into corporate conversations. It came from a report issued two years earlier by the United Nations. After a three-year effort chaired by the prime minister of Norway, Gro Harlem Brundtland, a committee defined "sustainable development" as "development that meets the needs of the present without compromising the ability of future generations to meet their own needs."

The so-called Brundtland Report marked the beginning of a new era for multinational companies. For long-term, environmentally responsible development, "sustainability" became the new ideal. No one was quite sure how to make the concept work in practice. At Herman Miller, people would debate the idea for hours. But the notion lent itself directly to responsible forestry: "Sustainable" logging would allow loggers to keep cutting so long as they cut in a way that would allow forests to regrow for more cutting, for generations to come.

Foley and Johnston faced a decision of what to recommend to company executives. As they did, a group of about a dozen roving leaders across Herman Miller started to get together regularly to coordinate the company's environmental work. Foley and Johnston were among them, and they started to report their findings to the group, often using it as a sounding board. The question they now put out for discussion: Should we just stop buying rosewood?

At that point, Foley had personally seen enough. And his opinion, based on more than a year of research, influenced everyone. As far as he was concerned, sustainably harvested rosewood didn't exist. "It was an endangered species," he says. "From the purest of the purest points of view, it seemed like we shouldn't be using it."

Foley was preaching to the choir. The group of roving leaders, including Johnston, backed him wholeheartedly. They all agreed to support a ban.

THE DECISION BECAME A watershed moment. As clear as it seemed to the environmental leaders, it spawned a heated debate that quickly reached well beyond the group. By taking a stand on the environment, the group seemed to be taking a stand against a hallowed design. After all, the fate of the Eames lounge chair was at stake, and the product, internally known as 670, was not just Herman Miller's flagship product but a symbol of its identity.

To architects and designers the world over, the Eames lounge chair represented Herman Miller's design preeminence and quality. When sales people wanted to show what buying from Herman Miller meant, they pointed to the Eames chair. Customers who outfitted their offices with Herman Miller furniture associated it with the best. The Eames lounge chair was so celebrated it won a spot in the permanent collection at New York's Museum of Modern Art. To talk of changing materials in the Eames chair was like talking about swapping gems in the crown jewels.

And that created a dilemma for people in the company: Do we ruin a wonder of modern design or a wonder of nature?

Charles Eames died in 1978. He could not rule on whether a change to his design was acceptable. Bernice "Ray" Eames, his wife and lifelong design partner, survived him, and she agreed that the company should cease using an endangered wood. Still, many people didn't like the idea. What's more, the issue of Eames's acceptance was caught in a tangle of other issues—namely, business ones. What would the effect of dropping rosewood be on company sales, design reputation, and the satisfaction of repeat customers?

Events in fall 1989 would force the conflict to a conclusion. *Interiors*, an influential furniture-industry magazine, was preparing to run a story in December. The editors wanted to know: What is Herman Miller's policy on the use of tropical woods? The request landed on Johnston's desk and he didn't have much time to put an answer together.

Johnston's hardwood-industry contact, Keister Evans, would take part in helping shape the response. Evans was seeking a solution to the bigger conundrum of how to manage all tropical forests. To get beyond the politics, he urged the Smithsonian Institution to organize a workshop on tropical woods. He figured that only the Smithsonian would offer the credibility to come up with a solution everyone could live with.

The Smithsonian invited 12 world-renowned experts, from industry, academia, and environmental groups, to sit and debate the outlines of a solution. The goal: come up with a consensus opinion. The meeting took place at the Smithsonian in October, 1989. In spite of four years of heavy press about tropical-forest ruin, the timber-trade and environmental experts had never even met. Predictably, arguments over what to do raged. The biggest was over the issue of banning trade in tropical woods. The timber people said bans would put them out of business. The ardent environmentalists said that only bans could save the forest.

In the middle of the arguments were the academics. The extreme views on either side, they believed, were untenable. At one point, a professor from Harvard started pounding the table to gain attention. He finally quieted the ardent people. Banning the teak trade in Thailand, he pointed out, had destroyed the value of the Thai forest. Once the ban went into effect, squatters cleared the worthless timber to make way for farming, and rains swept away the soils. The lesson: A ban wouldn't save the forest. It would trigger its demise.

The group, chaired by scientist Thomas Lovejoy, moved at that point to outline the basis for sustainable use of the forests. A member of the Smithsonian, Lovejoy wrote the consensus, which said in effect: If people can't earn money from the wood, they will clear the land for other uses. Blanket bans and boycotts are a bad idea—both for the health of the forests and for the people who live there. To preserve the forests, the timber must be given value.

And so the consensus opinion of the group was this: The only way to save the rainforest is through forest management.

The opinion by the 12 workshop experts influenced Johnston and others at Herman Miller deeply. It reflected the wisdom of people ranging from the Harvard professor to a World Wildlife Fund activist to a Georgia–Pacific Corporation executive. It also gave Johnston just the authority that he needed to devise corporate policy. So when Herman Miller gave its policy to *Interiors* magazine, it could comfortably say it agreed in principle that, in the future, it would develop veneers only from woods harvested sustainably.

What did this mean for rosewood? There was yet no answer. In the fall of 1989, however, another event took place. Activists convinced the U.S. Fish and Wildlife Service that rosewood was indeed an endangered species. The Service then proposed listing it as endangered under the 1973 agreement known as CITES, the Convention on International Trade in Endangered Species. If the U.S. authorities approved the listing, trade in rosewood would be illegal, punishable by fines of up to $50,000 and a year in prison.

For Johnston, the proposed CITES ban forced the issue to a new level. "When that came up," says Johnston, "[the veneer on] our signature product, the Eames Lounge chair, the most visible icon of furniture that exists in North America, was being proposed for the endangered species list. How could we not make a decision to do something?"

Johnston, who worked just down the hall from CEO Dick Ruch, kept the boss informed as the story of the tropical wood unfolded. At first, Ruch, the successor to Max De Pree, didn't even know what Johnston was talking about when he said "sustainable forestry." And when he was told that Herman Miller shouldn't make rosewood Eames chairs anymore, he insisted otherwise. "That was a shocker to me," he says, "because Charles Eames...was a very autocratic designer, damn good, but it was his way or no way at all. And he said, look, that chair has got to be made in rosewood."

Eames was a design giant. He was named the most influential designer of the century in 1985 by the World Design Congress. The company reversing a design decision by one of America's greatest industrial designers was like a Venetian merchant telling Michelangelo to change the pigments on a work of art. It was by championing such design—and protecting it zealously—that the company had prospered for forty years.

As Johnston prepped the boss with ongoing developments, Foley requested a meeting with Ruch. Arriving with plenty of documents, Foley told the story of rosewood's life cycle. The cutting of just one rosewood tree, one of the world's most coveted woods, ripped a gemstone from the fabric of nature, Foley said. The forest, riven by logging roads, then unraveled into cattle pasture. Herman Miller, in good conscience, could not carry it.

Ruch looked at Foley and said, You're really convinced on this, aren't you?

Absolutely, answered Foley. The Eames chair might adorn offices in the most vaunted firms in the world. It might provide an envelope of warm-grained wood so alluring that buyers would turn a blind eye to rainforest decimation. But the wood should not be used in Herman Miller's products.

I'm worried about the damage this could do to the product line, said Ruch. Changing the veneer could kill sales of the chair.

Well, I think the product line can stand on its own with other materials, said Foley. It would actually look beautiful in cherry.

In cherry!

Foley held his ground.

Ruch, in the end, didn't argue. To be sure, Ruch knew how critical rosewood was to the development and the success of this chair. An executive who had started with the company in 1955, he had actually been with Eames when the designer said the chair *had* to be made of rosewood. Still, says Ruch, "It didn't take long for me to change positions, because it was a strong argument: You're wiping out forests and when they're gone, they're gone. Once I got my feet on the floor and understood what was happening, it was not too difficult a decision to make."

With the buy-in of the boss and other top executives, Johnston, Foley, and others crafted an official policy on tropical woods, aided by viewpoints from both sides of the environmental aisle: Friends of the Earth and the International Hardwood Products Association. And on March 16, 1990, just before the twentieth anniversary of Earth Day, Ruch announced the decision publicly. Herman Miller would buy wood—all its tropical wood—only from "sustained-yield forest sources."

"The rain forests will survive only if we add value to them by encouraging their productive use rather than destruction," said Ruch in a statement. "We believe our influence and the influence of those who are working with us will create policies throughout the world that are for the benefit of both the environment and mankind." Within months, Herman Miller would offer the Eames chair only in alternative veneers like cherry and walnut.

THE REACTION FROM COMPANY outsiders came quickly. Ruch had the privilege of receiving many congratulatory letters from the public. One even came from a theologian who praised the action. Legislators also weighed in. Michigan Senator Donald Riegle introduced a Congressional resolution: "Business leadership like this is essential in our efforts to slow the destruction of . . . tropical forests . . . .[Herman Miller's leaders] are to be strongly commended." When the press started running articles over the next three months, a dozen magazines published stories giving Herman Miller positive press.

Taking the high road paid dividends, or at least so it seemed, as if a happy ending was coming to a story of corporate responsibility. But the decision didn't sit well in some quarters. In fact it put Johnston crosswise with just about every outsider he had talked to for the previous year. When environmentalists saw the term "sustained-yield forest sources" they told him the decision was not good enough. When importers saw the term, they asked him, what the hell does that mean? All along they worried about job losses. What was this going to do rainforest loggers?

The importers reminded Johnston of Lovejoy's consensus statement arguing against bans. So what's this ban all about? they demanded to know. This will wipe out the value of the wood. One man from the industry told Ruch that the decision had done more harm than good. And even Herman Miller's closest contact with the industry, its hardwood veneer buyer, was dismayed. He kept his mouth shut but felt nobody seemed concerned about the livelihoods of Brazilian forest workers.

Johnston was in a bind. The company taking a leading stand on tropical woods was, at least behind the scenes, getting jabbed by people he had worked with for months. He had come to value his many relationships with experts across the spectrum. But now he was a target of loathing.

On the way into a meeting of hardwood importers in San Diego, he felt the gaze of contempt. He waved to a placard-carrying protestor from Greenpeace who had earlier advised him.

What are you doing here? she shouted from the crowd.

Once inside, he suffered the same scorn from industry representatives. At a meeting of the International Hardwood Products Association, he says, "I personally took a lot of heat from wood importers. I was viewed as a heretic. People came to me directly, and were very confrontational about the decision." They worried about jobs. They worried about the press smearing their good name indiscriminately. And as far as they were concerned, they had lost a business relationship with Herman Miller. The company had broken their trust—had cut them off.

THE ONGOING FALLOUT FROM the decision stung Johnston. But the criticism made him determined: Whatever problems have to be worked out, Herman Miller is going to take part in solving them. If we only buy wood from sustainable forests, he vowed, we have to ensure logging takes place sustainably. The decision had to be followed by real execution.

Johnston and Foley both took to the job. The ban would start in June 1991, and by then the company needed a replacement for rosewood. Foley contacted the Woodworkers Alliance for Rainforest Protection. The group developed indigenous sources of sustainable wood. It also tried to figure out a labeling mechanism to certify the sustainability of tropical wood sources. As Foley's research had showed, Herman Miller needed both.

Johnston, in league with Keister Evans and Thomas Lovejoy, helped found the Tropical Forest Foundation to foster sustainable forestry practices. With Evans as executive director, the foundation spearheaded the building of a demonstration model of sustainable forestry. The model combined selective cutting, minimalist roads, and logging equipment that went easy on the landscape. The foundation eventually started training loggers across the globe, from Indonesia and Gabon to Guyana and Brazil.

Johnston meanwhile lobbied for legislation in Washington, D.C., to preserve access to sustainable wood. Provisions in some bills, by Senators Al Gore of Tennessee and Tim Wirth of Colorado, actually made access harder. While Herman Miller urged the banning of endangered species, it didn't urge a blanket ban. Johnston had to explain how a complex issue deserved a complex answer. In a letter to a customer at Bank of America at the time, Johnston summarized Herman Miller's position.

"The Materials Research, Purchasing, and Corporate Relations areas for the company were involved in more than a year of work examining the issues in use of tropical woods. In that examination, we learned quickly that we could sidestep the issue by refusing to use any tropical woods. That policy, however, would not have helped improve the timber management situation in tropical countries. Instead, we opted to become involved in forestry management issues and to use our influence to stimulate improvements."

"...Herman Miller is acting responsibly in choosing its tropical woods. Currently we are offering, as recut veneers, mahogany, mahogany dark, ash, and innertone. Recut mahogany, mahogany dark, and innertone are produced from a tree called obeche. Ash is...produced from a tree called ilomba. Both of these trees come from sustained sources in Cameroon...."

Johnston finally got some relief from the criticism coming from all sides by early 1991. The Business and Institutional Furniture Manufacturer's Association, or BIFMA, the industry trade association located in nearby Grand Rapids, took Herman Miller's position. Arch competitors Steelcase, Haworth, and other office-furniture makers would also cease buying rosewood. Once again, it looked like there would be a happy ending to a story about corporate responsibility.

But this was not to be, at least not yet. The challenge this time came from within the company. On February 4, Johnston talked by phone with board member J. Laurence Kulp. Kulp was displeased by the tropical wood decision for his own particular set of reasons: The time Johnston and Foley spent on the issue diverted them from regular business. The decision appropriately rested with the board of directors, not management. The countries with tropical forests should set logging policy, not Herman Miller. And Herman Miller should guide decisions based on its own views, not the views of politicians and environmentalists.

Johnston, having struggled with the issue for two years, told Kulp a part of his story, saying in any case that Congress and customers forced Herman Miller to act.

Kulp, one of the sharpest of board members, wasn't mollified. He asked Johnston to send him relevant memos, letters to suppliers, or other materials.

Kulp, a onetime Princeton acquaintance of Albert Einstein, had a formidable intellect. Formerly a geochemistry professor at Columbia University, he was head of R&D for wood products behemoth Weyerhaeuser. He had often contributed to major decisions at Herman Miller, including guiding the company into building its environmentally attractive waste-to-energy plant nearly ten years earlier. But Johnston was worried that Kulp would try to overturn the tropical wood decision based on forest principles alone.

Johnston sought help from CEO Ruch, who with a memo from Johnston in hand, phoned Kulp on February 12. In spite of Kulp's objections, Ruch sided with his roving leaders. Herman Miller would not sell products made of rosewood. Afterwards, in the margin of a memo, he wrote, "Larry may be old school of forestry. BIFMA has taken our position."

BUT KULP WANTED TO make a point to company decision makers—that the environmental leaders hadn't adequately assessed the facts. He phoned an executive who had oversight for the group of green-minded leaders that included Foley and Johnston. Kulp barked: Who's behind this stupid idea of sustainable woods strategy?

When Kulp heard that the company's environmental leaders all backed the strategy, he demanded an audience. By this time, the group had organized into Herman Miller's official Environmental Quality Action Team, or EQAT. So the entire team of environmental leaders assembled on March 28, 1991. Some of the group thought Kulp was there to give them pats on the back, to compliment their solidarity in backing the tropical-woods decision.

They were disappointed. Kulp pulled out a white collapsible pointer and displayed overheads and charts. He had come to lecture.

While going through a litany of forestry facts, he told the group: You are following your emotions, not the science. You should follow the lead of the governments on policy, not usurp the lead yourself.

The group listened.

You can't possibly have enough scientific data to support your opinion, and you need to reconsider it. You need to make a good, rational decision about logging practices.

The group listened still.

You're threatening the men, women, and children of the rainforest—did you ever think about that? You're taking their livelihood away by taking away the value of that wood.

Kulp held forth for more than an hour. He allowed that the decision was probably the right one. But he questioned the environmental team's decision-making process: He was unhappy about their overlooking unintended consequences and was concerned that they were making decisions without enough science to back them up.

Kulp's argument had merit. The man knew the scientific method better than any of them. And three weeks later, the green-minded leaders assembled again. Many had been stunned by Kulp's comeuppance. But they resolved to rededicate themselves to facts and not emotions, in a decision that would become a guiding principle for much of the work by the environmental group for years to come. "Dr. Kulp's visit," the minutes reported, "may serve as a warning that it is critical to have all of the facts straight and be prepared to confront the challenges and decisions based on sound science."

Foley, for his part, remained certain that he could have defended every one of his points. He just didn't have the chance. He certainly wasn't arguing for a decision that had been based on emotion. He remained bothered that Kulp embraced a common refrain of the time when it came to environmental issues: "We need more research." Foley felt the demands for more research could become a corporate delaying tactic. "Nobody wants to make a decision," Foley says. "No one wants to make a stand, to do anything."

Foley felt there were enough good reasons to go ahead, reasons to easily outweigh the perceived consequences. "I'm not anti-capitalist," he says, "But it was just that exploitation of materials is just not a way to run a business—or to have a life. It makes no sense."

In the end the roving leaders would not see their decision reversed. They held their ground. And so did Ruch—acting on their knowledge of the right thing to do even as they took Kulp's lessons to heart. "It was a very visible action," says Foley, "that was based on a very long-term environmental conscience of the company—true stewardship of the earth."

AS THE CONFLICT OVER the decision died down, Herman Miller launched an aggressive public relations campaign to explain its position. In response to Kulp, it published a research summary, "The Search for Good Wood: Sustaining the Yield from Tropical Forests." And it trumpeted how it had worked with both opponents and allies—Friends of the Earth, the Tropical Forest Foundation, and the International Hardwood Products Association.

And to the environmental leaders' satisfaction, the decision played well in the court of public opinion. The Council on Economic Priorities, a New York City environmental nonprofit, awarded Herman Miller its Corporate Conscience Award for its tropical wood decision, among other initiatives, including the Kulp-inspired waste-to-energy plant built in 1981. Later, the Bush White House awarded Herman Miller an Environment and Conservation Challenge Award.

In midsummer 1991, *Business Week* sent a reporter to Zeeland who wanted to know: What makes Herman Miller a green leader in the furniture industry? Many of the environmental team members were interviewed, and when *Business Week* sent a photographer, the magazine wanted a picture not of CEO Ruch but of Foley, underscoring the role of roving leaders at Herman Miller.

The photographer coaxed Foley—who in pressed shirt, necktie, and polished black shoes wore the corporate uniform of the era—to recline in an Eames Lounge chair with his feet on an ottoman. The article then appeared with Foley's image alone. He sat in a Michigan field, reclining in front of a background of cottony clouds and leafy woodland. The photograph quickly became an emblem of Herman Miller's environmental leadership.

The virtues of the decision finally piled up for Johnston. The next year, 1992, CITES indeed named Brazilian rosewood an endangered species. In a poetic turn of events, the U.S. wood-products industry recruited Johnston as U.S. industry delegate to the International Tropical Timber Agreement, a document negotiated by the United Nations. By following Herman Miller's ethic of environmental sensitivity, a onetime journalist had turned into global trade negotiator. Johnston stepped into a privileged seat at tables in Washington, Quito, Yokohama, and Geneva.

Ironically, Johnston's work would reprise the themes hammered on by Kulp. As he sat across tables with delegates from around the world, he struggled with ardent environmentalists who took positions based more on gut-level emotions than facts. He found the emotional positions hard to negotiate with. "I was pretty green...in dealing with public policy issues at this level," he says. "I had to mature in order to stay at the table."

In the end, the rosewood ban by Herman Miller would join the collection of stories the roving leaders would tell for years to illustrate how Herman Miller would favor action, not inaction, on the environment. A company once caught unawares of its full impact now was caught up in a global effort to lead once again, based on science and values. In 1993, Herman Miller would formally adopt the United Nations concept of "sustainable development" as its goal. And once again, a magazine would give the signal that Herman Miller was on the right track with the public. *Fortune*, in its first listing of companies with the best environmental records in 1993, named Herman Miller to the top ten.

CHAPTER 2

Honest Design

On a hot July day in 1930, D.J. De Pree sat in Herman Miller's Grand Rapids showroom. Around the president and founder of Herman Miller sat handsome wardrobes and couches adorned with wood carvings and latticework. Like other manufacturers of the time, Herman Miller made reproductions—in the Louis XIV, Queen Anne, Sheraton, and other classic styles. The company imitated whatever buyers wanted for stocking their big-city stores in New York, Chicago, and Philadelphia.

De Pree could sit in a showroom of his own only because he had taken a chance seven years earlier. He had bought the company with his father-in-law's money. He even named it after his father-in-law, whose reputation was synonymous with quality and integrity. Following Mr. Miller's advice, De Pree made furniture with the best materials and workmanship—"made as high priced as we dared and as low as we could," he wrote. Some of his ornate bedroom sets sold for as much as $700, more than the price of a new car.

But that money, and the name, was now at risk. The stock market had crashed nine months earlier. Furniture sales had collapsed. With buyers ceasing to snap up such favorites as the Heppelwhite bedroom suite or the Louis XIV ebony suite, De Pree was grossing half what he had just the year before. Through the 1920s, his sales ran well over $300,000 a year. In 1930, they slumped to $144,000.

De Pree, feeling the situation hopeless, wondering how he would survive, engaged in soul searching. He had staked his life on the business. His wife had just given birth to his sixth child. "You are a young man, and you're responsible," he recalled thinking later. "You are a failure, you're bankrupt."

He had no financial cushion. He was out of cash. The company was undercapitalized, and always had been. By his figuring, bankruptcy was just a year away.

Surrounded by the bedroom sets, wardrobes, and couches in his showroom, he could see two things. The first was what made the company successful: The fine carving. The lush fabrics. The fancy inlays. The exotic woods. Herman Miller may have made period knock-offs, but it produced pieces of the highest quality. The second was what made the company unsuccessful: An industry in which all the firms competed in the same way, for the same business, to please the same big-city buyers. With so much competition, he had to compete on price. And wars based on pricing would squeeze him out of the industry.

De Pree, the son of Dutch Calvinists, had another concern. Even if he could survive the price wars, price cutting would force him to cut quality. To him, quality was the highest business objective. It was a moral imperative. He had rejected some of the fixtures of his upbringing, leaving the Dutch Reformed Church of his parents to join the Baptists. Still, he was cut from the local cloth in Zeeland, his hometown. He was brought up to read the Bible every day, and he still did.

As a youth, the son of a tinsmith, De Pree planned to go into law and politics. Circumstances led him to a job in accounting, and he brought the values bred into him to the workplace. So did a lot of people in Zeeland. Settled by Dutch immigrants seeking religious freedom in 1847, the people there were known for industriousness and quality mindedness. De Pree later said, "The people are dependable, cooperative, peaceful, and thrifty—and they are taught all that from the pulpit."

Since the crash of business, De Pree had rededicated himself to praying. At 39, he began regularly studying the scriptures. He admitted that when it came to his business travails, he had no idea what to do, how to develop an approach to secure the future of the company. And yet that was the challenge he faced, to develop a durable means to regain and sustain company prosperity for the next generation.

AS IF IN RESPONSE, into the Grand Rapids showroom walked a man who introduced himself as Gilbert Rohde. Rohde, a 36-year-old New York designer trained as an illustrator, was looking for work. He had shown his first furniture pieces in New York just the year before. He had designed a series of smoking and side tables with chromed bases and DuPont-made artificial tops. De Pree knew his name, had read about him and his *art moderne* pieces. De Pree also knew that, in the late 1920s, most such modern furniture met the same fate: It sold in closeouts.

Little did either man know, however, that Rohde would help De Pree meet the challenge of his survival. In fact, De Pree's encounter with Rohde would kick off a decades-long education in the principles of design and management. The encounter would also reverberate as many as 60 years later, as Herman Miller set out in earnest on the road to sustainability. By then, Herman Miller would have turned itself from a small maker of bedroom sets into a big manufacturer of commercial office furniture.

In 1930, however, De Pree had his doubts about Rohde. He figured Rohde came for a visit only after striking out at selling his ideas to every other Grand Rapids furniture maker. And though Rohde was new to furniture design, he was also arguing for a new kind of furniture, less ponderous, more utilitarian. He maintained that people of the day, with smaller houses and lower ceilings, needed something other than period reproductions. The reproductions, he said, just didn't fit the new market.

De Pree heard Rohde out. He later admitted, "I didn't understand what he [Rohde] was talking about, but I had a realization that he knew what he was doing." De Pree also knew, as he looked down the road to the prospect of bankruptcy, that he did not have a lot of options. "I was grasping at straws. A drowning man always grasps at straws," he said. "At this early stage of my life, I faced oblivion as a manager."

So, suspecting Rohde's appearance just might be providential, he asked: How much to design a bedroom set?

One thousand dollars, Rohde replied.

One thousand! That was three times the fee he paid the best Grand Rapids designers.

Or I'll do it for 3 percent royalty on the goods after they're shipped, offered Rohde.

Well, De Pree thought, I can't lose: I don't have the money to pay up front, and I can add the three percent later to the sales price. He told Rohde they had a deal.

Receiving Rohde's blueprints later, De Pree winced. Although Rohde had come back as promised with designs for two bedroom sets, the chests of drawers looked like simple boxes, utterly plain, with no carving and no inlay. Unadorned flat veneers ran from edge to edge. On the beds, headboards and footboards both looked as rectangular and plain as drafting tables.

De Pree rejected the designs instantly. "I wrote him that I thought they were manual training school design and they needed surface enrichment," De Pree said. A veteran of the furniture business, De Pree knew all the earmarks of fine furniture designed by seventeenth- and eighteenth-century masters. And he knew full well that Rohde's designs needed "eye value" to sell. The designs on the blueprints looked like closeout material.

Rohde wrote quickly back with a two-page letter. Reworking his designs was not acceptable, he said. You don't have to go through with this, he told De Pree. But if you do, you have to do it just the way I design it.

De Pree later recalled that at this point he realized Rohde knew more than he did, and that he'd better start listening to the man.

And so began the signature practice of D.J. De Pree: to listen to company outsiders who, as if providentially, appeared to grasp just the right way to revitalize his business. And, especially, to listen to a succession of industrial designers who ranked among the greatest of the era. De Pree seemed to have a knack for sniffing out just the right people. And he would learn from them not just about the perennial truths of furniture design: He would learn about the "design" of management.

De Pree gave himself over to schooling by Rohde, and he would soon have conversations that would stick with him for the rest of his life:

You think, said Rohde, that period design is the most interesting thing in a residence, don't you?

Yes, I guess I do, De Pree replied. I think period designs *are* the most interesting.

No, said Rohde. It's the people that live in the house who use the furniture that are the important ones.

That was "almost an earth-shaking statement," De Pree recalled later.

Rohde then elaborated: "You're not making furniture anymore; you're making a way of living—a lifestyle."

De Pree would recall and repeat this comment for years. Up to 1930, he had always produced for the store buyers. If he couldn't please the buyers, he couldn't get his furniture displayed. Rohde would have none of this slavish response to the middlemen. He designed for people in their homes.

De Pree took to Rohde's philosophy. He liked how it relieved him of courting the middlemen. He also liked how it played to the biblical themes of honesty and service to others. Rohde's designs also cost less to make, so De Pree would be able to price four pieces (bed, dresser, chest, vanity) at a reasonable $130.

Although De Pree continued to fret that Rohde's pieces were too plain, Rohde's first bedroom group sold right way. A New York furniture retailer bought 12 sets. In the first year, the New York store then turned its inventory 12 times, compared to an average of four times that was typical for Herman Miller. De Pree saw that Rohde was apparently onto something. And he became a Rohde advocate.

De Pree in effect embraced the philosophy Rohde had absorbed from Germany's Bauhaus movement, which cherished simple and function-rich design. Beauty, so Bauhaus thinking went, came from revealing—not hiding—joints, fittings, attachments, and materials. The Bauhaus philosophy ran at complete odds with the practices of furniture makers in West Michigan, where every company made period furniture and everyone used lots of ornamentation. Workers even "distressed" pieces to make them look authentic.

You're making new furniture, Rohde said, why not be honest about this? Don't make it look like old stuff.

De Pree began to agree that being honest with design fit with being honest in life. Carving, embroidery, and add-ons that covered joints and imperfections in workmanship added up to a form of dishonesty. "I began to see that function and simplicity were truth in design," he said.

De Pree's vision for the company became clearer. Designing to help people live better lives became the purpose of the business. De Pree eventually phased out design aimed solely to please dealers, buyers, and the people, like his father-in-law, who revered antiqued period pieces. By 1934, he offered eight Rohde lines—modern bedroom suites, dining groups, side chairs—enough for customers to furnish every room but the kitchen and bath. By 1943, Rohde's modern groups made up 23 of his 29 lines.

In 1944, however, the unimagined happened: Rohde had a heart attack. While at dinner in a French restaurant in New York, the 54-year-old leader of design died in his seat. He was three years younger than De Pree.

Certain that a top designer was critical for his survival, De Pree sought a successor, and he found one in George Nelson, another New Yorker, a Yale graduate, and the architect who won the Rome Prize in 1932. Nelson, after spending time in Europe sketching antique monuments, published 12 articles on European architects. Although Nelson had never made any furniture, his concept for "storage walls," outlined in an *Architectural Forum* article, caught De Pree's eye. The two formed an immediate bond, in spite of entirely opposite views on religion. In a meeting in Detroit—a meeting lubricated by Nelson's like of martinis—they sealed a deal.

Like Rohde, Nelson favored practical furniture for modern living, even though he worried over his total ignorance of the industry. Just a year after De Pree hired him as design director in 1945, he unveiled a line of products. Among the pieces were those destined to become classics. One was a waist-high wooden hotel cabinet. It featured an interior desk and an adjoining slatted bench. He also designed utility cabinets, platform benches, vanity stools, ottomans, and sectional seating. Nelson's designs fueled Herman Miller sales. When he started, company revenues ran to $554,000. In five years, they spurted threefold to $1.7 million.

Besides a boost in sales, Nelson gave De Pree greater clarity about what honest design meant. "It must be a solution for a living need," said Nelson.

This became a mantra for the company: Design must respond to a need. It had to solve a problem in work or life. Nelson said, "If any designers think you are going to be totally free creative agents, forget it; and if it should happen to you, which heaven forbid, you would have no idea of what to create. Social values provide the framework within which the designer does his job."

Nelson didn't feel that he had a monopoly on smart, problem-solving design, however. He had his eye on the man who won first prize in a design competition at New York's Museum of Modern Art in 1946. Charles Eames, 39, an architect and filmmaker, had, with a colleague, won the MoMA prize in part for his design and production of a molded plywood chair. The chair was simple, yet suave and comfortable, without padding or ornament.

Eames appeared to be traveling in a direction that fit Herman Miller's path. A resident of California who worked in a studio with Ray, Eames sought to find ways to mass produce and make chairs economically. The molded plywood chair was his masterpiece, a quintessential example of simplicity and function, a spare chrome frame supporting an elegantly shaped seat back and base. The chair would go on to become one of the most famous designs of the century.

De Pree agreed with Nelson to bring the Eames couple into the Herman Miller design fold. In doing so, De Pree for the third time revealed a unique capacity: he could give himself over to others. One observer would later talk about his "abandoning" himself to designers. The elder De Pree developed such trust that he gave away more authority and control than most company bosses could stomach. By doing so, he realized one success after another.

The Eameses, who also designed tables, storage units, stools, and aluminum furniture, reaffirmed and refined De Pree's thinking about honest, problem-solving design. Charles Eames scorned designers who talked about "style." "The extent to which you have a design style," he would say, "is the extent to which you have not solved the design problem."

Eames believed style came from a designer's investment of his or her unique self in the solution to a problem. It did not come as a fashionable flourish at the end. He felt that originality for its own sake was contemptible. With Eames around, people did not talk about "good design" or "nice styling." They talked about "solving the problems" of work and life.

When Eames heard someone utter the words "good design" in a New York show room in the 1940s, he reputedly said, "Don't give us that good design crap.... The real questions are: Does it solve a problem? Is it serviceable? How is it going to look in ten years?"

In focusing on problems, Eames's approach was as much analysis as art. Analysis required the identification of "constraints." It led to a list of dozens or hundreds of them. And when designers took all of them into account, they didn't compromise their way to a solution that gave them a little of this and a little of that. They instead solved a puzzle of immense complexity that gave them a design that won on all counts. Once interviewed on the topic, Eames made a number of comments destined to become company lore:

What constraints does design depend on?

"The sum of all constraints," Eames answered. "Here is one of the few effective keys to the design problem—the ability of the designer to recognize as many of the constraints as possible; his willingness and enthusiasm for working within these constraints: the constraints of price, of size, of strength, of balance, of surface, of time, and so forth. Each problem has its own peculiar list." Does design obey laws? he was then asked. "Aren't constraints enough?" To whom does design address itself—the greatest number? Specialists? Amateurs? A privileged social class? "Design addresses itself to the need."

SO SUCCESSFUL WAS EAMES at accepting design constraints that in 1956 he and Ray were invited to make an appearance on NBC's Home Show. Arlene Francis, the leading woman on talk television, opened the segment with close-ups of the Eames plywood chair revolving before the camera.

Francis cooed, "It was a revolutionary new chair and I must say it caused quite a flurry."

Eames, in his signature bow tie, often gazing down to reveal a flattop of hair, looked bashful.

"...And the designer Charles Eames has become almost a household word," Francis added. She took Eames's hand and walked him through a gauntlet of his molded-plywood, wire, and fiberglass chairs.

"We're in New York to introduce a new chair for Herman Miller," Eames began. A chiffon veil lifted from a round dais, lit like an alcove in a church. Symphonic music played. The new Eames lounge chair and ottoman emerged into the light. "It's rosewood plywood and it's black leather, and the insides are all feathers and down."

The television network could hardly have given the Hope diamond more dramatic staging. All told, Francis gave the chair, Charles and Ray Eames, and in turn Herman Miller, ten minutes before a prime audience, the pivotal decision makers in home consumer purchases across the United States.

As Herman Miller gained celebrity through the Eames' successes, De Pree lauded Charles Eames's triumphs. In the September 1956 *Arts and Architecture* magazine, he praised Eames's "aesthetic brilliance and technical inventiveness." Eames showed that the makers of ponderous hand-made reproductions represented the opposite of honest design. He wrote: "With one stroke he [Eames] has underlined the design decadence and technical obsolescence of Grand Rapids."

By the mid 1950s, De Pree's worries about the company's survival had waned. He rode to prosperity on the design thinking of Eames, Nelson, Rohde, and textile designers like Alexander Girard. Herman Miller's yearly sales hit $4 million. The business was appealing enough that two of his sons, Hugh and Max, joined. The eldest, Hugh, began to take over much of the company's management. D.J., in turn, spent more time championing a design philosophy that would serve the company for years.

In a course for training plant managers, D.J. covered a dozen design principles: simplicity, cleanliness, unity, coherence, balance, beauty, feel, comfort, honesty in function and materials, and so on. "More with less; less material, less weight, less mass, less cost"— those became his bywords.

Echoing his earliest learning from Rohde, D.J. stressed an unflagging belief that design should take into account human values— what a piece "does for and to the human being." De Pree by this point had discovered two things for certain. He could depend on the principles and values of problem-solving design to guide his business. And he could count on abandoning himself to mavens of design to get the work done.

AS DE PREE SOLIDIFIED his thinking on design as a management cornerstone, he also came to clarify his thinking on the handling of workers. The management of the work force had long bothered him. Since the late 1930s, workers and management in Michigan, home of an infamous 1936 sit-down strike at General

Motors in Flint, had fought intensely. "Unfortunately, the business takes the attitude of 'the damn union,' and 'the damn union' takes the attitude that it's 'the damn management,' which causes problems," De Pree said later. "Then an adversary relationship is created."

Herman Miller was not unionized, but De Pree and son Hugh wanted a better relationship with workers. D.J. called "priority number one" the people who used his furniture, but he called "priority number two" the workforce that built it. He also wanted a way to boost productivity. At the time, the plant ran poorly. Deliveries ran as much as 26 weeks late. So little trust did De Pree have in his workers fixing errors in manufacturing that both he and his sons, Hugh and Max, spent time inspecting items as they left the plant.

On the lookout for a better way to handle the workforce, the De Prees ran into a man hailing from MIT who preached a new way of treating and paying workers. Carl Frost, inspired by labor organizer and MIT lecturer Joseph N. Scanlon, urged managers to allow shop-floor people, on their own, to assume responsibility for quantity, quality, and costs. Frost, a professor of management at Michigan State University, believed workers could help a company succeed by disciplining *themselves* to do needed work. He didn't feel workers needed constant badgering by their bosses. They could take full control of their work and relieve management of continuous oversight.

In 1950, the De Prees convinced him to help them bring this new way of managing to Herman Miller. Frost's plan, the "Scanlon Plan," had two main parts. The first was to set up worker committees that met monthly to help make decisions. The second was to start paying monthly bonuses for suggestions adopted from workers for productivity improvements.

From the start, Frost insisted that workers owned the entire payroll. Given that the payroll then amounted to 32 cents of every dollar the company spent, workers should always get that percentage, Frost told De Pree. If the workers could shrink their cost as a percentage of sales to, say, 27 percent, they should still get the entire 32 percent share of total spending.

In fits and starts, the Scanlon Plan took root. Though the workers were mistrustful at first, they came to like "participative management." Each of them had the opportunity to play a role in the business by making suggestions and contributions, and by improving performance. They also liked the money. Coached intensively by Frost, they earned on average a 10 percent bonus. Said De Pree later, "The spirit of the factory was so wonderful!" Wonderful enough, in fact, that grateful workers took a pool and bought Frost, a far from wealthy professor, a new car.

For the De Prees, changing the way they supervised people was not easy, even if they thought it was the right thing to do. Like people pursuing a life change, they often went to their guru for guidance, but they struggled to stay with a program that was hard to execute. "For management, he [Frost] was often like an office chair that would not swivel -- an irritant that forced correction and change," Hugh wrote later in his memoir. "He served as a spur, an advisor, a confessor."

But the De Prees revered Frost as they did Rohde, Nelson, and Eames. The new participative management became another cornerstone of the company philosophy. The workers no longer had the bosses looking over their shoulders at every turn. They started to take ownership of their work and the future of the business.

"If you really believe that the worker is so important, then you must begin to take him in as a partner," D.J. said later. "He may not be a stock holder, but he's a stakeholder in the company. And he's a stakeholder in that he gives his working life to the company.... He decides, 'This is my place of work,' and his wife and family begin to get a feeling that this is his factory."

AS THE DE PREES gained confidence in their growing management capabilities, a new problem began to emerge, and it threatened the company's growth and stability. Hugh De Pree, soon to take the reins from his father, called it a crisis. In spite of a catalogue of classy products—sofas, coffee tables, bubble lamps, cabinets, shelving, pedestal tables—Herman Miller was succeeding mainly by solving the problem of seating. Sales were growing, but the company had largely turned into a chair maker.

"This was fun, it was simple, it was profitable," wrote Hugh in his memoir. "But it wasn't long before we were fretting about what would happen if the bottom fell out of our chair business. We were vulnerable." In the language of the company leaders who would come after him, De Pree worried that Herman Miller had failed to build a broad, and thus sustainable, product line.

The solution to this crisis followed a circuitous course. At first, the De Prees began by falling back on the venerable approach used during the era of Rohde, Nelson, and Eames. As they continued to sell the earlier designers' pieces, D.J. and Hugh searched for another giant of design to take them into the future.

In 1958, they hired Robert Propst. Propst was an inventor, had been an artist, sculptor, and teacher. In his Denver studio, he had developed concepts for a spring cushion and furniture mold. The De Prees saw in him just what they needed: a man who could identify new problems to solve, who could come up with concepts for solutions, and who could take Herman Miller well beyond chairs. In a sense, Propst was another Rohde, a designer the De Prees would follow back to growth and stability. But he was also a designer who could take them into new markets.

Son of a Colorado rancher, Propst, like George Nelson, was a furniture-industry outsider. His interests ran in every direction of the industrial compass. Soon after his hiring, he was at work on 32 projects that indeed targeted new markets—a waffle spring, heart valve, squash-ball caster, a livestock identification program, and a laser projector. For almost two years, he and his research lab poured forth new ideas. "The first year and most of the second," wrote Hugh, "was a time of excitement and joy: of visions of a new Herman Miller."

But by 1961, the De Prees saw that Propst's train of invention was outrunning the tracks of execution. What did Herman Miller know about designing, marketing, and selling so many new things—everything from health devices to livestock equipment? What kind of investment would it take to get up to speed? Herman Miller couldn't follow through on all of Propst's concepts—in fact, not even a small percentage of them. They had gone overboard in their expectations for reinventing their business.

In early 1962, the De Prees had no choice but to rein in their run at diversification. They issued a "restatement of purpose." They slashed Propst's project list. They retreated to a position of strength—furniture.

Fortunately, in spite of his mandate to diversify, Propst had taken a keen interest in the problems posed by a new customer that needed a lot of furniture—the managers of white-collar businesses. Propst had become obsessed with the problems of how paper, material, and ideas flowed—or didn't flow—through organizations. So deeply did he delve into researching these problems that he hired psychologists, architects, mathematicians, and anthropologists to help him.

Propst asked: How can we design solutions to enable people to work more efficiently and effectively—with joy, health, interest, and productivity?

His answer would start to define a huge new market for Herman Miller. Although the company had made pieces for the office since Rohde designed an executive office group in 1941, it had never aimed to sell office furniture in volume. The prospect of making a big splash in that market struck the De Prees as a natural new direction for the company to take.

The move seemed to go well at first. Working from Propst's concepts, Nelson designed a handsome set of freestanding pieces—desks, storage units, display tables, and shelves. One of the desks was of the stand-up, roll-top variety. Another was a carrel for phone calls and notetaking. Customers in offices at the time sat at metal, flattop desks, often painted linoleum green. In comparison, Nelson's designs were works of art. They had elegant chromed legs and were edged with wooden sideboards.

When Herman Miller introduced "Action Office" in 1965, the press raved. So did dealers, architects, and customers. Stories about the new line appeared in *Business Week* and the *Saturday Evening Post*.

But customers yawned. Many felt the pieces were overpriced, hard to assemble, hard to figure out how to use, and didn't make a complete office. To Propst's mind, they didn't even reflect his original concepts. On top of it all, they cost too much to make, were hard to ship—and they wobbled.

What the De Prees wanted was another "bell cow," a term used by Eames for popular, profitable, and singularly successful new designs. Bell cows led companies—and industries—into new pastures. The Action Office of 1965, however, came out as a lame cow. It was a commercial flop.

Hugh reacted quickly. In September, he ruled that Herman Miller would make an economy version. It would sell to middle management for half as much money. It would make a "system," comprising a small set of highly tooled components. And it would sell the system either as separate pieces or as an office landscape of mobile walls. Herman Miller needed a product that served the mainstream market and made money.

The path forward was still not smooth, however. As Propst and his people struggled for perfection, it appeared as if they would never deliver the new Action Office—as much as Hugh insisted they do so. Part of the holdup was that Propst had always thought of himself as a "searcher." He disliked the word "researcher" because it implied he was looking backward, not forward. But a bigger problem was that one of the company's most venerable management traditions—giving a giant of design unfettered rein to bring a product to market—was not working.

PROPST'S DEDICATION TO RESEARCH would remain an article of Herman Miller faith. So would innovation. Propst would later write, "The outside world is ruthless about embryonic innovation. It is devastating. In its early stages, innovation is very fragile. It is toddling around. It does not know how to stand up, and it can't say anything very well."

Hugh tried to protect this toddler. He would continue to believe in the power of solo virtuoso designers. But he hit his limit in September 1967. At a seminar in Chicago, sponsored by *Office Design* magazine and called "Open Plan in the Office," he caught a view of his industry's notion of the future. It looked an awful lot like Propst's concept. Hugh feared another company might get the concept to market first. Could Herman Miller fall to the trailing edge in office furniture?

"I came away shaken to my boots," Hugh commented later.

By this time, Propst had been working on office concepts for eight years. His concepts were ahead of their time. A man without peer in defining a design problem, he created concepts for personal space enclosures, "workstations" tailored to personal needs, shelving and desks that put documents at hand. His office layouts guided traffic, screened desks for privacy, triggered chance meetings to make for breakthrough thinking by coworkers.

Propst foresaw well before others that the office was on track to kill productivity if the problems he saw emerging went unsolved. He worried about information overload, communication failure, suppressed creativity, sedentary-worker illnesses, paperwork bottlenecks, and the explosion in the numbers of office gadgets. And yet, as he worked on inventing solutions, which stressed portable, changeable systems, he was burning up months of time.

Hugh, realizing he had let things get out of hand, couldn't wait any longer. He decided that the new Action Office was more than one man, or one innovative group, could handle. The market had become more demanding, technology more complex, manufacturing more sophisticated. As a system of products, "Action Office 2" demanded a team of people to commercialize—to engineer, test, manufacture, and sell.

On October 3, 1967, Hugh issued an edict to remove Propst as the leader of the Action Office 2 project. He assigned commercialization to Propst's operations chief. In a memo, Hugh wrote, "Problems to be solved before we can introduce it are in Design, Engineering, Manufacturing, Costing, Controls, and Marketing."

In one stroke, Hugh found a way to get things back on track. He engaged the hearts and minds of a much bigger group within the organization. "I think that was the first time we recognized that some other people might have input into all this," Hugh wrote. Up to then, despite the company's Scanlon-inspired participative management, designers held total sway during product development. If Eames or Nelson created a design, engineering didn't alter it.

"This was a defining moment for Herman Miller," remembers Dick Ruch in his memoir, "since most people thought that innovation was the province of a few highly gifted designers and inventors." Ruch, who would years later become CEO, was a member of the new team.

"We were closing a period in our history—'designer as God'"—wrote Hugh. When Herman Miller developed a product now, he saw that many more people would have to be involved. Though a single wunderkind designer would still spearhead a project, a team would take over and execute the production. This would be a team populated by those "roving leaders" Max De Pree would eventually write about.

AS THE NEW TEAM jumped on the project, the approach to completing Action Office promised to educate the De Prees about a more sophisticated way to manage and design. The new approach required more attention to costing and pricing in order to bring the product in at an affordable price point. It required engineering and manufacturing engineers who acted as if they owned the process to assure not only a durable, reliable product, but one that the company could mass produce.

At the end of development, Action Office 2 (eventually just called Action Office) did indeed fulfill these requirements. In so doing, it supplied a new answer to the principles of honest design, marking the birth of mobile walls and panel systems. In a departure for the company, the "aesthetic brilliance" typifying Eames pieces was missing. Inside Herman Miller, factory people, fond of crafting the classics from Nelson and Eames, fought the new product. So did some managers. Sales people ridiculed it. Eames called it "honest ugly."

In fact, Action Office 2 was ultra rationalistic. People would later call the product "office cubicles." It was a practical solution in the extreme. Herman Miller was not just introducing a new product. This was a solution for a problem few had articulated and nobody had solved. Herman Miller no longer made just piece parts—chairs, desks, tables, shelves—for the home. It made systems for the office.

And the sales potential of the new systems was revolutionary. Herman Miller's target customers, who continued to bulk up their white-collar workforces, needed office setups that bridged the gap between two traditional extremes—fixed corridors with a name-plate on each door and bull pens with a nameless person at each desk. Action Office 2 was the answer. As a partition-based system, it suggested moving to something altogether new: doing away with interior walls and using furniture in their place.

Herman Miller introduced Action Office 2 in July 1968. Within a few years, sales started to turn Herman Miller from a marginally profitable, family-run furniture maker into a big-time, publicly owned firm. In 1970, the year after D.J. De Pree retired and left the CEO post to Hugh, Herman Miller went public to raise cash to fund the product. A company workforce of 230 brought in $25 million in sales. By 1980, the year Hugh retired, a workforce of 3,000 brought in $230 million.

Following the same approach to management, in the mid-1970s Herman Miller made another big advance in its product line. It introduced its first ergonomic desk chair, the Ergon. At the start, the design, proposed by another top designer, Bill Stumpf, didn't meet all the new constraints, as viewed by sales, marketing, and engineering. It could not be made at a price that had a market opening. Glad to stay open to the comments of the new team of leaders, Stumpf reworked it.

Ironically, as if reprising the reaction to Action Office, some people chided the company over the chair's new look. One customer said it looked "like two hemorrhoid pillows put together to make a chair."

But the Ergon would eventually become a steady seller, and along with robust sales of Action Office, company revenues climbed smartly. As Max De Pree took over from Hugh in 1980, revenues continued to rise in spite of the worst recession, 1980–1982, in the last half of the twentieth century, when unemployment in the United States hit 10.8 percent.

And the company's success came from pursing the same course. Herman Miller no longer just sold furniture. It sold design that solved problems of people in work and life. Gilbert Rohde remained the fount of inspiration. As Hugh De Pree wrote: "Rohde's continuing thesis was quite simple: Forget about public taste and trends. Forget about producing what you think will sell.... Concern yourselves instead with researching and answering certain human needs."

And design that met those needs no longer relied on solo giants like Rohde and Eames and Nelson for refining fresh, bestselling concepts. It relied on a company filled with roving leaders, energized by the responsibility given them with participative management. These roving leaders, though facing unforeseen constraints, could solve an endless string of riddles that would lead to new products, processes, and ways of managing.

As Max De Pree would write, "If you want a corporation to be truly effective, you will need to help corporations be open to giants at all levels."

By the time Dick Ruch took over as CEO from Max in 1987, one of the new constraints facing these leaders was safeguarding the environment. That meant relying on people like Bill Foley and Bob Johnston to root out unsustainable materials. It meant relying on leaders who would emerge from the new environmental team, like Paul Murray, to rework factory processes to prevent harm to the planet. It meant redesigning products to make them green. The list of challenges for these roving leaders was new; the challenge to diligently employ honest problem-solving design, the same.

CHAPTER 3

Magic Zero

From the moment Paul Murray was hired to run the solvent-based wood-finishing line at Herman Miller, memories of his son's run-in with solvents came rushing back. He could see Matt's hives, the swelling, the choking. He could remember how the reaction happened just seconds after Matt brushed against his clothing. Murray would never again think of xylene and toluene in the same way.

Murray was joined by others at Herman Miller who were having troubling thoughts stemming from environmental hazards. These memories shaped the values of many roving leaders at the company, including Bill Foley and Bob Johnston. Among this group were also people who would figure into other environmental decisions the company would make—Joe Azzarello, Jim Gillespie, Tom Ankney, and Willie Beattie, among others.

Behind each name was a story. Beattie, who worked for Murray on the wood-finishing line, had started his career at General Motors in the 1970s. A self-professed "geek" and "factory rat," he spent his days in a precision machine shop making fuel injectors for diesel engines. Though he loved life in the shop, he began to have trouble breathing.

A doctor put him on the powerful steroid prednisone. Over time, he had more breathing trouble. He had to take leave—for three months.

With lungs recovered, he returned to the shop. But he lost his breath again. The doctor pointed to hydrocarbons as the culprit. Beattie and his shop mates sprayed a fine mist of oil on everything, a mist that hung in the air, casting a blue haze across the plant floor. The mist apparently led to his respiratory system faltering again in 1977. He lost 40 pounds and 20 percent of his breathing capacity. On some days, he couldn't lift his head from the bed. It took him three years to recover.

Not every roving leader went through such personal trauma, but they all shared the story that came with their generation. For some, that story began on the first Earth Day, April 22, 1970, when 20 million Americans worked to reverse the harm from oil spills, factory pollution, raw sewage disposal, toxic dumps, pesticides, and loss of plant and animal life. For others, it began in their own neighborhoods as factories turned the sky orange, and trucks poured waste into marshes. For all of them, it was heightened by the prospect of the ruin of critical ecosystems, including the rainforest that made the oxygen to sustain life on earth.

Each of the leaders at Herman Miller had to come to grips with the reality of his or her job: They were working for an industrial enterprise. Though it ran in a perfectly legal way, it released solvents into the atmosphere, churned out hazardous waste, created heaps of scrap, and sent thousands of tons of trash to landfills.

The De Prees had always believed that Herman Miller had a moral constraint to "do the right thing." D.J. De Pree's statement in the 1950s, "Herman Miller will be a good steward of the environment," remained a mantra. Every employee learned about D.J.'s insistence that no more than half of each company property could be developed. The other half had to be left green. Environmental stewardship became a given.

But as the rosewood episode showed, the standard for the right thing in taking care of the environment kept changing. Green standards of the past no longer met the expectations for the future. Herman Miller could wrap itself in a green flag, but the fact remained: The byproduct of manufacturing was waste and pollution—neither of which seemed like the right thing to produce.

In the late 1980s, the volumes of waste became harder to ignore. With the passage of stricter landfill laws, city and town dumps across the United States started shutting down, unable to meet new groundwater standards. Three thousand of them locked their gates between 1982 and 1987. The airwaves and newsstands were flooded with stories that America would run out of landfill space—and in places it did.

In the most infamous incident, a barge carrying 3,168 tons of garbage, medical refuse, old tires, cardboard containers, and other trash from New York City embarked to dispose of its waste in North Carolina. Over six months, in Alabama, Louisiana, Texas, Mexico, and Belize, the "garbage barge" failed to get authorization to stop. Ultimately, New York took its waste back and incinerated it. But the story became a symbol for the American public: People were dumping too much garbage into the environment—more than the planet could handle.

The debut of the Toxic Release Inventory (TRI) became emblematic of another problem. Provided for by the Emergency Planning and Community Right-to-Know Act of 1986, the TRI program required every company to report releases of more than 300 toxic chemicals to the Environmental Protection Agency (EPA). For the first time, in mid-1989, the EPA published the results. Just about every company that made anything in the United States was on the list. And just about every newspaper in America reported releases. Reporters had a field day. They enumerated one poison after another spewed into the air and water in cities and towns across America.

Herman Miller was not spared. It ranked among the top ten polluters in Ottawa County. Its Zeeland plant alone sent 100,600 pounds of pollutants into the air in 1987 (reported in 1989). Among them were 26,300 pounds of xylene and 12,100 pounds of toluene. To be sure, the company's releases were little more than a case of industrial bad breath compared to other companies. One Dow Chemical plant across the state in Midland sent 3,946,375 pounds skyward in the same year. Still, the Herman Miller tally shocked the senses.

The TRI and other ugly environmental facts of the era faced the environmental leaders at Herman Miller. With the public anxious about company transgressions, and with the press hungry to blacken company reputations, the demand for action was urgent. It was particularly urgent for people working in a company whose culture obligated it to do the right thing.

Murray's evaporating solvents—collectively known as VOCs, or volatile organic compounds—contributed to the TRI. He faced a dual challenge. The first was a manufacturing one: Figure out how to run his line so that, as solvents dried, the line produced a stream of product with fewer blistered surfaces. The second was the environmental job: Over the long term, figure out how to run the line without solvents at all.

Murray worked with Beattie, who had started as a line supervisor in 1987. By tinkering with the line they inherited, they succeeded in reducing the blistering, cutting yearly scrap rates by 95 percent, or $145,000. But progress didn't go quite as smoothly on the environmental side. Owing to regulations enforced by the state, Murray had to get a new emissions permit for a proposed new line. When he went through company records, however, he discovered that the existing line had fallen out of compliance. It released more than its permit allowed.

Herman Miller had stepped over the legal line, and the discovery made Murray uncomfortable, to say the least. When he applied to the Department of Natural Resources for a permit for a new line to improve paint performance even further, officials told him he had to first correct the permit for the existing line. He applied for a variance—and he received it. But the experience left him chastened. "The liability for this oversight could have been bad," he wrote in a memo at the time, "with both penalties and jail terms. We must not duplicate this error ever again."

Murray still couldn't get a permit for the new line, however. State officials wouldn't accept his application. He had calculated the new line would emit 100 tons of solvent a year at normal production levels. This may have been an acceptable level before, but with the toughening of the Clean Air Act by Congress, officials said it would not be acceptable in the future. They told Murray he would have to add equipment that would destroy VOCs.

Though sympathetic to the health impact of solvents, Murray did not, in practice, have a way of eliminating them from the stain and clearcoat used on the Herman Miller line. He knew the technology well. He had until 1988 worked for the paint manufacturer PPG Industries on solvent-free coatings. Cured under ultraviolet (UV) light, liquid plastics made of 100 percent solids emitted nothing. But neither PPG nor any other company made solvent-free coatings that met Herman Miller's quality standards.

That left Murray in the same place as all the other people in the band of roving environmental leaders: ill-equipped to quickly erase environmental impacts. He and everyone else in the company faced a question larger than their jobs: How do we make environmental responsibility a part of the way things work at Herman Miller? At the time, they were part of the problem, not part of the solution.

DRIVEN LARGELY BY ENVIRONMENTAL zeal, people across the company started to take action. No environmental czar existed. Middle and front-line managers launched initiatives on their own, emboldened by Herman Miller's history of participative management. Murray would later call this local activism "the power of one." "Many of our environmental achievements," he says, "come as the result of one person saying, 'I know we can do better.'"

One of the earliest environmental leaders at the Zeeland plant was Joe Azzarello, a former engineer for coal, nuclear, and gas plants at a Michigan utility. Azzarello, a plant engineer who had revamped the waste-to-energy incinerator, had started tracking Zeeland's waste stream in the late 1980s. He then looked at ways to shrink it.

In the late 1980s, tired of Styrofoam packaging, Azzarello called a meeting with the supplier. He had a tense conversation. Azzarello said: Take the used Styrofoam back, and sell us something recyclable.

Recycling isn't possible, the supplier responded. Nobody does it.

Azzarello wasn't convinced. After the meeting, he found another supplier that indeed recycled Styrofoam. He then called another meeting with the original supplier, telling him: Your contract runs out soon, and we're not going to renew it because we found another supplier that can do everything you said you couldn't.

The supplier, shocked, asked Azzarello to give him a week. I'll get you another proposal, he said.

Azzarello agreed. After all, the contract was worth nearly $1 million, and it was the man's biggest.

The supplier came back as promised. We can do everything you asked, he said, and at an even lower cost.

Azzarello jumped at the chance to get such good service for even less money.

Another leader was Jim Gillespie, a maintenance supervisor. Gillespie had found many ways to divert waste into useful products, so much so that he was nicknamed "the king of recycling." In one instance, he talked with a plant supervisor who had a truckload of scrap foam-rubber pieces. The supervisor wanted it sent to a land-fill, and pronto, to free up space for more disposal. Gillespie, figuring that landfilling would cost $345, got on the phone. He found a buyer nearby, with a truck, eager to scoop up the waste.

In the end, Gillespie won doubly. He spared Herman Miller landfill costs and snagged an $850 check from the buyer for material that was worthless to Herman Miller. All told, he boosted Herman Miller's bottom line by nearly $1,200. The foam pieces were recycled into low-grade carpet backing.

Having found cash in cushion waste, Gillespie went after it elsewhere—in fabric, wood, sawdust, plastic, vinyl, aluminum, and waste oil. Herman Miller had been paying $1,000 to dispose of each excess barrel of foam-making liquids, called *isocyanates*. He found a buyer in California who bought off-spec product and ended up selling him opened barrels for $25 and unopened ones for $50—and the buyer paid for shipping. Where did the liquid go? To a Mexican business to make foam for coffins.

Yet another leader was Tom Ankney, a product safety engineer. In the early part of the 1980s, one of Washington state's new facilities experienced a notorious case of sick-building syndrome. People fell ill from working in the building's tainted air. The state shut it down and reconditioned it, but the mitigation didn't work. The state had to turn the building into a warehouse, and it then issued standards for levels of formaldehyde and VOCs emitted from furniture and building materials.

When Washington prepared to construct four new buildings, Ankney faced up to a new and hot environmental impact: furniture offgassing from freshly manufactured products. What was the effect of the emissions from furniture and panels on indoor air quality? To stay in the running as a supplier, Ankney had to figure out how to evaluate offgassing and how to answer the state officials' questions.

In one exercise, the state asked Ankney to coordinate a test at Herman Miller. The officials picked products coming off a Herman Miller line. Workers tagged them, put them on pallets, and shrink wrapped them on the spot. The officials observed as the workers put them in a locked trailer and the driver departed for an Atlanta, Georgia, testing lab. In Atlanta, Ankney and the officials met to unload and verify the tagged product came out of the trailer. The lab then put the products in a sealed chamber to test for releases of formaldehyde—verifying that they met state of Washington standards.

People throughout Herman Miller entered the environmental fray in the same in-depth fashion. Driven by a latent energy by a growing environmental consciousness, they thirsted for action. As for Murray, he and Beattie felt the burden of 100 tons of solvent emissions coming from their finishing line. How would they reduce that waste? State officials suggested a solution that was simple—but costly. Buy thermal oxidizers, or furnaces, to burn the VOCs—in other words, use incineration to turn the solvents into carbon dioxide and water.

Murray found a thermal oxidizer maker in Germany. Using natural gas to fire the combustion chambers to 1,325 degrees Fahrenheit, the furnaces destroyed 96 percent of the VOCs. The quality of the air exiting the furnaces would be cleaner than the air outside, since Zeeland was downwind from industrial cities like Gary, Indiana, and Milwaukee. Out of the ovens would come tough, stain-resistant coatings, a quality finish for the flat desk and shelf surfaces Herman Miller needed by the thousands.

Murray was sold on the solution, but the decision on the project was not his. It needed approval by the board of directors owing to the $1 million price tag. Complicating matters was the differing approach of a competitor with a similar line-renovation plan. The competitor had decided to fight the state's demands—a fight it would win, enabling it to delay the same expense for three years. That would give the competitor a market advantage, as Herman Miller would have to apply paints at a greater cost.

IN SELLING HIS IDEA, Murray first faced a committee made up of the company's CEO and senior vice presidents. He had looked at various furnaces. He had visited Harley-Davidson, which was using them on its paint lines. He had taken into account the advances of coating technology, and he figured water-based coatings would not reach Herman Miller's standards until the mid-1990s.

Will the furnaces work? one of the committee members asked. What do *you* think we should do? asked another.

Murray assured the executives the furnaces would burn the VOCs almost entirely. And with the new Clean Air Act provisions kicking in by 1995, he said, Herman Miller would need the furnaces soon.

"And I live downwind," Murray added, "and I think we should do it."

The senior leaders signed the request. They believed it was the right thing to do.

But the decision was not final. CEO Dick Ruch took the proposal to the board. The directors put him through the wringer over the cost. The furnaces were not even required yet—Herman Miller could, like its competitor, fight the state's request. But Ruch argued that buying the furnaces was ethically correct.

The board went along.

Ruch did recognize that the decision was open to question from an economic viewpoint. He knew he could be stepping out of line when it came to return on investment. But, as in the rosewood decision, he was won over by the logic of the request. For one thing, it went along with Herman Miller's values as a company. For another, the technology was the best out there, and besides, Herman Miller could always sell the furnaces later.

Murray was pleased. So were the other environmental leaders, who felt the decision reaffirmed the company's pattern of stewardship. The decision "really showed the commitment of the company early on; this was some place different," says Murray. "Even though we knew we could not justify that $1 million [from a business perspective], we could do the right thing for the environment and still make money."

Once installed, in November 1990, the new line and furnaces got immediate press in *Furniture Design,* an industry trade magazine. More importantly, in 1991, the first full year of TRI reporting after furnace installation, the Zeeland site's total releases of VOCs fell by more than 40 percent, to 56,400 pounds.

DESPITE THE ENVIRONMENTAL PROGRESS the company had made up to this time, successes continued to come mainly from solo bootstrappers. Murray had recognized the helter-skelter nature of the effort in 1988. That prompted him and others in Zeeland to propose a coordinating committee. The group would come from middle management and include most of the roving leaders of the late 1980s, like Foley and Johnston from the rosewood work. With CEO Ruch's blessing, the leaders got together for the first time in Holland in 1989.

The new team, essentially a corporate "green team," worked informally at first. And for a time the team members served more as a mutual support group for further bootstrapping than anything else. Their work did take on fresh urgency as the public's call for the greening of industry became louder. Along with the passage of new legislation, like the Clean Air Act Amendments of 1990, Earth Day 20 came around on April 22, 1990. Two hundred million people in 141 countries took part.

The zeal for action by the nascent green group ramped up. Azzarello, finding that Herman Miller landfilled 800,000 Styrofoam cups a year, arranged to eliminate them. He replaced the throw-aways, which took 700 years to degrade in landfills, with 5,000 plastic mugs. And he waxed eloquent about the effort. "We want to leave as soft a footprint as possible," he said to a reporter. "It's not just a dollars and cents issue. It's also preservation of the earth for our children and grandchildren."

Gillespie helped organize a recycling event, at which West Michigan businesses could buy and barter unwanted materials to avoid dumping them. In one instance, he ran across the perfect swap. One business owner had excess cardboard to get rid of; another, excess pallets—and each needed the other's surplus. Their swap not only saved them money but saved the community a heap of landfill space.

Despite the innovative work by the informal green team, by early 1991, Herman Miller's top executives agreed that the company needed a formal structure for coordinating its environmental work. They chartered the Environmental Quality Action Team "to ensure that we are and will remain in compliance in putting initiatives in place that will put us in the leading edge of being environmental citizens."

The group started gathering regularly for day-long meetings at the company's lakeside retreat, Marigold. Marigold was a fitting site for the group. On Lake Macatawa, a finger of water connecting to Lake Michigan, it occupied a peninsula groomed with the lawns and gardens first created by an early twentieth-century industrial-ist. Complementing the gardens were rooms outfitted with design classics from Herman Miller, including the Eames lounge chairs and popular Eames stool, an elegant pedestal of pure walnut turned on a lathe.

The group set to work on its new structure and responsibilities. It created work teams. It reviewed progress reports. It drafted a mis-sion—it took more than three days to nudge all the right words into place. It shared tips and tricks from the field. Because it was an officially chartered team, its members gained confidence that Herman Miller could win the industry leadership position on the environment.

AND THEN THE TEAM received a report on the company's green status. Ordered by the team early on, it spelled out all of the expected issues—water use, air emissions, hazardous waste output, and landfill volumes. The team wanted to know: What is Herman Miller's overall tally of impacts?

One impact stood out from all the others: 41 million pounds of landfill waste.

The roving leaders had made a lot of progress in tackling waste, and this number was down from earlier years. Azzarello was keeping track. He reported recycling of 20,000 tons of materials per year, including plastic, paper, corrugated, fabric, fiberglass, Styrofoam, metal, and chemicals. He calculated "total materials saved" in a two-month period in 1991 as 357 trees, 9,921 gallons of oil, 1,662 cubic yards of landfill, and $7,908 in disposal costs.

But for all the activity, Herman Miller still wasn't exactly a green enterprise. True, following the earlier rosewood decision, it had scooped up the "Corporate Conscience Award" given in April 1991 by the Council on Economic Priorities. It was applying for—and would win—President George H. W. Bush's Environment and Conservation Challenge Award.

But Herman Miller was green only compared to other companies. And it wasn't green in the minds of some people: In the early 1990s, people calling themselves environmentalists didn't actually give companies awards. Herman Miller, for all its work, still had miles to go in meeting the new constraint of making itself sustainable as an environmentally sound business. The landfill waste was a whopping lot of material. In fact, it was enough to fill more than six garbage barges.

WITH THIS CHALLENGE LOOMING, Murray moved into the role of leader of the environmental volunteers in 1991. Although he was shouldering more green responsibility, he didn't feel he had a powerful means to make significant changes. The group had a company-wide structure, and top management supported it, but it didn't have a way to reap big-time results that would vault the furniture maker from an industrial-waste machine to a verifiably clean company. In fact, he felt the group was struggling.

Of course, the company had teams working on waste minimization, permit compliance, raw-materials management, and government affairs. They had taken bold moves, like banning unsustainable wood, which added sparkle to the company's name. They had also kept on with dozens of small initiatives. In 1992, Gillespie cut a deal in which Herman Miller recycled office paper and bought the same paper stock back as toilet paper and hand towels.

But to Murray's and other people's frustration, the gap between the right thing to do and the right way to achieve it still yawned wide. The question facing the green team was simple: How can we make good on our bigger ambitions—to vanquish some of our biggest impacts? "We need something big, really a rallying cry, to use to accomplish something significant," Murray recalls thinking.

At the time, quality management reigned as one of the most powerful management movements in Corporate America. In the 1980s, the Japanese had used quality practices to commandeer market share from U.S. firms, especially General Motors, Chrysler, and Ford. *Consumer Reports* had panned American-made cars, leaving consumers to favor imports like Toyota and Honda, and premium brands like Lexus and Acura. In response, many U.S. manufacturers had started taking crash courses in quality-improvement techniques.

One principle of Japanese manufacturing surprised U.S. firms. The Japanese didn't shoot for low defect rates and call it good. They strove for zero defects. In the practice of quality management, elevated scrap rates signaled systemic quality problems. Although factory workers could inspect products after production to catch faulty ones, the focus on inspection diverted their attention from the more critical job of correcting systemic failures. The systemic failures translated into persistent quality crises and high costs. Ironically, Japanese quality practices originated with two Americans who couldn't get the ear of Corporate America, W. Edwards Deming and Joseph Juran.

With conversations about zero defects rumbling through every U.S. manufacturing firm, the discussion among the environmental leaders naturally drifted to the notion of zero waste. Murray and Azzarello started to peddle the idea. Vice President Martin Dugan, who oversaw the environmental team and was eager to put an ambitious number on the scoreboard, nonetheless reacted with concern: "My first response was, 'Oh my god, that's impossible.'"

But experience in manufacturing had shown that giving people impossible goals had a paradoxical effect: It drove unimagined innovation and, in turn, unheard of results. Dugan was soon won over. He remembers thinking, "If we don't put a goal out there that's ridiculously crazy, what are we going to get done that matters?"

In early 1992, the members of the team were still talking over the zero notion when the new CEO, Kerm Campbell, took his post. They invited Campbell to a meeting at Marigold. Unsure of themselves, they floated the zero idea. Nobody knew how they would ever get to zero. On the other hand, they didn't know how to defend any goal but zero. Accepting some level of waste wasn't acceptable— for quality, for the environment, for business.

Campbell, a chemical engineer from Dow Corning's executive ranks, liked the idea. He said the company could set a target of reducing waste by 50 percent, or 80 percent. But the workforce needed a "stretch" goal. And stretching for zero made the most sense to him. "So we embraced zero," recalls Beattie, "like embracing a porcupine."

SOMETIME THEREAFTER, CAMPBELL INVITED Murray to ride with him to a speech in Dearborn, Michigan, about three hours east of Holland. Murray had since been singled out as the company's future full-time environmental manager. With Murray moving into the new role, Campbell wanted to get his take on the state of the company's environmental work. What was Herman Miller's biggest impact? How was the environmental team doing?

Murray admitted that one of his biggest worries was the mountain of landfill waste. Other impacts concerned him, from air emissions to hazardous waste to energy usage. But the landfill goliath commanded attention like no other.

With that in mind, Campbell launched into his speech at the Henry Ford Museum. The museum, situated just outside Detroit, showcased a bit of everything from the American experience, from classic Ford cars to pop-up campers to dioramas of mid-century motel rooms. Murray had heard much of what Campbell talked about. The new CEO, a member of the museum's board, spoke of the traditional strengths of Herman Miller. He touched on quality, the environment, the future.

The audience, comprising mostly architects, was particularly interested in what Campbell was saying about the environment. Architects and other design professionals had embraced the addition of environmental factors as an architectural constraint early on. The American Institute of Architects had started the Committee on the Environment in 1990.

Then Campbell said something Murray had not heard before— and had not expected to hear. To this crowd of design mavens, Campbell said Herman Miller would deliver zero waste to landfills by 1995—just three years away.

Zero. By 1995.

The number and date rang like an alarm in Murray's head. Campbell had just elevated the green team's secret ambition into a company goal. Not only had he made the pie-in-the-sky goal public, he was trumpeting it from a podium to a pivotal audience— professionals who could swing the million-dollar furniture-buying decisions of Herman Miller's biggest customers. No other furniture company had breathed a word about such an idea, but Campbell was announcing it officially. True, the environmental leaders had been talking about it in hallways and on the lawn, at Marigold. But they had never confirmed that the goal was actually within reach.

Campbell's announcement meant at least two things: First, Herman Miller actually had to deliver results. The company's good name was now on the line. Second, Murray and the environmental team were going to have to devise something radical to make it happen—and Murray, as he was becoming the leader of company's environmental efforts, would be charged with succeeding. The challenge for Murray was huge because, to date, the roving leaders had cut back on cardboard packaging, banned Styrofoam, recycled everything from shrink wrap to gypsum board. But landfill volumes, companywide, had fallen by only enough to fill a few tugboats.

Campbell's announcement was a natural for the CEO. Owing to his long tenure at Dow Corning, another Michigan chemical company, he had the religion of zero bred into him in another area: plant safety. In the same way that quality management stressed zero defects, safety management stressed zero accidents. At Dow Corning, workers routinely handled harsh chemicals. Says Campbell of his onetime employer, "We don't have a goal of one lost-time injury per year. We don't have a goal of one death per year. We have a goal of zero."

At the same time, Campbell was not by nature a reserved, left-brain engineer. A tenor soloist who had performed operettas, he acted on his gut—sometimes impulsively. When he came to Herman Miller, he felt that people didn't have enough freedom. In the first two months, he disbanded his group of senior vice presidents, because he felt they killed good ideas. He had banners hung around the company: "Liberate the human spirit." He now intended to liberate the spirit of the environmental leaders.

Though the announcement was a surprise to everyone, the green team knew the public outing meant they had to try like never before to reach their environmental ambitions. Outsiders would be watching—and not just fellow employees but the public, outside designers, customers, and even neighbors. For the first time the zero goal was completely real.

Up to then, says Murray, "We had not publicly acknowledged that to anybody." The act of going public now forced a new level of accountability—especially for him. After all, Herman Miller had now set an impossibly tough goal, highlighted by Campbell's public commitment, and Murray's name was on it.

DESPITE THE NEW PRESSURE, zero did feel suddenly liberating. Murray and the green team saw that the CEO was giving them latitude to transform things. In the same spirit that roving leaders had transformed the company through design in earlier years, they could transform it for the sake of the planet in coming years. As the group kicked off its zero campaign, it handed out coffee mugs inscribed with an environmental logo and a quote from Buckminster Fuller: "On spaceship earth there are no passengers, only crew."

As the new goal drew widespread attention and injected fresh energy into the group's work, so did the drift of world events. The zero goal came at a time when environmentalists were focused on what would become the biggest global environmental meeting of the century: The so-called Earth Summit in Rio de Janeiro. One hundred eight heads of state and thousands of other organization leaders would attend. For the first time, in June 1992, global leaders would signal that they all agreed on at least one thing—the primacy of saving the planet from the depredations of man.

With the implicit backing of global leaders in the offing, work on the environment took on a new air. Murray, who soon added Gillespie and Beattie to his staff, turned to a glaring problem in Herman Miller's waste stream: corrugated cardboard. A weeklong study showed that thousands of tons of it were going up in smoke at the company's energy plant. At the time, cardboard was fetching $30 per ton. The obvious question: Why was Herman Miller burning what it could sell?

Murray wrote a proposal to buy machines that could bale cardboard on the factory floor. That way, Herman Miller could recycle all of it. He cut a contract with a local recycler to split the take on cardboard, the more she could recycle, the more she—and Herman Miller—could make. The deal would drive both the recycler and Herman Miller to recover as much material as possible.

Although everyone knew about the zero goal, Murray, Gillespie, and Beattie didn't at first receive a warm welcome when they took their idea to the factory floor. Supervisors told them they didn't have the space for balers, and that they couldn't spare anyone to run them. They had a lot of work to do, and the balers would be a nuisance. "We got thrown out," says Beattie. "Manufacturing didn't want to talk to us because that just meant more work for them."

The group cajoled their way into a pilot, however, in the Zeeland plant, the company's largest. In place of carts that filled with cardboard roughly every fifteen minutes, they placed a baler that filled every eight hours. Instead of tugs pulling away five or more carts per hour, hi-los periodically removed the compact bales. All told, the balers cut the waste-processing area by half. And with the money the balers promised to bring in, the machines would pay for themselves in a year. Although the baler effort moved slowly forward, plant supervisors saw that the zero goal cleaned up the plant floor, and they soon embraced it.

Still, the clock was ticking for Murray on the zero landfill goal. Tabulations showed that by the end of 1992 the company had sent 40 million tons of waste to landfills. By the end of 1993, the tally was almost the same. The balers had won backers, especially after the initial pilot in Zeeland brought in $11,383 from the recycler, but with 1995 not far away, the progress toward zero was, for all practical purposes, close to zero—even as Gillespie, Murray, and Beattie pressed on with other waste-reducing work.

To better focus their efforts, Murray and his group decided to study waste as it left the plants. Gillespie and Beattie, joking about new careers as dumpster-diving detectives, followed trucks to the landfill. They took Polaroid pictures and estimated volumes. Their work revealed corrugated to be a persistent waste monster—2,000 tons of it a year. To spur people to take stock of how much this was costing the company, they took their evidence to front-line bosses on the plant floor.

The bosses said they would do better, but Murray saw that to slay the landfill goliath he had to figure out how to guide his attack in a new way. He just wasn't going to get the cooperation or achieve the progress he needed to meet CEO Campbell's zero goal. One day, while he was jogging, it hit him: Why not go to the janitors? Ask the people who throw things out what they are putting in the dumpsters and why – especially why corrugated still remained in the waste mix.

Assembled in a meeting, the janitors chuckled over finding themselves in a conference room with plant engineers. They had plenty to say, however. A lot of waste that looked recyclable just wasn't. In one case, they had to trash heaps of boxes because foam was attached to the cardboard. The boxes were used for packing painted black tiles for mounting on office panels. Finger-like Styrofoam sleeves, glued to the box interiors, prevented tiles from getting banged and scratched.

We can't get the foam off the corrugated, one of the janitors said, so we can't recycle the boxes.

A quick discussion among the engineers ensued. Well, since the foam and corrugated cannot be recycled together, why don't we make those sleeves a little beefier, they said, and then just bind them together with stretch wrap? Let's dispense with the box altogether.

This led to an epiphany for everyone: Significant waste cuts—and cost savings—would not come from changing the way they handled cardboard. They would come from not buying cardboard in the first place.

Gillespie liked to tell the story about then teasing the company's purchasing people:

We just realized, you guys buy 100 percent of our scrap.

Oh, come on! the purchasing people would protest.

Well, you buy everything that comes into the plant, he replied, and what's left over, we have to get rid of.

To be sure, recycling would remain part of the answer to cutting down landfill volumes. So would burning at least some waste in the company's energy plant. But buying components with no packaging materials at all promised the great leap forward. Get rid of the cardboard, the foam, the plastic.

Local teams of janitors, engineers, and plant-floor employees across the company began to work on cutting back shipments to landfills from each site. In short order, Gillespie, Beattie, and Murray found themselves in a new position. Having finally figured out the right way to tap into the hearts and minds of Herman Miller's participative workforce, they did less persuasion and more guidance and cheerleading. Progress took off.

Says Beattie: "It was an issue of how do you manage a stampeding herd. It was magic."

As they reaped gains with the landfill work, they pushed harder on other initiatives, such as those for recycling fabric, stretch wrap, and plastic banding. Outsiders and many competitors still felt Herman Miller's zero landfill goal defied reality, but the press and customers loved it. When *Fortune* magazine named Herman Miller to its list of environmental stars, it noted the company's waste-reduction efforts. In 1993, Hewlett-Packard, a major Herman Miller customer, awarded Herman Miller a perfect 4.0 score on its environmental policies.

The benefits to the environment added up, and if those didn't catch the attention of people working on the shop floor at Herman Miller, the dollar benefits did. Murray became a champion not just of adopting green business practices but also of conducting a green business profitably. "The model we've worked on from day one is that it's not bad to be sharp business people," he says, "Let's be a little cheap here and let's make sure it's good business."

By 1994, Murray had made sure that Herman Miller installed a scale at every plant to accurately weigh waste volumes. By the end of the year, landfill volumes were down forty percent to 24 million pounds. To Murray's disappointment, the company recycled less than 2 million pounds of its materials. But participation in the effort kept growing as plants started competing with each other. Managers also gave employees incentives to cut waste. In response, one woman kept the compactor she ran under lock and key: Waste only went to the landfill that passed her muster.

With waste volumes declining, the stampeding herd thundered on in 1995. Alas, by the end of the year, it couldn't get to zero. The number stood at 9 million pounds. Much more work remained, though this was down from 41 million pounds a the start of the decade. More work also remained on other green efforts. Murray and Beattie had unfinished business with solvents. The TRI for the Zeeland plant was sharply down, to 17,800 pounds, owing to the finishing-line's thermal oxidizers. But Murray was not satisfied.

Still, with the company having declared sustainable development as its goal in 1993, conducting business in a green way was becoming part of the definition of success at Herman Miller. The effort had achieved three feats that Murray felt were essential: The environmental leaders had the CEO's support. They had a management structure for driving progress. And everyone had discovered the magic—if not perfection—of setting a goal and letting a stampeding herd drive toward zero.

CHAPTER 4

The Teacher

Ed Nagelkirk, a tall, quiet-spoken construction manager for Herman Miller plants and offices, had worked for the company for 20 years. He had run around its facilities for even longer. As a child, he crawled along and rolled down Herman Miller conveyors. He drove orange, battery-operated carts across warehouse floors. He grew up in the company's plants, offices, and warehouses because his father, also Edward, was a construction manager before him. "There wasn't a day in my childhood when there wasn't a prayer for Herman Miller," he says.

Like his father, Ed Nagelkirk was a keeper of the Herman Miller architectural-design flame. Though not one to flex his muscle, he held a front-line position on architectural standards. And at Herman Miller, the architecture of buildings stood on the ladder of veneration right next to the design of furniture. George Nelson was an architect. So was Charles Eames. Nelson had designed three of the company's headquarters buildings. Problem-solving design in architecture held almost as high a place at Herman Miller as problem-solving design in furniture.

Herman Miller had long cultivated aspirations to go beyond straightforward problem-solving, however. Whether it was the

De Pree family or the Nagelkirks, everyone who worked in facilities management took as an article of faith: Herman Miller would use architecture as a means to raise the company to the "next level." Going with the status quo, even if respectable, was not acceptable.

In 1993, raising the company to a new level in architecture came to encompass environmental issues. People in the construction business ranked the impact of buildings as one of the biggest environmental problems the company could solve. In the United States, buildings used a third of the country's energy and two-thirds of its electricity. They consumed billions of tons of raw materials and trillions of gallons of water. Herman Miller could not go to the next level if it didn't include sustainability as part of its new architectural standard.

Nagelkirk, 39, saw a threat to moving in this direction. In just a few years, the company's Phoenix Designs subsidiary had grown into a juggernaut. Based in Holland, Phoenix remanufactured used Herman Miller furniture and sold both refurbished and new Herman Miller products. By 1993, the unit's sales were spurting 35 percent a year, in spite of a recession, fueled by customers' demand for the unit's express ordering and shipping expertise. Bix Norman, the president, needed two football fields' worth of new plant space. And he wanted it in less than a year.

The motto of Phoenix Designs told the story: "simple, quick, and affordable." Not only did Norman make that promise to customers, he managed the unit that way. Less than two years before, he'd had to expand his space by 102,000 square feet. After completing the project in just four and a half months, his people boasted of the speed: "In following with their marketing plan," said a report, "the buildings that house this fast-paced growth operation likewise needed to be simple, quick and affordable. A pre-engineered metal building was chosen to fill those requirements."

A pre-engineered metal building. That was a good solution from the standpoint of sustaining the unit's momentum. But in Nagelkirk's mind, it didn't fit the architectural ambitions of Herman Miller. Whether it concerned a new chair, building, or table setting for a customer luncheon, the Herman Miller ethic was clear: Don't sacrifice design—use design as a tool to solve problems. And a pre-engineered building did not serve as a premier example of problem-solving design in an age of increasing social consciousness.

And yet here was Phoenix Designs, whose number one business goal was speed. "Go fast because speed is exhilarating" was one of its slogans. To keep up the unit's run of business success, Norman worried less about running afoul of architectural standards than running out of space. As a rule of thumb, for every $50 million in new sales, he needed 100,000 square feet of space. And he expected to capture that extra burst of sales within a few years.

The first question on Norman's mind was how that space should be added. Should he build another addition on the current site? Should he build another 100,000 square feet in a new building? Should he consolidate the whole operation in a new 350,000-square-foot building? Whatever the answer, he didn't see why he couldn't get it on a compressed time schedule.

Nagelkirk and other company leaders, above all Nagelkirk's boss and the leader of the environmental team, Martin Dugan, didn't want to slow Norman's blistering sales growth—or his unit's speedy service. Under Norman's guidance, Phoenix had won praise for short turnarounds. In an industry where most companies took 12 weeks to fill furniture orders, Phoenix filled them in under four.

But the building leaders had no appetite for cutting the design process short. They winced at the thought of earlier mistakes, when the company had hastily put up buildings to meet sales spurts. The resulting structures—among them one attached to headquarters— had failed to take the company up a level.

THE MISTAKES IN HERMAN Miller's building design dated to 20 years earlier. In late 1970, Max De Pree returned from several years of work in Herman Miller's European business. Accustomed to the hallowed architecture of Britain, France, and Germany, he was distressed with an addition at the Zeeland headquarters called "Building E." The explanation for the new bare-bones building was simple. The construction manager had delivered the only structure possible within CEO Hugh De Pree's budget. To keep a lid on costs, he spent most of his money on good walls, a decent floor, and a durable roof. The 80,000-square-foot structure had little insulation. It had windows along the roofline only. It was made from concrete blocks without a brick veneer—on a site where everything else boasted red brick. And it only had a rest room for men.

Max complained to his older brother, who suggested that Max tackle the architectural design issue himself. Thus, Max became the guardian of Herman Miller architecture, a role he kept even when he took over as CEO in 1980 and retained for as long as he remained chairman, until 1995. Max helped draft a series of statements about architectural philosophy. The most influential appeared when the company set out to build a new plant in Bath, England, in 1975. Max refined his writings in what became known as the "Bath Brief," a set of guidelines that documented the company's architectural values and beliefs.

The brief contained a number of memorable passages: "Our goal is to make a contribution to the landscape of an aesthetic and human value." "The environment should encourage fortuitous encounter and open community." "The space should be subservient to human activity." "The facility must be able to change with grace, be flexible, and non monumental."

When it came to the environment, the younger De Pree wrote, "We wish to . . . reflect the company's commitment and reputation in environmental arenas . . . be constructively involved with the neighborhood . . . [permit] maximum relation of work spaces to the outdoors."

Despite episodes of backsliding, Max De Pree rededicated the company again and again to its principles. He often spoke of architecture with civic high-mindedness, as in an interview in the early 1990s: "Once a building is up, it's publicly owned. It's there. We can't avoid seeing it. So it either blesses us or embarrasses us. People who build buildings don't have the right to behave only in their own interest. A building is either an environmental asset or an environmental problem."

Max eventually added to the Bath Brief a significant new guideline. His realization that he needed to amend the guidelines actually dated back to the 1950s. At the time, he had asked Charles Eames to design a home for his family. As Max recalls it, he and Eames met for breakfast in downtown New York. Max, starting to describe what he wanted, was stopped by Eames.

Let's approach this another way, said Eames. Tell me about your family.

Eames then asked a long series of questions. How many children are you going to have? What does your family do? In a lesson echoing the teachings of Gilbert Rohde, Max realized Eames wanted to know all about the lives of the people who would live in the structure, not about the structure itself. "It didn't take me too long to realize that I was in the hands of a teacher," he says.

Max came to a similar realization when he hired A. Quincy Jones, a Los Angeles architect. When Jones came to Zeeland in 1971, in the wake of the Building E affair, he rose early and ate in a local Holland diner. He asked questions of other patrons to learn about the local people. He left the diner in time to see workers arriving at 6:30 A.M. to start the day shift at the company's plant.

Max had never seen an architect take such detailed interest in the habits of everyone in a building. Jones watched as workers arrived in the morning and staked out their turf with their lunch buckets. He noticed that some later ate together, some played cards, some prayed together. De Pree later remarked that Jones had taught him and others at the company about their own employees, about how they worked and lived. Why hadn't the executives learned as much on their own?

By 1993, after long hours logged with many architects, Max saw that the company needed to add to the guidelines. So a new principle appeared: "The most important criterion in selecting an architect is our potential to learn from them more about architecture, ourselves, our customers, and about the importance of good design." Later he said, "We work with the person who we think can teach us the most."

ALL OF THIS WAS front of mind for Ed Nagelkirk and other facilities leaders in the early 1990s. Many of them had in hand drafts of a book by Jeffrey Cruikshank and Clark Malcolm that documented this architectural legacy, due out in 1994. Malcolm, a writer for Herman Miller since 1983, worked closely with CEO De Pree and understood his philosophy down to the last detail.

Nagelkirk kept a photocopy of part of the manuscript in his files. One passage read: "When a corporation begins to think about putting up a new building, it has the chance to learn a great deal. It may learn how little it knows about itself. It may discover how poorly or how well it treats its employees. It may find out that its attitudes toward the community are not what they should be."

Nagelkirk created an informal one-page fact sheet based on material from the book. He handed it out to architects as a primer on the Herman Miller way of designing buildings.

One of those architects was Holland's David VerBurg, who in 1989 designed Herman Miller's Midwest Distribution Center, a 355,000-square-foot warehouse on a new 161-acre site by Interstate 196. Everyone was happy with the building. The company even held its annual stockholders meeting there. With 19,000 square feet of glass, VerBurg had found a way to bring daylight deep into the structure.

Bix Norman, the Phoenix Designs chief, agreed to hire VerBurg in late 1993 to start work on his new building. VerBurg produced the Phoenix building's initial "programming" which included a description of goals, intentions, and building features. Familiar faces from the green team appeared on the design team, notably Martin Dugan, who, in addition to overseeing the environmental group, was vice president for Herman Miller facilities, and the executive Keith Winn, who worked for Dugan.

In January 1994, the design people met with Norman to discuss options. Norman set an aggressive timetable: Give the board of directors an overview by March, a detailed plan in May, and finish the building in June 1995. They all agreed on one option—putting a new building on land next to the Midwest Distribution Center. Norman preferred a single consolidated operation, where he could further speed up manufacturing and shipping times. He also, according to his finance people, liked the way the new building would save money compared to staying in an expanded leased space.

The project group met a month later, by which time VerBurg's programming stressed that the building should contribute to, not harm, the surroundings. It should take advantage of winter and summer sun, winds, and views. It should minimize energy consumption and environmental deterioration. It should "encourage employee personal expression." The group settled on a single building of 270,000 square feet.

Norman was most keen on features that would further the way his operation ran. In fact, he wanted to bring back a small-company interplay between hourly and salaried employees. He felt this interplay had faded at Herman Miller despite its participative management and the Scanlon bonus that went with it. He wanted to permanently break the barrier between office and plant workers, so people up and down the ranks would work as a team. As he liked to say, "We have a pecking order but no pecking is allowed."

IN MARCH, NORMAN TOOK the proposal with VerBurg's simple plant footprints to the board. The cost of the new plant and land would run $11.6 million. The board approved the project, but everyone looking at it, including CEO Campbell, agreed: Here was an opportunity to advance their learning as a company to a new place—especially when it came to green building. And the concepts for the Phoenix building did not hit all the marks of sustainability.

The project, in other words, was moving the company forward but not up. The environmental leaders had taken sustainability to heart by this point. The year before, a couple of them had gone to Washington to talk about setting up what would become the U.S. Green Building Council, a nonprofit group dedicated to green building practices. They even talked Herman Miller executives into paying the $20,000 to help the launch. In spring 1993, Herman Miller became one of the council's founding members—only the second corporation to sign on. With this growing commitment to green building, they were not inclined to let the Phoenix plant became another architectural compromise.

In August 1993, another event highlighted the company's green commitment. Paul Murray organized an environmental conference of people from different plants. The cross-company confab amounted to a coming-out party for the leaders of sustainability. One of the outside speakers, Paul Hawken, set the tone for Herman Miller's aspirations—high aspirations indeed.

Hawken, an entrepreneur and activist who had founded a natural-foods wholesaler and garden-supply company, had just written his third book, *The Ecology of Commerce*. Destined to become a standard business-school text on business and the environment, it turned a lot of business thinking on its head. Hawken wrote, "As generally proposed the question is 'How do we save the environment?' As ridiculous as it may first sound to both sides, the question may be 'How do we save business.'"

At the conference, and in the book, Hawken argued for something more ambitious than an economy based on environmental principles. He sought a "restorative" one, with systems and companies able to heal the harm already done to the environment. "The restorative economy," he wrote, "unites ecology and commerce into one sustainable act of production and distribution that mimics and enhances natural processes."

Hawken introduced the environmental leaders to three principles underpinning his ambition. First, "waste equals food": That is, every industrial (or consumer) waste stream should feed as a raw material into new industrial or consumer products. Second, "nature runs off current solar income": People and business should fuel their lives and work with the power and products of sunlight. Third, "nature depends on diversity": Everyone should recognize that the life-support system on earth depends on restoring the planet's web of plant and animal communities.

Music to the ears of people at Herman Miller was Hawken's belief that the solution was design—or rather redesign of economic and business systems. Business, the only force powerful enough to do the job, had advanced too often by breaking environmental constraints rather than respecting them, he said. The challenge to people at Herman Miller was plain—not to compromise but to find solutions within constraints, the same challenge articulated so well by Charles Eames.

Hawken's constraints, to be sure, posed almost impossibly high hurdles. But like no other activist of the era, Hawken could put a green fire in the belly of corporate environmental leaders. And that's just what he did to the roving leaders at Herman Miller.

These leaders had Hawken in mind as they looked at Bix Norman's initial board-approved plans a few months later. Norman hadn't so quickly taken to the environment cause. Though sensitive to design—he owned two Eames molded-plywood chairs given to him by his father—he was less interested in greening his building than in greening the income statement. That was his job, and that was the source of his success at Phoenix Designs—still the fastest growing unit in Herman Miller's business.

On the other hand, Norman was also successful because he believed in "the art of the possible." He recognized the company's leanings—even if his soaring profits gave him license to push his own agenda. And he took pride in not letting stubbornness get in the way of the best decision. He would later say the greatest compliment he ever received was this: "I've never known anyone who, when presented with a different viewpoint, can change directions so fast."

Norman began to change his mind quickly. A greener operation dovetailed with the desires of his customers, some of whom valued the recycled Action Office parts sold by Phoenix Designs. It also went over well with his many young employees, who engaged in everything from recycling to food-scrap composting. So when the green leaders argued that, for just a little more money, they could build an environmentally friendly building, a building that could even be more efficient over the long term, Norman became an advocate.

NAGELKIRK, DUGAN, AND OTHERS had gotten the green light to move ahead—and up—with Herman Miller's architectural design ambitions. Everyone then shifted to talking about bringing in a leader to advance the cause of sustainability. As architect, VerBurg had already moved the company's architectural standards up a notch on the last building. Herman Miller was now in the market for someone completely different, with strengths and views not yet brought to company.

"Sometimes an incumbent architect is on a losing track with us," says Nagelkirk.

The group already had a name in mind. A number of members of the roving band of leaders—Joe Azzarello, Martin Dugan, Keith Winn, Bob Johnston—had helped launch the U.S. Green Building Council. They had mingled with architects in the American Institute of Architects' Committee on the Environment. They had started a green-building committee as part of the environmental team now led by Paul Murray. Everyone pointed to Bill McDonough, an architect from New York City who had spoken at an environmental team meeting in November 1991.

McDonough was a 42-year-old Yale graduate. He would become professor and dean of the School of Architecture at the University of Virginia. As a student, he had read the Whole Earth Catalog and designed a solar home in Ireland. He later won renown by building a green office for the New York-based environmental group Environmental Defense Fund. He was now a rising star in the green architecture movement. An outspoken environmentalist with a talent for coining new concepts, he often contrasted eco-effectiveness with eco-efficiency. Eco-efficiency, the goal of many companies, meant following economic laws to improve environmental behavior. Eco-effectiveness, his passion, meant following nature's laws to improve economic behavior.

In one of his landmark assignments, in 1992, McDonough worked for the city of Hannover, Germany, to formulate principles for an environmentally sound Expo 2000, the upcoming World's Fair to be held in the city. McDonough and partner Michael Braungart drafted nine guidelines for promoting sustainability, dubbed the Hannover Principles. Among them was the idea that mankind must live off natural energy flows. He introduced the "solar income" notion preached by Hawken.

McDonough had started to develop a signature talent for offering business people new ways to think about the value of the environment. He often did it with financial metaphor: Imagine that the earth is a corporation, he would say, the resources of which are its capital. If the earth is to prosper, people have to husband those reserves, not use them up. What they *can* spend is the income the earth receives every day—income from solar energy. That income includes direct energy, solar heat and light, and indirect energy, namely plants, trees, and organisms that grow and regenerate from solar energy.

An orator-cum-visionary, McDonough could turn environmental antagonists to activists in an hour-long speech. His grasp of design concepts captivated people—he had given lectures on the power of the geometry in the "golden rectangle." He offered elements of green philosophy in analogies that played to his audience: Plant life, he said, was the currency of solar income. Trees were an extension of the sun. Architects could use wood to avoid using earth's non-renewable capital and instead build from its income.

McDonough often mingled with various people from Herman Miller in New York and Michigan. He had several times pushed the idea of Herman Miller buying a forest and marketing chairs made of its own, branded, responsibly grown wood. He had dabbled with the idea of designing furniture himself. He knew dozens of Herman Miller insiders, including CEO Kerm Campbell, who had hired his team in April 1993 to design a home in northern Michigan.

As grand as his reputation was becoming, McDonough was not just waiting for clients to come to him. In fact, in the early 1990s, he was on the lookout for big American companies to adopt his ideas. Herman Miller, a design icon, ranked at the top of his list. So when people at the company called him to talk about a new plant project, he didn't hesitate. "I had designs on Herman Miller. And they had designs on me," he says.

McDonough visited Holland on March 17, 1994, in a trip arranged by Nagelkirk. For all practical purposes, McDonough was coming for an interview. Bix Norman and his team wanted to meet him and size him up. Nagelkirk and the other facilities people wanted to do the same. They were both looking for McDonough to prove himself—to prove Herman Miller had something to learn from him.

When McDonough arrived, Nagelkirk and he drove to the 37-acre site chosen for the new plant, a flat dome of land next to the Midwest Distribution Center. The two men walked to the highest point.

I've got it, McDonough exclaimed.

You've got what? Nagelkirk asked.

McDonough drew a serpentine-shaped building. It followed the contour of the ridge. It will be a "stealth" building, McDonough said. It will blend so well with nature that no one will see it.

Okay, Nagelkirk said, holding his judgment.

McDonough then gushed with a fountain of ideas: We could build the plant with timber—so we use a sustainable material. We could replant timber on the site—so you have replacement material when you have to rebuild. We could restore the native habitat to bring back traditional plants and animals. We could build new wetlands to filter storm water from the roof and parking lots.

Nagelkirk marveled at what he heard. "That was the first day I met Bill" for the project, he says, "and I thought that there was really something here to get people to think. I didn't know another architect on the planet that would suggest building a 300,000-square-foot structure—an operations building—out of wood timber." The notion was impractical.

Impractical yet fresh. That's what Nagelkirk was thinking. And that's what Norman and his project people thought when they walked the site with McDonough later. McDonough again described the native landscaping and serpentine shape. He called for walking paths for employees. He talked up native habitat to suit the site's bluebirds. Facing west, he urged siting the building to reap the heat of Michigan's winter sun, which passed in a low arc across the horizon from November to February.

Bright, analytical, urbane, McDonough played well to a group that favored novel thinking and quick action—even if his measures of success, like drawing songbirds back to an industrial site, struck people as far-out. The entire Phoenix team liked him right away. As McDonough talked, they could see he was clearly excited. And the enthusiasm was infectious.

At day's end, Nagelkirk took McDonough to dinner. They drove ten minutes to the Lake Michigan Coast, past the docks and boat-storage warehouses along Lake Macatawa, into which the water from the new building would flow. At the Ottawa Beach Inn, a local restaurant with restrooms marked "buoys" and "gulls," McDonough started in again: Serpentine shape. Native landscape. Wooden timbers.

McDonough pressed Nagelkirk: Let's just go to Kerm's house and sign this deal.

Nagelkirk held him off. He was imagining wooden timbers. "We're going to have the highest infestation of termites in the world," he thought, "and no insurance underwriter is ever going to allow this." Still, he liked McDonough's rarified perspective. Although the architect might not pass a practicality test, he certainly had ideas students of architecture could learn from.

Within a matter of days, they worked out a deal. The building would require two architects. McDonough came from out of town, arrived with exotic thoughts, pushed for things the company probably couldn't do. VerBurg came from Holland, developed working drawings quickly, and had excellent relations with local trades people and building authorities. So Herman Miller asked McDonough to partner with VerBurg. Herman Miller would then get the best of both: The visionary with the flamboyant ideas and the seasoned, local practitioner who had a track record for turning those ideas into results.

Time was short. Owing to their intent to try so many new things, they chose not to follow the typical process—creating a design and bidding it out to contractors. They had to run a fast-track process, with many experts involved up front. In some ways, they had no choice. They couldn't come up with all the answers on their own. So Nagelkirk arranged for a meeting that convened both the architects and the owners and vice presidents of Michigan-based building, electrical, heating/ventilation/air conditioning, landscape, glass, steel, interior design, and other firms.

Getting everyone together so early posed a test for McDonough. He was expected to prove himself to the group. Could he coordinate people to come up with a concept for a practical, sustainable structure? Could he move the company not just forward but up? Could he really play the role as a teacher? Says Nagelkirk: "We expect our architects to stand in front of our people and explain: What value does this building bring to the community and to ourselves? Why is this going to be better for our employee experience? Why is it going to be healthier?"

ON APRIL 11, 1994, Nagelkirk gathered nearly 30 people at Phoenix Design's plant on Chicago Drive in Holland. Among them: McDonough and associate Chris Hays, Nagelkirk and his boss Dugan, VerBurg and Herman Miller designer Winn. Also on hand were all the key subcontractors—the interior architect, construction contractor, and subcontractors for air and heating, electric, glass, and metals.

McDonough led the group through his concept. What captured people's attention were his architectural metaphors. Bix Norman needed a factory. He needed space to receive materials, make things, ship things, do paperwork. The structure was not a museum or glitzy office mall. It was a Midwest manufacturing facility. But McDonough, borrowing from biologist John Todd, called it a "living machine." A living machine, McDonough argued, would come alive and respond to the people inside and the weather outside.

McDonough embraced the living-machine concept—as opposed to Le Corbusier's "a machine for living in." He went further and talked about conceiving a building like a tree—a building that was alive. He said people should feel connected to the outdoors. The more connected, the more productive, the more inclined to happiness they would be. People should even feel as though they had spent the day working outside. They should feel outdoor air as it enters the plant and sweeps across the plant floor, free from the VOC emissions so typical of buildings full of manufactured materials, paints, and carpets. And they should see the light shift and waver as the sun crossed the sky.

As for the building's exterior, it should blend with nature, not stand out like a monument. He argued for humility. He disliked flat roofs. Better to have curved ones that mimic the rolling landscape. Better yet to cover the roof with turf. Best of all, blend the roof so well with Michigan's farmlands that birds flying over it do not realize it's there, indeed mistake it for their own habitat.

Some of the people who listened to McDonough hold forth struggled to keep doubts at bay. A few rolled their eyeballs and giggled. "Who is this guy?" was the initial reaction. As for the turf roof, no other factory in the United States had such a thing. The skeptics couldn't help but joke: "That's a great idea, but how are we going to mow it."

McDonough, however, benefited from thinking in much the same way as Bix Norman. His unconventional ideas relating to the natural environment fell in line with Norman's unconventional ideas relating to the human environment. Norman wanted a factory that took advantage of light, views, and air flow—that brought a feeling of the outdoors to the inside. He felt they all could benefit from the feeling of casualness, comfort, and fun.

McDonough's vision was in some ways no more fantastical than Norman's. They both wanted to get people thinking beyond building a manufacturing plant. They both wanted the new facility to celebrate the environment—both human and natural. McDonough said: Imagine a building that made people want to come to work, want to spend a day putting screws in a panel, stay excited about getting up on Monday morning.

In his charming way, McDonough brought the team around to a new definition of success in environmentally minded building design and construction. The team signed onto the principles: The structure would blend with a landscape rich in biological life, would be heated and lighted by the sun, would supply abundant fresh air to everyone, would be completed with local materials to cut down on energy consumption, would shed rainwater into wetlands for natural filtration, and would restore the habitat, rather than smothering it.

All the while, McDonough's audience worked with pens and pencils on paper, markers on whiteboards, their hands painting pictures in the air. The work of the group, he felt, should be a "fierce commotion." He posed a lot of hard questions, and he often came up short with the needed answers. Instead, he got the entire group to start questioning and teaching each other. The subcontractors pitched in with knowledge only they could have. Ideas flourished.

One of Norman's project leaders, Del Ensing, says he'd never had so much fun at work in his life. He recalls, "You felt like you were on the cutting edge of everything."

William Caudill, who had been an architect and a board member for Herman Miller years earlier, had said, "Great buildings...stretch human potential through inspiration." The same can probably be said for great architects. Everyone was electrified by McDonough's brazen appeal to stratospheric, sustainable goals.

Nagelkirk recognized that he had tapped into just the teacher the company needed. McDonough couldn't have won the assignment if the roving leaders hadn't thought he could bring people alive. In a sense, however, McDonough had done more than jazzing people. He was providing an answer to an exalted question raised by the De Prees: How would the project—and McDonough—help Herman Miller and its people better realize their potential?

Though the new building wouldn't contain the wood timber design McDonough had floated at the start, his outsized aspirations assured that he would provide an answer to Max De Pree's challenge from years before—to create a structure that would bless the company with an environmental asset. But Nagelkirk saw that their hiring of McDonough went beyond getting a teacher that provided answers. They were getting to see the wonders of design that come from hiring an outsider who inspires passion.

"For every person that comes through that door, he [McDonough] has to ignite a flame, and get them excited," Nagelkirk says. "He was able to do that"—and do it over and over again.

A COUPLE OF WEEKS later, McDonough and Hays sent Nagelkirk and others a draft of the proposed building's "brochure." Similar to a coffee-table art book, the brochure exhibited large drawings and images of the building and its grounds. The most prominent feature was the building's indoor, mall-like avenue covered by an arcing roof of glass. To the side of the pictures ran captions of intriguing text.

Although it was a brochure in that it had a pretty layout, the unbound document amounted to something more: It was a manifesto for the cause of green architecture. The text alluded to the Hannover principles: "Living in sustainable architecture is nothing less than an appeal to accept our place in the world, mediated between human and natural processes." It went on to reinforce themes from the design meeting: The building would allow "people to experience cyclical changes, such as, from day to night, from season to season or simple weather changes...[and] have multiple views and have easy access to operable windows....the goal is to put all users of the building back in touch with their environment."

"The curve of the building," it added, "follows the natural ridge of the site. The building grows out of the earth.... The character of the landscape reflects the rolling hills and vegetation of the Michigan landscape. . . . Not only is the building linked directly to the land-scape, but the landscape infiltrates the building."

In some ways, the brochure amounted to an outline of topics for a course in green architecture, a list of Professor McDonough's classes on sustainability: the grooming of interior and exterior landscapes; capturing sunlight as heat and light; filtering air to clean out particles like pollen; choosing materials that caused no environmental harm in their extraction, manufacture, and dis-posal; assessing material energy use, toxicity, offgassing, recycla-bility; and even buying local instead of faraway materials to save energy.

Understandably, this syllabus was a product of a visionary mind. Was it also the product of a practical mind? Could Herman Miller pay for all this?

A meeting of the board was less than a month away. Nagelkirk, Dugan, and other leaders kept asking the architects: Can we bring this in at $48 per square foot? Although the typical cost for plant space for Herman Miller was $40 per square foot, the board had agreed to add 20 percent to get new architectural features related to sustainability.

Bix Norman took the final draft to the board on May 18. It retained most of the aspirations from the design specs. It also met the cost constraint by cutting a few features, such as dropping shelves to reflect light from outside the building in. It nixed perhaps McDonough's most favored feature as well, the turf roof. Not only did the green roof cost more; it was an unproven design. A single-ply membrane made of recyclable material was substituted.

When Norman pitched it to the board, Kerm Campbell and Max De Pree both backed the plan. McDonough and the Herman Miller team had indeed developed a design for an environmental asset. The board voted it through, and VerBurg and McDonough plunged ahead.

Ever the unsatisfied professor, McDonough kept trying to ignite the flame of even higher aspirations. In July, Chris Hays faxed to Nagelkirk a summary of the pros and cons of a green roof. In the face of Herman Miller's resistance, he argued that it would advance Herman Miller's environmental agenda, save heating and cooling money, help purify stormwater, and ease roof maintenance—along with furthering the "stealth" nature of the building.

Nagelkirk and others wouldn't go for it. Where the professor kept faith with his ideals, the construction managers kept their eyes on the budget. Done with a six-inch depth, the roof would cost another $1.10 per square foot; to a 12-inch depth, $3.15 per square foot. Yearly upkeep would run a few thousand dollars. Nagelkirk finally told McDonough: We're not going to talk about his any longer, although Nagelkirk did agree to a structure strong enough to add a turf roof later. McDonough, who liked to tease Nagelkirk, called him the "one-point man"—the guy watching over every tenth of a cent.

They broke ground in mid-September. The excavations shaped ponds, berms, and swales to mimic West Michigan's environment. Successive stages revealed the features from the brochure—"the street" under specially glazed glass, the 66 skylights that brought daylight to the entire plant floor, the café shared by workers and management. Fourteen months later, in November 1995, Bix Norman and his team moved in.

Having worked within the constraints adopted from the start— for operations, sustainability, and cost—Norman had the building he wanted. Along with the green features, the building did produce the atmosphere of play he sought. He and one of his top managers even hung bicycles outside their offices. They rode them down the street and out the door for lunchtime exercise. To symbolize the unit's speed and teamwork, they hung a bright yellow racing scull over the cafeteria.

As for the green leaders, they basked in the light of praise from the press. Articles lauding Herman Miller for moving ahead of the pack appeared in *Fortune* and *Business Week, Architectural Record* and *Environmental Design and Construction.* If the atmosphere of the build-ing wasn't enough, the savings proved the advantages of going green: Energy costs fell $35,000 a year compared to the old facility. Natural gas costs dropped 7 percent; electrical, 18 percent; and water and sewer, 65 percent.

Not everything went well, of course. In the summer, the building overheated, and the sun cast too much glare across the work floor. The ozone-friendly chiller didn't have enough cooling power and its refrigerant and logic controls had to be replaced. And then the cost went over the original target budget, albeit with the board's blessing: The all-in tally came in at $52 per square foot.

But as Norman had hoped, higher productivity and happy workers helped the Phoenix Design unit's sales (now renamed Miller SQA) continue their breakneck growth. Social scientist Judith Heerwagen compared the old and new facility. Her study showed that productivity in the nine months after the move didn't dip, as it usually does after a corporate move; instead, it rose slightly (0.22 percent). She also found that roughly a third of workers *felt* their performance was better, although the number of workers who said that they looked forward to working in the building fell somewhat for the second and third shifts. Meanwhile, the rate of on-time deliveries edged up to 99.53 percent and quality performance to 99.23 percent.

In the end, Bix Norman, who in 1993 had sought to win a game of the art of the possible, won much more. He brought to his unit a reputation for the art of green leadership. Ed Nagelkirk, Martin Dugan, Keith Winn, and the rest of the green leaders did much the same. They had indeed moved the company up a level, creating an environmental asset at a reasonable cost.

"While it is almost impossible to make an environmentally perfect building, this facility has changed the way buildings will be constructed at Herman Miller," said Nagelkirk at the time, "What we did here was set a new standard." A standard of green design, to be sure, but also a standard for hiring designers who could stir a passion for advancing the state of the art.

The building's ability to advance that art reached beyond the confines of the company. Over 700 firms a year sent delegations to tour the facility, eventually renamed the GreenHouse. CEO Mike Volkema, Kerm Campbell's successor, saw a fresh opportunity: Using the building to convince these visitors of the wisdom of green practices. Volkema wanted to show even hard-nosed CFOs that companies could spend—and should—so long as green efforts across the company, taken as a whole, yielded a good return.

Volkema also stimulated a debate on the board about more green spending on buildings. He guided the members of the board to what many observers considered a landmark decision: In 1998, they concluded to make all Herman Miller buildings meet at least the U.S. Green Building Council's second-highest level of certification: silver.

CHAPTER 5

Thirty Questions

Along the eastern shore of Lake Michigan runs a string of state parks and miles of fine-grained freshwater beach. There is Holland State Park and its creamy plain of sand. There is Saugatuck Dunes State Park and its mountainous 200-foot-high dunes plunging to the shore. There is Grand Haven State Park with its sentinel red lighthouse and pier. These natural wonders draw people from Zeeland, Holland, and Spring Lake, the hometowns of Herman Miller.

One of the visitors to the beaches in the early 1990s was Bill Dowell, Herman Miller's computer modeler, the man who, when computers barely had the power, modeled the way people sit, creating a program called Hermanoid. On the beach, Dowell would seat himself in the shell of a plastic Equa, an ergonomic office chair Herman Miller brought to market in 1984. In the shell, without cushion, pedestal, or base, Dowell could rock easily back in the sand.

What was on Dowell's mind in the early 1990s was news coming from Germany, where legislators were proposing that companies take back their worn-out products. Though livid over the new rules, German businesspeople had started to prepare. Volkswagen had figured out how to design its Golf—the European version of the Rabbit—so it could strip it down in just 20 minutes for recycling.

The news from Bonn was an awakening to Dowell. Herman Miller had already started to sharply cut waste from its plants, guided by Paul Murray's team of roving environmental leaders. But what about the waste from customers who would eventually dispose of worn-out Herman Miller products? Dowell wondered about the chair he was sitting in. What would happen to it at the end of its life? Not everyone would be willing to turn their old Equa into a beach chair. Was its destination the landfill? Was the landfill the destination of all that Herman Miller made?

Dowell, nearly 40 and a self-described "old hippy," joined Murray's group early on. Before starting at Herman Miller in 1983, he wrote a controversial editorial in a company newsletter: He argued to fellow employees at Clark Equipment for a no-growth economy. To a corporation full of members of the United Auto Workers—mostly men who drove trucks—he was arguing a radical green idea. The United States is blessed with both a powerful economic system and abundant natural resources, he said. The country needs to take care of both.

Tall, modest, prone to understatement, Dowell didn't actually have any responsibility for environmental work at Herman Miller. But he, like other roving leaders, had passion for the environment. His time spent contemplating take-back of the Equa shell brought his biggest concern into focus. Herman Miller had sold the chairs for most of a decade. During manufacture, workers finished the shells with paint. One of the environmental problems: The paint made them—tens of thousands of them, sold all over the world—unrecyclable.

Dowell wondered what Herman Miller would do if it had to take the Equa shells back. In turn, he wondered what the role of people who created new products should be in making take-back easier: What should the designers be doing? What should the engineers be doing? What should *he* be doing?

Dowell, the only person from product research, design, or development on the green team, felt Herman Miller wasn't doing enough. The other environmental leaders, in the vanguard of new thinking in U.S. companies, agreed. Paul Murray and Joe Azzarello felt responsibility for environmental impact shouldn't start and end at the plant gate. It should reach upstream to people who sold raw materials to Herman Miller and downstream to people who bought products.

In the early 1990s, employees in many companies felt that their prerogatives for green action lay within the company. But at Herman Miller, thinking of the company as just an isolated segment in a global chain of economic transactions ended with the rosewood decision. People felt they should take responsibility for products from "cradle to grave." In 1992, Murray sent a letter "upstream" to all Herman Miller suppliers: Stop using the trichloroethylene in your plant processes, he said. Herman Miller doesn't want to do business with people using the solvent.

When it came to product developers, however, the cradle-to-grave thinking was an unknown concept. Few engineers in U.S. companies at the time knew much about the greening of product design. Even in firms with environmental programs, the designers worked outside the sphere of green action. Researchers at MIT had found in 1992 that half of all surveyed companies engaged in environmental life-cycle work, but almost no product developers were involved.

As Dowell watched other people at Herman Miller make their marks in protecting the environment, he became frustrated that he wasn't making any mark at all. "I would go to these meetings and [have] feelings of inadequacy because I wasn't contributing," he says.

Murray, Jim Gillespie, and Willie Beattie would tell stories at these meetings of gunning for a landfill goal of zero. But when it came to efforts in research, design, or development, Dowell couldn't tell stories about any green action at all. "I didn't really know what to do about it," he says.

In 1972, Hugh De Pree and Action Office designer Bob Propst had met away from the office to define Herman Miller's distinguishing characteristics. "A few organizations (i.e. Herman Miller) have a different concept of problem solving," they wrote in their notes. "It is based first on the idea that society is moving and aspiring to new goals and that solutions should focus on new positions." That concept still distinguished Herman Miller 20 years later, and Dowell was wondering by what means the designers could be moved to those new positions.

DOWELL STAYED ON THE lookout for a chance to get involved. When he was named to work for two renowned chair designers, Bill Stumpf and Don Chadwick, he wondered if he had found his chance. The two men, Stumpf from Minneapolis and Chadwick from Santa Monica, had started work on a new chair project, code named Echo. The duo had designed the Equa chair ten years earlier, and although Equa was a design milestone and sold well, they had bigger ambitions for their new project.

Dowell joined the team as the ergonomist. He was charged with researching posture support, pressure distribution on the seat and back, kinematics (movement) of the seat with the sitter, anthropometrics (sizing), and the heating/cooling properties of the seat. As the designers came up with new approaches, he gave them the experimental data to validate their aims and refine successive prototypes. In this case, they were aiming to create a chair that gave people of all body types support in all work postures.

Dowell was the expert on "human factors." The success of the chair depended on the minutiae of his experiments. As part of his work, he made a series of pressure-point maps, or "butt prints," of people of various sizes and weights. He also measured the height and weight of scores of people to create a bell curve of people's size distribution. He even put sensors on people's buttocks and backs to record changes in skin temperature over time.

In the temperature experiment, he showed that a mesh system proposed for the Echo seat and back could offer unrivaled skin comfort. For people who spent long hours at a desk, the system would even have health benefits. The mesh gave an airy skin sensation akin to that from the cane seats Stumpf recalled from street cars in St. Louis. Dowell's experiments showed that, on the mesh suspension, people's buttock temperatures over time remained steady. On the same seat made with foam and fabric, temperatures spiked 12 degrees Fahrenheit in 20 minutes.

These experiments led Dowell to the green opening he was looking for. Serendipitously, he ran across an article in the September 1992 issue of the *Economist* magazine. Amory Lovins, founder of a "think-and-do" tank for developing efficient and green technologies, was touting mesh seats on desk chairs to cut air-conditioning bills. According to the *Economist*: "...Rocky Mountain Institute claims that, if everybody started using chairs that were ventilated rather than upholstered, investment per American in air-conditioning and electricity-generating equipment could be cut by as much as $300."

Dowell was at first concerned to see that Lovins was working on the same technology as the Echo team. "It was like he had seen what was going on behind our closed doors," says Dowell, "and I said to myself, 'I have to go talk to this guy to find out if he had actually seen this, or if these were just his ideas.'"

Dowell phoned Lovins.

No, Lovins replied, I don't know anything about Herman Miller's work.

The polymath scientist, a dropout from Harvard and Oxford (where he became a don), told the story of how he came to investigate ventilated seating. He had just written a six-volume set of books on how to save electricity. A self-made expert in an astonishing range of technologies, Lovins knew every detail of how to save electricity on lighting, appliances, office equipment, water heating, space cooling, air handling, drive systems, fans, and pumps. The mesh seat was just one of his thousands of energy-saving ideas.

A man with a bookish demeanor and a shoe-brush mustache, Lovins had been trying to solve a bigger mystery as well. Why, he wondered, had U.S. companies spent, by his calculations, $1 trillion on unneeded air-conditioning equipment and power supplies to run it? Why had they not taken advantage of the thousands of existing technologies to scale down or eliminate cooling (and heating) capacity?

A big believer in the efficiency of the market economy, Lovins further wondered: How had the market misallocated so much capital?

The answer to that mystery gradually became clear: The people who chose and installed the equipment were not the ones who paid for running it. A onetime pianist and composer, Lovins could not wave a baton and solve that market failing. In fact, he and others would work on the problem for years with only modest progress. But he could detail the technology to make change happen. One of his simple investigations involved seat cooling.

Using indices for predicting thermal comfort—namely, a construct called Fanger's Comfort Equation—Lovins showed how a mesh chair could reduce costs by lowering air-conditioning demand. In a research report he sent to Dowell, he showed how companies could save 10 to 20 percent in air-conditioning capital costs just by letting people wear casual clothes in the office instead of suits. Simply by letting men dispense with neckties, companies could save $43 in capital per head. In other words, American firms could pocket big savings in two ways: buying smaller air-conditioning systems and using less electricity to achieve the same comfort level.

Dowell was enthralled—and he began to see how green thinking could dovetail with ergonomic thinking. Not only was the new Echo mesh suspension more comfortable, it also had the bonus of helping the environment and making a good business case. And that gave him an opening to learn much more from one of the leading environmental scientists of the time. Though Lovins was never signed on as a consultant, his normal procedure, he became an advisor to Dowell and the Echo team. He was the expert who, even if not originating the team's green ideas, provided the authority to confirm that they were on the right track.

ONE ISSUE DOWELL DISCUSSED with Lovins was plastics. Since early 1992, Dowell had urged the Echo team to rethink the use of hard-to-recycle thermoset plastics. Thermosets can't be simply remelted and reused. The Equa chair was made of polyester (PET), the material used for soda bottles, mixed with 30 percent glass fiber. The glass made the polyester much stronger, but no good channel then existed for recycling the composite (and there was none at all if it was painted).

Dowell thought that designers and engineers would be better off choosing materials based on ease of recyclability. He had a basic guideline for this in his head: aluminum (great), steel (good), biodegradables (good), thermoplastic (okay), thermoset plastic (bad). As it turned out, designer Stumpf favored aluminum parts, so the team could buy recycled aluminum for making most of the Echo chair's components, and customers could recycle all the aluminum in a worn-out product. Dowell thus urged the team to replace thermoset plastic parts with aluminum wherever possible.

Lovins took a different view. To save massive amounts of energy in transportation, he had invented the idea of hypercars in 1991, and he was working tirelessly to sell the concept to automakers. Hypercars' success hinged on being made of strong, lightweight composites—the only way to make ultralight, superefficient, ultralow-drag cars with tremendous mileage. At that time, and until a decade later, the preferred resins were thermosets. The big question was, if auto engineers specified the use of thermosets, would the auto companies later have a process for recycling them?

Although there was no ready recycling channel for the plastics in 1992, Lovins had worked out how the car companies could recycle thermosets via long-proven, low-temperature catalytic processes called pyrolysis and solvolysis (typically *methanolysis*). A recycling market would surely develop in the future, he believed. Once the car giants started recycling millions of thermoset-laden cars, they would create an enormous recycling channel on which Herman Miller could piggyback. An unrecyclable material would then become readily recyclable.

Lovins gave Dowell and the Echo team a new way of looking at their options. The advantage of fiber-reinforced plastics was that they allowed companies to pursue a relatively new concept called "dematerialization." Lovins argued this way: Make your furniture smaller, lighter, able to do much more with much less. Cut the raw materials. Cut the energy input. As for aluminum, it is not always preferable: You can recycle it easily today, but aluminum recycling consumes many times more electricity than recycling other materials.

Lovins didn't know which car company would pick up his hyper-car brainstorm. But he was confident one would. He could sound idealistic, but in fact, he simply had faith in the steady advance of technology. Unlike most environmentalists, he relentlessly argued for pragmatism. He showed how a thousand small steps—with existing technology—could lead to giant leaps for the economy. He had done the calculations to show he was right: One trillion dollars of wasted air-conditioning investment!

The Echo team embraced Lovins's message. They could design a product that won on all counts: comfort, greenness, and profitability. That, of course, was the message of other visionaries, like Paul Hawken and Bill McDonough. But Lovins had all the particulars worked out. He could describe what to do with an indisputable grasp of technological detail.

TO DOWELL FELL THE task of transferring Lovins's message and technological thinking to the designers and engineers on the Echo team. He took a common-sense approach. As the team built a list of components, he broke out the materials by weight and volume. He then graded each as "earth-friendly," "neutral," or "negative." If a plastic was hard or impossible to recycle, he asked whether aluminum could be substituted. Despite Lovins's plan for the future, the team still viewed aluminum as greener than plastic.

The group took a fresh look at the advantages of durability, long a tenet of honest design from the De Pree years. They asked: What if we can delay the Echo's entry into the waste stream? What if customers could replace parts without dumping the whole chair? What if the chair lasted so long the customer never needed to buy another? If the chair could last a lifetime, that alone would create a whopping environmental benefit.

In its kickoff, the team didn't take Lovins's math-intensive approach. It focused on three green-design mantras: recycled content, recyclability, and ease of disassembly. Designers, engineers, and the purchasing agents who bought from suppliers would hear from Dowell again and again: Don't specify virgin material. Don't specify hard-to-recycle materials. Don't bond dissimilar materials because they will be hard to take apart and instead end up in a landfill.

AFTER FOUR YEARS IN development, the Echo team brought its chair to market. The brand name chosen was Aeron. Introduced in Europe in October 1994, and in the United States in June 1995, the Aeron had 50 parts. Stumpf did insist on aluminum to take advantage of both its recycled content and recyclability—even though using aluminum cost perhaps $10 more per chair. By weight, the chair was composed of 35 percent aluminum, 27 percent plastic, and 24 percent steel. Over two-thirds came from recycled plastic, aluminum, steel, and foam. For its time, the chair was an environmental breakthrough.

Ironically, in 1995, most customers didn't pay attention to the Aeron's environmental pluses. Facility managers, the people at companies who bought chairs by the hundreds or thousands, just weren't calling for green products. Marketers at Herman Miller actually debated how to soft-pedal the environmental story, not highlight it. One marketer joked, "I'm not sure people would pay that much for recycled beer cans."

The group also fretted over the risk of selling a dematerialized product. It was lighter, more transparent. How do you tell customers they're paying more for what looks like less? So marketers told the environmental story but gave it a light touch. Leaving aside the beer can joke, they instead focused on how the chair frame recycled more than 20 two-liter soda bottles.

The chair was also a breakthrough in furniture design—which at first posed a problem. The chair had a radical look. It was a see-through skeleton with a disembodied tilt mechanism. And as with Herman Miller's design breakthroughs of the past, the Aeron didn't sell explosively at the start. Echoing the early reaction to both Action Office and the company's original ergonomic chair, the Ergon, some Herman Miller board members panned the Aeron. One, as the Aeron team requested money for tooling, was quoted as saying, "I don't know who is going to sit in that chair, but none of the people in my business would ever sit in one."

The chair's team had braced themselves for ridicule. Product manager Robert Hieftje told a story about running into a salesman months earlier who had admitted, when the Aeron was still top secret, to getting a glimpse of the "stealth chair," as salespeople called it. "But don't worry," he had told Hieftje, "it was just a shell."

"I didn't have the nerve to tell him," says Hieftje, "that was the whole chair."

But the chair had plenty going for it: It came in three sizes, to fit different body types. It tilted backward *and* forward to move with the body in all kinds of work positions and tasks. It featured a comfy, air-cooled suspension, sculpted to support good posture and fit a bell curve of backsides. On top of all that were the green-design features, which trend watchers at Herman Miller were convinced would soon rise in appeal.

As for the recyclability of the plastics, most of them appeared in the chair back, frame, and mesh seat, and each was made of the kind of plastic Lovins was advocating, namely, glass-filled polyester. Though it was not easy to recycle, as were the pure soda-bottle polyester plastics, the seat would be recyclable in volume when channels for recycling thermoset plastics matured. In the meantime, the plastic ranked higher than other materials because its strength and light weight enabled the unprecedented dematerialization.

The plastic in the frame represented a breakthrough of another kind. Recognizing that the Aeron might be slow to win a market, Herman Miller had in early 1994 put a team of 20 people on a project to redevelop the ten-year-old Equa. The goal: to produce it more cheaply and make the design more ergonomic—with an improved tilt mechanism, adjustable arms and seat, a posture fit—and of course, greener. Ted Venti, one of the roving leaders of the environmental team, was named manager of the project.

Venti hit the obvious roadblock: the unrecyclable plastic shell of the Equa. Long made of plastic from DuPont, the shell had to be painted in each of the colors Herman Miller wanted to offer consumers. Venti wanted to dispense with the paint and ask the supplier to instead pigment the plastic. But owing to impurities in the plastic called *ligomers*, pigmenting would weaken its structure.

AlliedSignal, another chemical company, stepped in to solve the ligomer problem in its competing plastic. It reformulated its glass-filled resin to get rid of the ligomers. Herman Miller's part supplier could then pigment the plastic during blending, just before injection molding the part. The seats no longer needed paint and could be recycled. They also cost roughly $10 less to make, and Herman Miller could offer them in a range of colors.

The Aeron team won in this process. Herman Miller used the new AlliedSignal 30-percent glass-filled Petra-brand resin on both the Equa and the Aeron. The Aeron was also thus launched in a variety of colors, red, blue, black, green, gray. A chair that might have been largely unrecyclable would now be mostly (60.5 percent) recyclable.

All told, the advances in green design gave a heady feeling to Dowell and the company's roving environmental leaders. As for Dowell, he had spearheaded the integration of green thinking into the design and development of the company's leading new product. He had gotten his team to look both upstream and downstream in a way they never had before. And now everyone else was looking to Dowell to guide the green-design efforts farther.

DOWELL HAD NOT REACHED everyone in research, design, and development, of course. To do so, he took a new role at the end of 1993, leading the Earth Friendly Design Task Force. The task force, about a dozen people, sought to raise awareness of green design, guide project teams in choosing green materials, and cajole designers and engineers into weighing environmental impacts of all Herman Miller products.

Defining what "earth friendly" meant stymied the task force at first. Just how far up- and downstream should they look? How many issues should they embrace? What were the boundaries? As for looking upstream, scores of questions arose. What were the impacts of the processes for extracting raw materials? For aluminum, did Herman Miller go upstream to bauxite mines? And what about the process for converting aluminum ore to usable form—electrolysis? As for other materials, which ones would require the least energy to make? Which were plentiful and which scarce?

Which materials, in other words, would they rate as the "best"? And how would they do so?

The task force got a boost from influences outside the company. At Herman Miller's second annual environmental conference, architect Bill McDonough spoke about the importance of green design. He gave an example to illustrate the ideal, describing how to "grow" plastic with "solar income." The plastic could be made out of plant-derived starch and sugar. It could then be coated with a glass film, and the coated material could be used to make containers that would replace steel cans. The cans, in turn, could be burned as a renewable fuel, and the ash and silica could be safely used in concrete.

The task force got a boost from politicians, as well. President Bill Clinton signed an executive order requiring government agencies to buy "environmentally preferable" products. He also created the Council on Sustainable Development, which included powerful personalities like Georgia Pacific CEO Pete Correll and Ron Brown, Secretary of Commerce. In 1995, the council took a cue from legislators in Europe and started to look into holding electronic-goods makers responsible for their products' lifetime environmental impact. Businesspeople across the country began to wonder if, and when, take-back would come to their industry.

As the world nudged corporations toward green design, the environmental leaders at Herman Miller threw even more support behind Dowell. In a May 1995 meeting in which they brainstormed a slate of upcoming initiatives, they ranked environmentally friendly products, design for disassembly, and product take-back high on the list. When the team voted on the top three initiatives for the next three years, it put "design and deliver environmentally friendly products" as number one.

Dowell and his task force responded by working to get product developers to adopt new green-design tools. The first was life-cycle analysis, or LCA, a new technique, still in primitive stages, that could inventory the impacts of a product from cradle to grave. An LCA for the Aeron, for instance, would include an assessment of the impacts of aluminum from the bauxite deposit to mill to chair-assembly plant to customer to recycling center.

The green team had been looking at LCA for some time, triggered by the tropical wood controversy. Tom Ankney, who had done the State of Washington offgassing study, had been the first to start asking questions. If our use of rosewood veneers could unravel nature's web in a rain forest, he wondered, what else might Herman Miller's materials choices do? What happens at the mine, in the forest, at the oil rig?

Ankney piloted a LCA for the Aeron chair, which fortuitously confirmed the wisdom of many choices the team made. The value of LCAs looked so promising that Murray's environmental team set a goal for doing LCAs of all new products by the end of 1998. The LCA seemed to be the tool of choice.

But the team struggled to progress. LCAs raised endless imponderables: What boundaries do we use? What assumptions? What method—of several competing ones—do we adopt? As it turned out, just about anyone could pick holes in someone else's LCA by questioning umpteen elements of the analysis. The cost of LCAs raised another question, as did the months of work demanded. At the time, a rule of thumb in industry held that a single LCA could run $100,000.

Dowell had more luck with a second green-design tool. As Herman Miller engineers received training in using the quality tools of the era, they embraced a matrix for sorting out competing demands. On the left side of the matrix, engineers listed product features required by customers. Across the top, they listed company capabilities needed to deliver the features. In a capstone grid cross-linking the two, they marked conflicts—where engineers had to exercise the most creativity to find workable solutions. The tool was called the "house of quality," owing to its roof-like cap.

The engineers embraced this quality tool. And with its help, Dowell made sure that, not only his main responsibility—ergonomic features—figured into it, but that green design did as well. The house then produced a record of goals, priorities, decision making, and questions to answer. With green issues on the matrix, Dowell could keep green design alive in product-development discussions.

DOWELL AND THE TASK force had high hopes that the momentum from Aeron would inject a zeal for green design into product-development everywhere in the company. But that was not to be. The Aeron chair was a green-design success largely because it was a high-end product, listing for $1,200, and its price could cover the costs and time needed for extra green development work. The team also had over four years to get the chair out the door.

The Aeron did not fuel broad interest in green design within Herman Miller. Dowell and the task force worked for a couple of years to educate designers and engineers about green design practices. But they ran into the reality of product development work: Time pressures often drive out any unessential work. After the Aeron was finished, for example, developers turned to the rest of the chair line. But executives had no intention of spending the same time and effort on the three other chairs in the works, the Equa ("Equa 2"), Ergon 3, and Ambi (a new and more modestly priced seat). The required turnaround was just 18 months.

"When you we're working on a premium product like Aeron, doing it the right way, even if it takes a little more time or costs a little more, is okay," Dowell says. "But when you were working on a more economical product, both time and money were more important. And I met resistance on these other products."

Plenty of attention was given to Equa's new plastic. But other parts and materials got shorter shrift. In the end, none of the three chairs, launched with the Aeron in 1995, was marketed on its green features. Green engineering wasn't even mentioned. Nor did products other than chairs get a thorough greening.

Adding to time pressure, technology could pose a barrier. One of the toughest issues was bonding. No engineer wanted to have his or her boss come back and say, "This part needs reengineering because it breaks all the time." So if engineers had to fasten and adhere two parts together, and the most reliable bonding technology was solvent-based glue, they specified the glue. Durability, an age-old Herman Miller point of pride, won hands down.

Members of the design task force would go to engineers and argue for fasteners that made products easy to take apart, and thus easy to pop into the industrial waste-recycling stream. But many engineers thought Dowell was living in too much of an ivory tower. "People were always saying, 'We can't do this, we can't do that.'" recalls Pat Laurie, a member of Dowell's task force. " 'We've been making furniture for 100 years,' they'd say, 'and we just can't do it that way.' "

Progress on green design didn't halt, of course. New leaders of the green agenda surfaced all the time. One of them on Dowell's task force was Catherine Bragdon. A fabric designer, Bragdon knew that when it came to upholstery fabric, the company threw away about 30 percent of the material it bought. Using traditional cut-and-sew methods, workers would buy cloth in 54-inch-wide rolls, place a pattern on the cloth, cut out the needed piece, and toss the excess. Bragdon introduced three-dimensional knitting for the Aeron; now new machines knit armrest covers to fit, ending waste altogether.

Still, the design task force struggled to think broadly about environmental stewardship. "There was a point where I became disillusioned with whether we were making headway," says Dowell. "We'd ask ourselves the tough questions...but we were pretty easy on ourselves in how we answered them."

Dowell had always imagined himself at the end of his career doing product disassembly for a recycler. "I'm going to be taking these things apart," he says, "and I want to make sure I don't have to pry them apart." And yet, here he was talking to people who were designing parts that he *would* have to pry apart—in a company that had declared sustainability as its goal.

IN THE FACE OF this resistance, Dowell and his task force set out to create another tool: a simple set of guidelines for earth-friendly design. If designers and engineers were to think green from the birth of a product to its disposal, what would they take into account? If purchasing people were to buy materials that had low impacts from birth to disposal, what would they think about?

Dowell's task force started by enumerating venerable Herman Miller design principles. A product had to serve a need, for example; otherwise it was waste by design and environmentally unfriendly. To the age-old principles, they added thoughts from the three mantras: high recycled content, easy recyclability, and design for disassembly. They then added specifics that applied to materials they often worked with, for example, urging the use of polypropylene plastic and water-based finishes.

Dowell took the growing list to the new-product engineers. He wanted their input, and he got plenty of it. One debate concerned polyvinylchloride, or PVC. Engineers had specified PVC for years. It was cheap, easy to use, and durable. Studies had started to show that PVC disposal was dangerous, however: Burning PVC produced cancer-causing dioxins. And the task force leaned toward getting rid of it. But that comment always prompted an argument by the engineers: It's in our old products. Why does it matter in our new ones?

Another debate arose over recycled steel. The guidelines urged the engineers to specify steel with at least 28 percent recycled content, the average in recycled metal. Dowell and the task force wanted to see recycled steel become much more common. But the engineers hesitated to specify it because they worried it might deliver inferior performance. They wouldn't consider any material that might break—in spite of industry assurances that the recycled steel was almost as good as the virgin stuff.

IN MARCH 1996, DOWELL gave engineers a draft of the new set of guidelines. He urged them to pass it along to fellow engineers, designers, and the purchasing people. The document, though just three pages long, was a milestone. For the first time, the company had a green guide for everyone who specified how to make Herman Miller products.

The guidelines did not take the form of strictures. In some ways, they amounted to a tip sheet, thoughts from people who had considered in depth how Herman Miller products could harm the earth from cradle to grave. On the other hand, they offered a simple set of questions—30 of them—that collectively defined environmental responsibility as a constraint in honest design.

Some items were modest, but others obligated engineers and purchasing people to ask some surprisingly invasive questions of their suppliers, in particular, about earth-friendly manufacturing processes: Do you emit VOCs in making Herman Miller parts? Do you have a gray-water system that recovers nonsewage waste? Do you reduce worker exposure to formaldehyde?

When he issued the guidelines, Dowell said he knew they would not be easy to follow. He admitted that even he had trouble following them in simply getting them printed. He wanted to print them on paper with 50 percent recycled content. But, he wrote: "Similar to product specification...it took a little time to find some, and it felt like I was making someone do extra work to get it. It was kind of a pain. I know that some of the suggestions that the 'Design

Guidelines' make will be kind of a pain also. Is it worth the effort? I'm convinced that it is."

Up against the daily grind of meeting budgets, delivering against milestones, and finding alternatives to trusted engineering habits from the past, developers struggled with the guidelines. One tug-of-war that persisted was over PVC. Dowell and the green leaders did not have the authority to issue an edict to prohibit it. They tried to persuade the engineers that the company shouldn't be using it, but in the end they only asked in the guidelines that engineers at least specify recycled PVC, and make sure that it remained recyclable by keeping it free of labels and additives like fiberglass.

Another persistent point of contention was bonding. Glue still often won out as the best technology for holding things together. At the time, Dowell pointed to the company's biggest product, the Action Office system. The scrim on the panels—the foil and fiberglass cover needed for sound-deadening and fireproofing—was glued together. It couldn't be recycled.

After five years of working on earth-friendly design, Dowell began to doubt if it would ever become a permanent fixture at the company. Did it matter beyond a few new marquee products? Would they ever make progress on the much larger set of traditional furniture? Were designers, engineers, and purchasing people really looking beyond their doors, taking the effect of Herman Miller's product in the larger world into account?

Dowell's pessimism was not shared by many people. Where he saw a glass as half empty, others saw it as half full. Paul Murray, for one, would call Dowell's guidelines a signal achievement. The thirty questions formed the foundation for what the company would start calling "Design for the Environment," or DfE. Making DfE a part of the product-development culture would take years. But environmental sensibilities *were* becoming part of a new set of design constraints. They reflected the company's long-held view of the environment as an asset.

DOWELL REMAINED UNCONVINCED OF the progress. The dialogue was advancing in fits and starts. After so many years of pushing the green-design rock uphill, he began to ease up his efforts. He didn't want to abandon his campaign, but he didn't want to burn out, either—and he felt he *was* burning out.

Then a couple of things surprised him. First, his boss, Don Goeman, approached him in the late 1990s for environmental advice. Having all along paid attention to the green-design work, he wanted Dowell to evaluate the greenness of a new panel concept called Resolve. Dowell was a seating expert, and he had not paid much attention to systems products. But he welcomed the request.

Once he took a look at Resolve, Dowell felt that more progress had been made than he had realized. Designer Ayse Birsel had departed from traditional frame construction of systems like Action Office. She had drawn up instead a post-and-beam concept, stretching fabric between steel pillars. The system had no aluminum and fiberglass scrim, and no wood panels. Following the aspirations of modern design, Birsel had cut bulk and weightiness. She added openness and transparency. She had dematerialized the panel system.

Dowell did a comparative study of Resolve, Action Office, and another system called Ethospace. Resolve won on all counts: It used recycled steel, required no rugged, yet hard-to-recycle, thermoset plastic pieces, reduced weight, and was recyclable at more than twice the rate (60 percent) of Action Office. Resolve took Herman Miller miles down the design-for-the-environment road.

In a second development, CEO Mike Volkema pressed his campaign to turn Herman Miller into a restorative company. This convinced Dowell that the company really had changed. In an open letter, Volkema wrote, "Our world is a gift shared by all God's creation. We must never forget that we are not possessors of the environment but only a part of it. . . . Our earth is too precious and fragile for us to be anything but true stewards of it." Volkema, in league with Murray, committed publicly to "design for the environment"—announcing the company's goals in print and on its new website.

Through it all, Dowell wondered: Was the Aeron his "peak" along the journey to green design? Was the fitful lead-footed uptake of earth-friendly ideas his "trough"? Was the long slog to persuade engineers his slope of enlightenment? And was all this now leading to a more realistic and pragmatic plateau of green-design productivity?

Hindsight would show that it was. Behind the scenes, Volkema in 1998 was listening to appeals by architect Bill McDonough to take green design much farther. Product-development chief Goeman and research chief Gary Miller had started to consider hiring new green-design people. The leaders in Murray's group pressed ahead, evaluating several life-cycle design methods that had matured since those used in the early 1990s. They hired a scientist to use one system to evaluate 22 different furniture products.

Then, too, the green leaders actually laid out the program Dowell had been thinking about from the start: product take-back. In a June meeting, they declared their intention to "close the loop of the entire product line." If they succeeded, they would finally move toward full, lifetime responsibility for Herman Miller products.

The group even floated a plan for kicking off the program. The company would start by taking back product made as many as 20 years before, gradually raising the take-back percentage. In 1999, it would take back 2 percent of product produced as far back as 1979. By 2003, it would take back 25 percent from as far back as 1983. "This de-manufacturing process," said the minutes from the meeting, "would be a first for our industry."

The take-back program never went beyond the brainstorming stage. That stemmed in part from Dowell and others realizing the age of professionalizing design for the environment was dawning. He and his task force were not the experts who would lead the next phase. The age of green design driven by evangelism was ending. The thinking and even the tools were passing them by. New faces would soon appear among the environmental leaders. And the new people would move the plateau of green performance higher.

Dowell held out hope that take-back would one day become a part of it. In reality, only a vote by lawmakers in Bonn or Paris or Washington could make that happen. The entire industry would have to get in on the act, driven by a change in economic and marketplace rules. But when it did happen, Dowell would have his fingerprints on the thinking and concepts that started it all. And maybe at that point—before Dowell quit using the beaches on the shores of Lake Michigan—he would see people returning the shells of their Equa chairs to Herman Miller.

CHAPTER 6

Dollar Sense

The tenure at Herman Miller of Kermit Campbell ended abruptly on July 11, 1995. An outsider brought in after the mild 1992 recession, Campbell served as chief executive for three years. In his third year, he let people do many creative things—too many things, as it turned out. Spending zoomed ahead faster than sales. Capital outlays for new equipment and buildings jumped 50 percent.

The result? Although Herman Miller's sales soared to $1.1 billion, its debt doubled, and profit nosedived 89 percent.

Brian Walker, 33, a certified public accountant and acting chief financial officer, likened the management of spending to a game of pick-up football. A lot of smart people went to the quarterback with an idea for catching a pass. The quarterback said, Great idea, go with it! Soon everyone was out for a pass, and nobody was on the line.

The result? The play ended badly, and the quarterback got sacked.

To be sure, Campbell aimed for future profits. But the number of projects and the money they cost—from the launch of all those new chairs to the construction of the new Phoenix Designs building to

the complex palette of colors for the Aeron chair—took the financial
wind out of the company.

Ironically, it was just the year before that Herman Miller had
declared its goal to be sustainable development. In a meeting at the
time, Paul Murray and other environmental leaders joked about the
definition of "sustainable." One of the people at the meeting said it
was pretty simple: A sustainable company is a profitable one.

Now that was no joke.

Walker, an alumnus of Michigan State University who had cut
his financial teeth at the former "Big Five" accounting firm Arthur
Andersen, saw that the element escaping the sustainability equation
in 1995 was indeed an adequate focus on profitability. D.J. De Pree
may have considered profit the lifeblood of a business—without it a
company could not contribute to the world's wealth and well-being.
But at Herman Miller, the results didn't provide the financial well-
being the company needed to thrive.

Herman Miller's record over the long term was in question. In
mid-1995, the stock peaked at $24.50 a share, not a dollar higher
than it had been ten years before, even though the company was
56 percent larger. Other than a payout of 1-percent dividends,
the company gave investors in the stock just about no financial
return.

By 1995, every full-time employee who had worked for at least
a year, from the janitors in the plants to the CEO, had become a
stockholder. The company referred to its employees as "employee-
owners." The employee-owners, like every other shareholder, saw
their company earn just 4 cents a share in 1995—compared to
40 cents the year before. Beset by such a bleak showing, CEO Mike
Volkema, who replaced Campbell, resolved to find a better way to
assure the company paid its way financially.

For Herman Miller and other companies on the road to genuine
sustainability, the achievement of long-term profitability remains
perhaps the hardest goal of all—and the question of how to deliver
it, the most compelling. Over time, many companies don't yield
any return for shareholders, in inflation-adjusted terms. The return
for the average company over the last 200 years comes to a modest
6.5 percent, according to McKinsey & Co.

Volkema recalls those dark days: "We had really gotten off track,
and for a lot of reasons, and we were going to break even in a year
when we really should have made a lot of money. That's when the

board became really interested [and said], 'We've got to do something really different.'"

That something different fell to Walker, whom Volkema would soon name as CFO. An enthusiast since childhood of an Okinawan form of karate, *Shorin Ryu*, Walker had left Arthur Andersen six years earlier for a post with Herman Miller in Japan. Thinking he would get to spend his spare time visiting martial arts schools, he ended up not visiting one, instead spending all his time in furniture showrooms and factories. After two years in Japan, he worked his way up the company ranks, spending three years in Europe along the way.

Walker didn't cut the figure of a sharp-penciled finance guy. Son of a road-building, heavy-equipment operator, crazy about the Spartans football team of his alma mater, he spoke in rambling sentences, often interrupting himself, working up to a point. And yet, in his affable way he combined the precision of a financial technician with the intellect and clarity of a leader guided by a steady internal compass. People trusted him and his capabilities.

WALKER KNEW THAT 1995 was not the first time Herman Miller had hit a profit slump. Dipping fortunes came and went over the decades, no different from the record of many companies. What Herman Miller relied on to survive was making the responsibility for profits not just the job of financial executives. The company depended on the financial acumen of the entire workforce— including the janitor on the plant floor.

That approach of shared financial responsibility dated back to 1950, when D.J. De Pree adopted the Scanlon Plan. Although the plan received updates over the years, with a major one in 1977 under Hugh De Pree, employee participation remained a linchpin. By 1995, the Scanlon legacy, nearly 45 years old, assured that people in the plants and offices understood more about how a business turned a profit than the average workers in America. Their knowledge spurred productivity-raising ideas of all kinds, including the green innovations like tinkering with paint-finishing lines and installing balers for corrugated cardboard.

In every case, the inspiration depended on what the De Prees came to call "business literacy." In the early days of the Scanlon plan, few workers had a white-collar education. Business literacy pertained as much to how to behave in a business-like way—even down to table manners, says Max De Pree—as to how to raise profits. He recalls how the company would hire busses to take workers to Michigan State University in East Lansing for a day of training, a football game, and a dinner at the Kellogg Center. At the time, many employees came from hardscrabble backgrounds, and most worked in the plants.

Business literacy also pertained to top managers, however, who sometimes had a more feeble grasp of finance than they should have. Hugh De Pree, who admitted that financial acumen was wanting, writes in his memoir about hiring the patriarch of a big accounting firm, Frank Seidman, to study Herman Miller, at a time when he felt that profits were too low. A week later, Seidman returned, saying, "Young man, I have only one thing to tell you. Any damn fool can give it away." The company was spending on things it couldn't afford, investing in things on which it couldn't reap a good return.

By the early 1980s, however, the company was not "giving away" so much money that its profits were low. In the ten years ending in 1985, it rewarded shareholders with a 48-percent annual compounded return (dividends included). One of the reasons for this success was that managers met regularly with their people and kept the focus on business literacy. In meetings, they reported company results and how business was going, a practice unheard of at most companies.

Besides the monthly factory chats, Max De Pree, CEO since 1980, held meetings in an auditorium to review results with employees. In one meeting, he explained how the job of improving accounts receivables fell partly to plant workers. When the company shipped product late, customers paid late. At the time, Herman Miller was having trouble with on-time shipments. It lagged badly behind the world-class manufacturers. Toyota Motor Corporation was reporting the ability to deliver with near complete reliability, and to the day. Herman Miller could deliver on time only 85 to 90 percent of the time, and then not to the day.

The CEO explained at the meeting that when Herman Miller delivered late, customers not only held up payment, they invoked a penalty clause in their contracts, forcing Herman Miller to cough up a discount.

Max felt that he'd done a good job of explaining how plant work connected to profits, but a couple of days later, a woman approached him on the factory floor. She asked, What was that again about accounts receivable? How come I'm accountable for accounts receivable?

Realizing he hadn't done such a good job the first time, Max went through the details again. Plant people, he said, could directly boost profits whenever they could find a way to get a wayward order back on track. It wasn't just the accounts-receivable clerks who could speed profit to the bottom line. It was everyone.

A common saying circulated at the time in the company reflecting the thoughts of management thinker Peter Drucker: "Profits are the cost of tomorrow." In a speech, one Herman Miller executive said, "If profits are truly the cost of tomorrow, you'd better not miss a payment. You wouldn't miss a mortgage payment would you? Profits are just as important."

With such analogies and explanations, Max and his executives helped people on the plant floor get a grip on finance. And each time the De Prees realized that business literacy within the company was on the wane, they sought to revitalize it. Max realized as much in the mid-1980s. The company hit a rough patch, not unlike the one in 1995, brought on by a slump in the computer industry and sharper competition. Profits in 1986 fell for the first time in 14 years. In an embarrassing development, Haworth Inc., an arch-competitor and neighbor in Holland, gained on Herman Miller based on price.

Max felt that a lack of literacy was the root of the problem. Herman Miller had made every employee a stockholder in 1983— and employees didn't fully grasp what that meant. In one monthly meeting led by De Pree, a worker stood up and declared: I see the stock went down two points last month, and I want to know what you're going to do about it! Max, of course, wondered what the man was going to do about it. As for what he himself would do, Max explained the company's strategy, deflecting suggestions that executives alone would take care of all the new stock owners' problems.

Max often said that, in a participative company—particularly one that had started to preach participative "ownership"— a manager's job was to "define reality" and to give everyone down to the lowest level an opportunity to own the business problem. In the 1980s, some realities were harsh. The decade had brought with it an explosion in hostile takeovers and restructurings. Many deals crafted on

Wall Street led to big employee layoffs and company breakups. That fate was on every CEO's mind.

Another issue on the mind of company chiefs was workers' common assumption of lifetime employment. Max was even asked in one monthly meeting, What do you think about guaranteed employment? Surprising some workers, he replied: Guaranteed employment requires guaranteed customers. We need to work hard to make sure we're producing the right things, serving the customers well, meeting their needs. That's the only way we can guarantee employment.

"My premise," said another executive at the time, "is that if 80 percent of your employees are business literate, you will have a decisive competitive advantage over the firm that only has 20 percent of its employees literate about the business." So Max's first challenge in the mid-1980s was not guaranteed employment; it was how to boost Herman Miller's literacy percentage toward that 80 percent.

TO GET THINGS BACK on track, Max launched a formal business-literacy program, complete with a steering committee and business-literacy strategy. The group charged with the effort aimed to teach people about the business's mission, direction, employee rights and responsibilities, and an understanding of economics.

Max favored defining literacy broadly. Asked by a top finance executive to share his vision in a meeting in January 1986, he listed traits characterizing, not just a financial mind, but an able working person: Genuinely understands the concept of the customer; knows the histories of company storytellers of the past; attends to the talents and gifts people bring to the job; grasps the realities of business and the results.

The goal, he said, was to have people know enough to work without a supervisor.

All employees went through literacy training in 1985 or 1986. If they didn't learn business numbers there, they could read about them in company publications. An issue of the employee newsletter published a business-literacy quiz. To score well, people had to define profit and calculate how many cents of profit Herman Miller made on each dollar of sales. Another issue contained a guide to the financial analysis of Herman Miller's annual report. It showed how to calculate the current ratio, stockholder's equity, net sales, long-term debt, earnings per share, book value, return on assets, and compound annual growth rates. It was a veritable how-to guide for novice investors.

The focus on literacy, especially on profits, showed up in a change to the Scanlon bonus calculation. Out went the system of paying people for meeting production goals or making cost-saving suggestions. In came a system for paying based on growth in sales, cost savings, return on assets, product quality, and the results of customer satisfaction surveys.

By the late 1980s, the new literacy push paid off. Earnings fell more in 1987, but by 1988 they rebounded handily, hitting a record $44.6 million. Sales grew to a record $714 million. By 1989 earnings inched up to $44.7 million, and sales, to $793 million. In 1989, *Fortune* magazine lauded Herman Miller in a story, "Hot Company, Warm Culture." It placed the firm ninth in its survey of America's most-admired companies. The magazine suggested the company had triumphed with its "too-good-to-be-true" management style. And it concluded, "After all the external and internal strife, Herman Miller is sitting pretty."

BUT IN 1995, WITH literacy sliding again, Herman Miller faced not a triumph but a tumble. This time *Fortune* published "Broken Furniture at Herman Miller," citing the near 90 percent collapse in profits, the recent firing of the CFO, and the subsequent departure of Kerm Campbell.

Some of the furniture had "broken" under outside forces. The industry had matured and growth had slowed. Analysts expected office-furniture sales to post no more than 5 percent yearly growth. Meanwhile, competitors were fighting for a piece of the market, so much so that Herman Miller lost its second-place ranking in the industry to arch-competitor Haworth, which overtook the company in 1995 sales by over $100 million.

Some of the furniture had "broken" from forces within, however. In internal documents, controller Dave Guy noted a long list of concerns: The culture had become paternalistic. People emphasized ideas at the expense of execution. Participative management (in which everyone gets a say) had become confused with democracy (in which everyone gets a vote). People's concern with performance dipped. Business literacy was "very low"—stemming from people not sharing information and from the company's mixed messages on the measures of success.

Walker and Guy joined in lamenting the perverse incentives given to top managers. As at many companies, managers negotiated performance targets with their bosses. Often, the targets of one person conflicted with those of another. Purchasing managers, for example, got rewards for driving down piece prices. If they could get suppliers to shave a nickel off costs in return for prompt payment, they earned extra pay. But trading 10-day payment terms for 30-day terms hurt company profits by forcing Herman Miller to put up more money earlier.

As Walker and Guy looked into the books, one financial failing galled them. The company, as they termed it, had "destroyed" millions of dollars of shareholder value. At the end of 1985, Herman Miller had a market value of $645.9 million and a book value (money invested minus depreciation) of $170.9 million. At the end of 1995, Herman Miller had a market value of $537.8 million and a book value of $286.8 million. Over ten years, management, on behalf of shareholders, had invested a lot more money but had a lot less to show for it.

The key facts were as follows: The capital on the company's books had gone up 68 percent. The market value of the company had fallen 17 percent. In a down economy, company executives could explain away such a poor showing by blaming it on things beyond their control. But in 1995, although the economy had slowed, growth continued. The stock market climbed at a steady clip, so much so that the next year Federal Reserve chairman Alan Greenspan would utter his famous warning about "irrational exuberance."

Walker said of this time, in prepared remarks to the board of directors, "You could have concluded at the end of 1995 that our shareholders had invested an additional $113.9 million in Herman Miller between 1985 and 1995, while the value of this investment decreased by $108.1 million. This means roughly that for every dollar they invested, they lost almost two."

The numbers were an embarrassment. But they left nonfinance people wondering, How could this be? How could a company that had grown so much not show a gain in its value? In almost every year, Herman Miller had reported profits. In almost every year, its assets in plant and equipment—including the marvelous Phoenix Designs building—had risen. What was holding back a surge in company worth?

Walker and Guy relied on the concept of "economic profit" for the answer—that is, profit after subtracting all capital and operating expenses. Since the early 1990s, Bix Norman, head of Phoenix Designs, had talked up the concept, as opposed to "accounting profit," as a new measure of results. Used across a business, it did away with conflicting measures of performance, misleading measures of investment success, and dysfunctional bonuses calculations. In 1993, he had adopted it for his 195 employees.

The concept of economic profit, aside from its calculation, was simple. It referred to the amount of money the company took in minus the amount it had to pay investors for the use of their money. If the old adage is, "It takes money to make money," the corollary is, "If you take money, you have to pay for it." The concept of economic profit took into account that, when a company uses someone else's money, it in effect owes that someone "rent."

Nonfinance people could be excused for thinking the "profit" reported by companies (i.e., "accounting profit") *is* economic profit. Why would companies report anything else? But "profit," or "net income," is a tally of the amount of money a company makes minus only the rent to lenders. It doesn't subtract rent to shareholders (except the amount paid as dividends). Therein lay part of the reason Herman Miller had posted profits but lost value: It had been paying only part of the rent. Remarkably—and this was true at many companies—it was also paying bonuses to people for achieving the incomplete profit measure.

Accountants have a good reason for not showing shareholder "rent" on financial statements. The company doesn't actually write a check for it—so accountants wouldn't properly record it on the expense ledger. But in practice, shareholders *do* expect the company to earn and pay that rent. They expect, in effect, to have whatever is not paid out in dividends reinvested in the enterprise. In turn, they expect to see the stock price climb as that reinvested money pays off. If the company fails to earn a payoff from that reinvestment, shareholders can't call in an IOU, as lenders would. But they can, and will, sell their stock—which of course drives the price down.

In the concept of economic profit, Walker and Guy saw a way to get Herman Miller back on sustainable financial footing. They also saw a missing piece in the definition of business literacy. If the people in the company learned to take only those actions that promised to create more economic profit, shareholders would get paid in full—and the employee–owners would win along with them. By adding the notion of economic profit, they could give the company a measure for true financial sustainability.

Herman Miller couldn't abandon traditional accounting. The law required it. But finance people could take the numbers in the books and adjust them by subtracting from net income an all-in charge for investor's money. In technical terms, they would subtract from net operating income after taxes an 11-percent charge for all capital employed. In practice, the calculation wasn't that elementary. But the lesson for both executive and plant employees was simple: Do only those things that add to economic income and stop (or change) things that do not.

The Phoenix Designs subsidiary had already learned the power of this approach. Its chief financial officer would go out on the plant floor and point to a line painted around a square foot of space. He'd then point to the annual cost of the investment for that square foot—all rent included. He would tell the employee-owners: Every time you can figure out how to rearrange your assembly lines to save that much space, we can stop paying that much rent—or save that much by avoiding a further expansion. A share of the savings, meanwhile, will show up in your bonus.

Walker and Guy became convinced that economic profit could make Herman Miller a more business-literate enterprise that would create more value for everyone. With Volkema's support, Walker drew up plans to launch a program in late 1995.

The leading voices on economic profit at the time were Joel Stern and Bennett Stewart at Stern Stewart & Co., a New York consultancy. Stern and Stewart had developed a sophisticated program to help companies install "economic value added," or EVA, their brand of economic profit. Stewart had detailed the concept in his 800-page book, *Quest for Value.* After meeting with Stern, Walker, Guy, and Volkema decided to hire Stern Stewart to help install the program. They needed help especially because they were in a hurry. They wanted to end the old bonus system in 1995 and start paying people based on economic profit in 1996.

Stern addressed the Herman Miller board for an hour and a half on January 3, 1996. An urbane former banker, columnist, and traveling professor with a persuasive way about him, Stern explained how Herman Miller would get four things with EVA: a way to keep score, a way to judge investments, a basis for incentive pay, and a guide to raising the stock price.

Pencil in hand, Walker furiously took notes, 21 pages in all. "The plan is designed so even a high-school drop-out can understand," he noted. "Included in their program is a 2-hour presentation to every employee in the company." "A positive side effect is an improved feeling of self-esteem."

Stern stressed how a focus on economic profit changed the way people at most companies acted. He told a story about Sammy, a 13-year-old delivery boy in South Africa, a child worker he had met while consulting with a big nationwide health-care organization. The foot soldiers in the organization, which retrieved blood samples for hospitals, were kids who rode scooters back to the lab. One of the child couriers was Sammy.

Stern met Sammy in Soweto while giving the last of 27 training sessions to 3,000 people. Around him on the floor sat Sammy and the other delivery kids. Also attending was the chief executive. Stern asked if anyone knew why an upstart competitor was stealing the health-care organization's market share. Stern had asked many other people in other training sessions but never received an answer.

From the crowd of kids this time, Sammy's hand shot up.

They make round trips! Sammy announced. We just do one way.

What do you mean? asked Stern.

They fetch samples in the morning and return results in the afternoon. They do in one day what we do in two.

How long have you known this?

A year and a half.

How come you didn't tell anyone?

Because the people in the white coats—they know I sit on the floor. They have no respect for me. They turn their faces and never say hello. I will never help them.

To the Herman Miller board, Stern was making a point essentially about participative management. The key to winning with economic profit was not just the measure. "It's not money; it's attitude," says Stern, "To get the right attitude, you have to have respect for people downstairs."

Stern said that during the Sammy episode, the CEO of the South African organization immediately grasped his failing. After the Soweto meeting, Stern urged the CEO and the committee managing the EVA program to invite Sammy to join. By getting the lowest rung of workers involved, the program triggered a turnaround.

Of course, this kind of participation was a Herman Miller forte. For an organization like Herman Miller, says Stern, "It's like going from a slipper to a very comfortable shoe." And the Herman Miller board was ready to put on that shoe. By the end of January 1996, the company signed with Stern Stewart. Walker tapped a team of a half dozen to help lead the effort, including Controller Guy and several others.

THE STERN STEWART TEAM was led by Justin Pettit, a whiz in financial analysis and strategy. The first job of Pettit's team was studying the finances of Herman Miller. Just what was hidden in the books? Pettit ended up delivering the kind of news people expected but didn't look forward to. He said in a report, "Herman Miller's recent operating (EVA) and market performance was quite poor, compared to other publicly-traded office furniture companies."

Out of ten companies in the industry, Pettit added, Herman Miller ranked among the bottom three. While the office furniture industry outperformed the market in that period, "Herman Miller consistently and significantly underperformed." Since 1990, in fact, Herman Miller had not earned an economic profit in a single year.

Pettit did report favorably on some items. Management of accounts receivable and accounts payable was "best in class." The company did a first-rate job issuing and collecting on bills. But on many other counts it ranked average or below. Its margins (net operating profit after taxes) ranked low, at 3.4 percent. One of its competitors (Knoll) was 70 percent higher at 5.8 percent.

Dick Ruch, chairman at the time, remembers receiving the results. Spending for new buildings had been high, so he knew the economic profit number would take a hit once the new capital charge was subtracted. Still, he says, "Some of our profitable years [were] merely breakeven... and that was a little humbling, because we thought we had had some great years there... but they were dampened down by this kind of analysis."

Managers had in effect treated capital from investors as free. One consolation was that Herman Miller wasn't alone in this respect. Many other "profitable" firms across U.S. and global industries had "destroyed" capital over the same period. That was one reason buyout capitalists could swoop in and buy them for bargain prices. They knew they could cut expenses, sell assets that didn't earn a return for shareholders, and make a quick buck.

DESPITE HERMAN MILLER'S DISMAL showing, Walker and his team now had the company on a new path. Adding to all the work on environmental sustainability, they resolved to in effect to restore financial sustainability. By adopting EVA, they would all at once stop the illusion of profit. The single measure would show if they made, or did not make, enough money to pay the company's way with all investors—lenders and stockholders.

Stockholders were the ones getting short shrift in the early 1990s. The main route to pleasing them was now clear: If Herman Miller gave them a return on their investment that matched what they expected, they would stick with their stock holdings. And of course, if the company gave them more, their friends would show up and snap up the stock, pushing up the price.

Adopting EVA also would offer a fresh way to teach business literacy—where capital comes from, how much it costs, where profit comes from, and what adds to or subtracts from it. People would win rewards for acting on this literacy. In the new bonus plan, finance people would each year calculate the EVA figure expected by share-holders. The number was derived from the market cost of equity. Employees would then receive a bonus if the company delivered that amount. If it delivered more, they would earn more—with no limit on how much they could get.

In March 1996, Pettit and his team from Stern Stewart began to train the top 150 company managers. Along with teaching EVA def-initions, calculations, and terminology, they tested people's under-standing. One question addressed the issue of inventory. What if you could cut raw-material inventory by $250,000 by having plant employees work overtime to receive material during a second shift? And what if that overtime cost $20,000 a year?

If the budget made no allowance for the overtime cost, managers in most companies would refuse to authorize it. If they did autho-rize it, their bosses would give them a black mark. But if they were trying to decide based on economic profit, they would probably act otherwise. At a capital cost of 11 percent, carrying the inventory would cost the company $27,500 a year. The after-tax cost of the overtime, at a 40-percent tax rate, would be $12,000. By paying overtime, the manager—though breaking the overtime budget—would earn the company $15,500.

To make the math simpler, the finance team created the "60/11 Rule," which converted pen-and-pencil calculations to a rule of thumb: Reducing an expense by $1 would boost EVA by $0.60—the savings after taxes. Reducing capital by $1 would boost EVA by $0.11—the charge in the EVA equation for the cost of capital. With the 60/11 rule, managers could estimate the gain on an improvement idea off the cuff. No calculator needed.

Managers took time during the training to brainstorm economic profit-producing ideas. In one of the first sessions, they came up with 40. Aside from cutting things like inventory, some surprising proposals came up. A marketing director suggested switching from issuing weekly to biweekly paychecks. Though perhaps of questionable popularity, the suggestion showed he had quickly grasped both sides of the 60/11 rule. The change would both reduce expenses (60 cents for each dollar) and delay cash outlay (11 cents on each dollar).

AS THE TRAINING OF top managers rolled out, Walker had time to consider training the rest of the work force. Time was running short. Only eight months remained until the bonus system would trigger EVA-based payments. The workforce had to become literate in the new program before then. Walker turned to Pettit. Would he be coming in soon with the rest of the training?

No.

Walker was surprised. "I'm paying you guys a lot of money" he recalls saying. "What do you mean no?"

Pettit, and others said the job was not theirs. It was Herman Miller's.

Walker objected. He said Herman Miller was paying Stern Stewart hundreds of thousands of dollars, and the training for the 6,000 employee-owners didn't come with it?

Nope. And it shouldn't. In fact, it wouldn't even make sense.

"That was kind of a fork in the road," Walker said later. The "spirited" discussion that ensued with Stern Stewart made him and Guy come to a realization: The training itself, not the measure, promised a way to make the company financially sustainable. If people without finance training educated other people without the training, the company would leap forward in business literacy.

"They really pushed us and made us embrace this whole train-the-trainer approach," recalls Walker. And "they were right on the money."

Walker admitted later that he could have chosen the wrong fork in the road, insisting on hiring outsiders as trainers. Instead, a plan evolved to build business literacy in economic profit by cascading the training down the chain of command. This would, of course, play to the company's history of involving people down through the ranks in participative management. The company's 500 directors, managers, supervisors and team leaders would carry the message down each level of the supervisory staircase.

But this came as a shock to some middle managers. Me? Teach finance? Me? Compute EVA? Anxiety levels jumped.

Understandably so. Among middle managers in most companies, a talent for finance didn't typically rank as a forte. Often promoted from engineering or marketing or product development, they usually didn't spend time reading and analyzing profit-and-loss statements and balance sheets. Few understood the theory or math for making decisions to invest capital. Among Stern Stewart clients, only the top 5 or 10 percent of people in a company would get EVA training from the consultant. Any other training was left to the company.

For most managers, the "cost" of capital mainly amounted to the blood, sweat, and tears of convincing someone in the finance department to give them money. These managers did not relate the cost to the dollars-and-cents expense of paying investors for the use of it. Walker, Guy, and a training expert built a curriculum to change that. As poor as the numeracy was in many companies, it would not remain that way at Herman Miller.

IN BUILDING THE CURRICULUM, they first put together a two-hour workshop called EVA 101. People learned about the theory of EVA, how to compute it, and how the measure determined their bonus. Giving them confidence was the fact that name-brand companies like Coca-Cola had adopted EVA much earlier. Upper-level managers also saw a video of Joel Stern telling his Sammy story.

In the training sessions, no bones were made about the company's sorry financial record in recent years. In an opening Q & A, the training handout said, "During the past 10 years, from 1985-1995, we did a poor job of creating value. In fact, for every dollar our shareholders invested in the company, we destroyed two dollars of value. That's like you putting $1,000 into a savings account and finding out next year [its] market value is $500. How happy would you be with your investment then? Would you put more money into that account, or would you take your money out and put it some-place else?"

Guy hinted at the frightening risks of staying on the path of destroying value: A venture-capitalist group might conclude that it could run the company better and make a bid to buy it. Could this happen at Herman Miller? Could harsh cost cutting and lay-offs follow? He showed slides of the value created (or destroyed) by three Herman Miller competitors. Herman Miller was far behind the value-creating leader.

Walker and Guy gave some good news during the training on the likely bonus. Had the company changed the system earlier, the companywide bonus over the previous 15 months would have averaged 18 percent, compared to the actual 15 percent. People had heard that the bonus calculation would change, and they imagined the worst. But the calculations in the training allayed their fears.

As people around the company attended EVA 101, Walker and Guy created EVA 201. Meantime, they reinforced the new focus in their talks, monthly videos, and lunchtime seminars. Though many employees thought EVA was no more than newfangled bonus arith-metic, they did learn in the videos how the number went up and down. And they did understand that by using the 60/11 rule, they could take action to earn more pay.

As the commitment to economic profit took hold, encour-aging results poured in. Among the executive ranks, people saw more clearly how costly factory and office space was. In the first 16 months, they cut space companywide by 15 percent. Shedding factories in California and North Carolina alone yielded savings of $23.1 million. Transfers of operations in Georgia and Grandville, Michigan, to other nearby buildings saved more. The amount of capital tied up in the Georgia plant shrank by over $10 million—the equivalent of lopping off over $110,000 in capital costs.

As for Herman Miller office workers, the purchasing people saw how they had been giving away value. For years they had ignored payment terms, favoring cash discounts as a way to get suppliers to lower prices. But when their job rating factored in EVA, they saw that paying bills too promptly gave away money that Herman Miller could otherwise hold onto for a while. In one case, they added $14,174 to EVA by changing payment terms for a $3.1-million purchase of aluminum from 15 days to 30.

As for people in the plants, engineers better understood the cost of equipment. Matt Campbell, a plant engineer, started thinking differently about whether to fix or replace machinery. A new boring machine would cost $325,000; a retrofit to fix a set of broken controls, $80,000. The new machine would work with nearly 100 percent reliability, the retrofit, 90 percent. The new machine gobbled up more capital at the start, but what about the cost of lost production? Only by putting all the factors together could he calculate that the retrofit would boost EVA more.

Bonuses quickly reflected these improvements. In the last half of 1996, the 3,500 employees working in Herman Miller's North American operations earned 28.6 percent on top of their base pay, compared to 14.1 percent the previous year. The bonuses, along with record sales, reflected the gains in shareholders' pocketbooks. Share prices rocketed from $7.72 at mid-year in 1996 to over $27.69 two years later, peaking at over $30.00.

Even workers nonplussed by the EVA math saw that actions promising to save money, boost sales, or reduce unneeded investment could gild their bonus. So enamored were people of the clear path to economic gains that the program spurred competition between units, including some zany challenges. In one of the company's biggest units, the vice president challenged his people to earn triple the targeted amount of EVA. If they succeeded, the boss said he would shave his beard—a beard he had sported for 20 years.

Walker enjoyed seeing the energy that came from the new economic-profit incentive. Although the unit trying to meet the triple-EVA challenge didn't make it, Walker gave the executive a consolation prize: the "close shave" award. And when the executive said he was going to try for doubling EVA the next year, Walker teased him about being a wimp. How about five times the EVA? said Walker.

What would you do if we hit five times? the executive asked.

Shave my head.

You're on.

Though his wife was appalled, Walker readily signed a document the executive had drawn up, had notarized, and then had copied and mailed to all his sales people. Everyone in the company heard about the challenge.

The unit, once again, didn't quite make it—although it only barely missed, hitting a remarkable 4.8 times the EVA goal. In a consolation this time, Walker had himself filmed with a skull cap and shaving cream covering his head. Dave Guy pretended to shave the CFO's scalp.

People throughout the company got the message: Anyone could help with EVA. In an example on the environmental front, when the company decided to move its Georgia operations to another building, Paul Murray was asked to review the new building's blueprints for environmental soundness. He zeroed in on the choice of a tar roof to save money —a solution that would save the company $120,000 in up-front costs. At a time of rising concern over global warming, Murray worried about fuel consumption. He asked the architect to calculate the added power needed to cool a building with a black, heat-absorbing roof. It came in at $108,000 a year. The cost for a bigger chiller added another $20,000. He didn't even need to compute the EVA to know a white roof was the smarter way to go both financially and environmentally.

A couple of years later, Murray and his people wrote a proposal to enroll Herman Miller in the EPA's Energy Star program. They sought to install more efficient lights in Herman Miller buildings. Walker reviewed the proposal, which asked for $40,000 a quarter, and summoned Murray to his office. Murray expected Walker to make him squirm for the needed cash.

Can you get by with $50,000 per quarter? asked Walker.

Excuse me? said a nonplussed Murray.

Look, this is going to boost EVA, said Walker. Can you go any faster with the replacement program?

Sure, said a surprised Murray, who needed a moment to grasp that the CFO was asking him to spend *more* money.

In an example illustrating the effect of EVA on company operations, in an April 1998 board of directors meeting, Walker, Volkema, and others reported on a range of continuous-improvement targets. In the seating unit, one target was to cut by 25 percent the number of past-due bills being carried on the books. Another was to improve the volume of chair shipments per square foot of manufacturing space by 25 percent. A third was to cut the number of mispackaged boxes by 50 percent. The executives could report that the unit met the last target and nearly doubled the desired gain on the first two. A fourth was to increase sales per employee by 20 percent—the actual was 10 percent. A fifth was to cut scrap per chair by 50 percent—the actual was 8 percent. All told, the gains across the board were enough to add up to a near tripling of EVA.

Alas, the heady times would not last forever. By the end of the 1990s, a time when the Aeron chair had become a totem of dot-com companies, sales sagged—and they would later plunge during the recession called the dot-com crash. After getting triple bonuses, workers would get none. Grumblings on the company's intranet would begin to appear. The board of directors, fearing widespread demoralization, would authorize a 100-share stock grant to every employee as a consolation.

To fight the dot-com freefall, the worst since the Great Depression, Walker and Volkema would start slashing jobs. And the best that could be said is that the EVA system would work as designed. As economic profit evaporated, so would bonuses. The plunge would cut payroll expenses by tens of millions of dollars, enough to slow layoffs. Volkema and Walker could thus limit the stretch of net-income losses to just one year, 2002.

The new level of business literacy, especially management's effort to "define reality" each step of the way, would help the company get through the trauma. Walker and Volkema would realize more clearly than they'd ever hoped that the EVA program would have a symbolic advantage at such times: Because everyone in the company earned his or her bonus based on the same measure, neither of them would earn bonuses while the workforce suffered—unlike executives at hundreds of other companies. They would earn the same bonus as everyone else: zilch.

The EVA system would remain a necessary force for economic sustainability, but it would not prove sufficient to stanch losses in a cyclical economic freefall. It would help achieve the bigger mission of preserving the company's financial health for the future, to allow the roving leaders to continue their work on all other Herman Miller ambitions. "Ultimately we are the stewards of someone else's money," says Walker. "We have a duty to make sure the enterprise can sustain itself, because if it can't sustain itself as an economic engine, it can't be a force for good in the broader sense."

On the Road to Sustainability

Business by Design Herman Miller's founder, D.J. De Pree (center, rear) staked the company's success on modern design. He turned away from long-popular period reproductions. Starting in 1930, a succession of distinguished designers won Herman Miller a reputation as a leader in modern furniture, both for the home and office. From left to right, Robert Propst, Alexander Girard, George Nelson, De Pree, and Ray and Charles Eames in 1975. Photo courtesy of Herman Miller, Inc.

Foundation for Sustainability Encouraged by successes with independent designers, company founder D.J. De Pree (center) formalized a progressive philosophy of management in the early 1950s. He had the help of management professor Dr. Carl Frost. The designers maintained that, through furniture design, they "solved problems" of people in homes and offices. De Pree in turn urged employees to do the same, eventually solving the problem of the corporation's role in society. De Pree's sons, first Hugh (right), and then Max, built on this legacy. Photo courtesy of Herman Miller, Inc.

The Corporate Activists In early efforts to advance sustainability, Herman Miller's "roving leaders" attacked mountains of landfill waste, led by Paul Murray (back, left). The group's goal in 1995: cut 41 million pounds of waste to zero. In time, the company quit landfilling over 2,000 dumpsters of waste per year. First row, left to right, Joe Azzarello, Vivien VandenBerg, Julie Lamer, Ted Stojak; second row, Jim Gillespie, Merrick Bacon, Bob Johnston, Greg Staskiewicz; third row, Bob Earnest, Murray, Willie Beattie, Bill Dowell. Photo courtesy of Herman Miller, Inc.

Earth-Friendly Designers Industrial designers played a leading role in making products environmentally friendly. Among them was Bill Stumpf (left), of Minneapolis, and Don Chadwick, of Santa Monica. The two men played pivotal roles in the design of the first "ergonomic" chairs. Stumpf's work included the Ergon (1976). The two collaborated on the the Equa (1984, components shown) and the Aeron (1995). With the Aeron, Herman Miller pioneered "green design." Photo courtesy of Herman Miller, Inc.

Birth of Green Furniture The Aeron chair came to market with two thirds of its content from recycled materials. It incorporated twenty 2-liter soda bottles in its seat back. At the end of its life, customers could recycle 60.5 percent of the chair. The kickoff to introduce the principles of green design came from Bill Dowell (earlier photo). Dowell sought to prepare the company for product take-back, an idea originating in Europe. Photo courtesy of Herman Miller, Inc.

Buildings as "Living Machines" "The most important criterion in selecting an architect," said CEO Max De Pree, "is our potential to learn from them more about architecture, ourselves, our customers, and about the importance of good design." In 1994, Herman Miller hired Bill McDonough to design the 300,000-square-foot "GreenHouse," in Holland, Michigan. The factory opened in 1995. It used the sun's heat and light, blended with the landscape's contours, emphasized sustainable landscaping and building materials, and filtered roof and storm water in manmade ponds. Photo courtesy of Herman Miller, Inc.

The Cutting Edge Over 75 years, Herman Miller earned a reputation for leaping to the head of the pack with new designs. Often it faced harsh criticism for leaping into the unknown. Research and development chief Gary Miller protected the "stealth" Aeron from project-killing talk by naysayers as early as 1990. In the 2000s, he would lead a group in developing radical concepts to make building interiors more sustainable. Photo courtesy of Herman Miller, Inc.

Eye on the Money   Herman Miller hit a rough patch financially in the mid 1990s. Though sales climbed, profits tumbled. Brian Walker helped rebalance company finances, restoring enviable profitability. Pictured here from the 1996 annual report, after he was named chief financial officer, Walker shows the energy and momentum of a company buoyed by financial rejuvenation. Later named CEO in 2004, Walker placed financial success securely in the equation for company sustainability. Photo courtesy of Terry Vine.

Mimicking Nature's Cycles When Herman Miller sought to eliminate toxic material in its products, it rethought product development. By the mid 2000s, engineers faced three new demands: use recycled material; use recyclable material; build products that come apart easily for recycling. The new "design for environment" program in 2003 yielded the Mirra chair, easy to disassemble in 15 minutes into 96 percent recyclable material. Photo courtesy of Herman Miller, Inc.

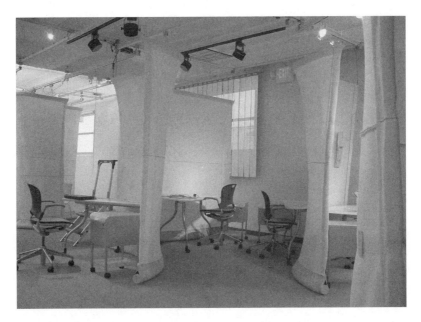

Designing the Future Working to re-imagine office interiors, Gary Miller (earlier photo) led the "Purple" project in the 2000s. His group created a plug-and-play infrastructure that slashed office-reconfiguration costs and renovation waste. A steel ceiling grid carried power, data, and tele-com. Lightweight, "dematerialized" walls, embedded with low-voltage lights and ports, hung from the grid. Office workers could reprogram devices with a two-button "wand." Shown is an early mocked-up office in Glendale, California. Photo courtesy of Herman Miller, Inc.

A Better World In the 2000s, Herman Miller expanded corporate sustainability to include creating "a better world." Top executives encouraged—and funded—volunteer projects through which employees could bring greater purpose to their lives. Executive Andy Lock led a trip to Tharangambadi, India, a village ravaged by the Asian Tsunami. Among a raft of restoration tasks, he arranged for the donation of a brick-making machine. Photo courtesy of Karen Kramer.

CHAPTER 7

Mister Ohba

L arry O'Keefe and Matt Long, two Herman Miller engineers, were on a mission to attack waste. This was not a mission they particularly wanted. They had been detailed from their Spring Lake, Michigan, file-cabinet-making plant to another company, Grand Haven Stamped Products (GHSP). O'Keefe and Long knew what most people at Herman Miller knew: Getting put on "special assignment" to another company was the kiss of death. Most people never came back.

But in late summer 1995, they updated their resumes and headed out the door. They did come back a couple of days later—they were only a couple of miles away—but not for long. The boss of their unit saw them in the lobby and told them they didn't have permission to be there. They were to spend the fall and winter on the plant floor at GHSP. O'Keefe and Long didn't feel so hot about this. They didn't even know if what they would learn at the local auto-parts maker would help them sustain Herman Miller's business.

But the challenge faced by their plant compelled them to go. Herman Miller's Integrated Metal Technology (IMT) subsidiary was exhibit A on the roster of operations that needed financial rehab. One of the reasons was that the unit's biggest customer, Herman Miller subsidiary SQA, was threatening to pull out, claiming it could get faster delivery and lower prices if it went outside the Herman Miller family. IMT faced a sales drop of 25 percent.

Nobody at IMT was sure they had the solution for their lack of manufacturing competitiveness. O'Keefe and Long's mission was to find that solution and turn the unit into a sustainable manufacturer. Although they didn't know it at first, the formula for their success would depend on cutting waste—more forms of waste than they had ever recognized, waste in inventory, in scrap, in floor space, in plant processes, in motion, and in waiting time by plant-floor workers. In cutting waste, they would become part of the company's effort to advance sustainability.

The two men, manufacturing experts, had been betting the plant's future on batch manufacturing. That was how their boss, and their boss's boss, believed they would win back business. They would increase their lot sizes and boost their inventories so they could gain economies of scale and deliver more quickly and cheaply. To make that happen, they would add space, take out workers, and add automated machines.

"Our dream was a 'lights-out factory,'" says Long. At the time, manufacturing experts widely believed in a batch-manufacturing axiom: You can't count on people, so you replace them with robots. And if you replace enough people, you can turn the lights out in the factory. O'Keefe and Long had even toured such a factory in Italy.

But nobody was entirely sure this was the best plan. The nature of the business was changing. Customers were ordering in smaller lot sizes. IMT once got orders for 500 or even 1,000 of the same "pedestal" file cabinet, the kind you put under a desk. Now they were getting orders for 100, 50, or just 25. Batch manufacturing, where cutting costs depends on running big lots without stopping, didn't work so well for orders of 25. It took 20 minutes to set up the line for each new variety, and with one 20-minute setup time piled on top of another, the plant couldn't run efficiently.

So O'Keefe and Long had to explore new options. Even before they went to GHSP, they had in mind the method they wanted to learn about. It was called "lean manufacturing." They also knew whom they wanted to learn it from: Toyota Motor Corporation. Toyota, venerated for the way it ran its plants worldwide, also ran a consultancy, in Erlanger, Kentucky, for its suppliers. Sometimes that consultancy took on companies outside the car industry to teach them the Toyota Production System, or TPS.

O'Keefe and Long's boss, Ray Muscat, had written Toyota asking for help. Muscat had also sent Hajime Ohba, the head of the consultancy, copies of Hugh and Max De Pree's books. Muscat figured the books showed how special Herman Miller, Inc., was. Muscat wrote Ohba not once, but several times starting in early 1995.

He didn't receive an answer.

Muscat's boss, Ken Goodson, then began placing calls.

No answer.

Goodson's boss at the time, CEO Kerm Campbell, began calling the president of Toyota to ask for a hearing.

No answer.

Months passed, and the IMT executives learned that, in their own neighborhood, a Toyota supplier was already an Ohba client. That supplier was GHSP, in Grand Haven, Michigan. The head of GHSP, whose entire factory was learning the Toyota Production System, heard about Muscat's efforts and agreed to take on two people from IMT to learn the system. One stipulation: Goodson and Muscat had to send their best.

That's when Long and O'Keefe learned of their assignment, and got an insistent push out the door. They were cast in the role of uneager apprentices to the nearest TPS mentors. Although they wondered if they were on a fool's errand, in time they would discover that they had become the roving leaders of a new manufacturing system at Herman Miller. The new system would be instrumental to sustaining the company's environmental progress.

O'KEEFE AND LONG WERE not novices. They had made their careers out of becoming masters of batch manufacturing. They had big plans to invest more in it—and those plans would proceed while they were away. Top of their mind at IMT was a proposal to add more plant space. The space, aimed at redoubling efforts to gain greater economies of scale, would underpin IMT's revival.

When they arrived at GHSP, they began to see things that cast doubt on their years of expertise. Their new mentors took them on a tour. Out in the back lot, they saw towering rows of racks for materials and inventory. The enormous storage capacity looked just like that at IMT—but the racks were empty. O'Keefe and Long's hosts said they had revamped the plant so they didn't need the inventory that had once been stored there. They suggested to the skeptical Herman Miller engineers that IMT could do the same thing.

Still, O'Keefe and Long didn't at first find their apprenticeship all that revealing. They joined a work team making BorgWarner shifter assemblies. Their first job was to standardize the work at each station. They also had to pace each station's work, so the assembly lines would run at the rate of customer demand, no faster. They had to change the way the way inventory flowed as well, by triggering upstream stations in the plant to make more parts on an "as needed" basis. They introduced a simple card, or *kanban*, to signal the depletion of supplies. No computer needed to alert workers to start replenishment, just the card.

Though the two men felt that a lot of the changes helped the plant, they also felt they were commonsensical. They were not convinced the new methods beat batch manufacturing. Neither were the 25 GHSP people they worked with. They also found the work frustrating. They didn't get any classroom instruction but instead took assignments from their supervisor. The changes they were told to make struck them as piecemeal, even arbitrary, and if they didn't get them done the Toyota way, they were sent back to do them again.

Over time, they occasionally caught sight of Mr. Ohba, who made periodic visits. Even before he arrived at GHSP, a fever of anticipation swept through the plant. "He's coming today!" people would say. Although Ohba had a bigger-than-life presence, O'Keefe and Long couldn't grasp what set people's minds on fire, even after working in the plant for almost three months. They simply felt Ohba was teaching the "tools" of the Toyota system—the way to standardize work, conduct kanban, pace the line.

The two men only started to see what excited people when they made a trip to the Toyota Supplier Support Center in Kentucky. There, consultants showed them the big picture, how all the tools could, together, enable them to entirely refurbish a dilapidated house of manufacturing. Up to that time, the men had only been rebuilding a manufacturing process brick by brick. They couldn't see what all the bricks added up to.

A core concept in the production system was *kaizen*, or making things better day to day, day in and day out. Better manufacturing came from cutting seven kinds of waste: unneeded movement of material, unneeded processes, extra inventory, overproduction, waiting, defects, and rework. Anything that didn't give customers value was waste—whether it was surplus manufacturing space, excess inventory, unneeded fuel, or too many forklifts for fetching parts. And the way to rid the operation of the waste was to follow the "plan-do-check-act" cycle—documenting a process, studying it for waste, making improvements, testing the changes, and making them better, ad infinitum. That was kaizen.

A light went off for both men. What they saw in Kentucky was the lean production system in action. With a model example before their eyes, they could suddenly take stock of the vast waste in their own plant—waste produced by batch manufacturing. When it came to inventory, they ran a factory in which racks for storing parts in process were stacked up to the ceiling. They also had filled 60 storage trailers outside—and planned to buy and fill more. "Fill the aisles!" was their motto. Of the plant's 200,000 square feet, more than 60,000 square feet were filled with storage racks.

And the racks didn't just waste space. They drove some people crazy. In one part of the factory, workers had a catchall space dubbed the "black hole," filled with the stray cats and dogs of unfinished pedestals. The frustration of trying to find parts in the black hole to complete an order, often while trying to wrap up work on a Friday, pushed people to the limit. More than one worker told his supervisor that he was leaving, announcing: "You don't want me to stay here, because I'm going to start throwing stuff."

To handle the chaos, the plant employed 50 people called "expediters" whose job was just to look for parts needed to complete orders. O'Keefe called the process a "scavenger hunt." Ironically, the excess inventory didn't provide a buffer the plant could naturally use up later. It led to overproduction because if the needed parts couldn't be found, the plant would make more—only to find the originals while doing quarterly inventory. So confused was the system that the plant actually lost—never to be found—an entire truckload of "wrappers," or unfinished file-cabinet exteriors.

The waste added up in other ways, as well. When it came to quality, the batch approach often prevented people from catching defects until they finished running an entire batch. In one instance, a worker dropped a welding fixture on the floor, and bent it unknowingly. The plant then had to throw out hundreds of wrappers that subsequently went through the welding and paint lines. Workers on the final assembly line couldn't snap the drawer slides into the cockeyed supports.

When it came to improving productivity, another form of waste crept in. In trying to realize the goal of the lights-out factory, IMT had installed a welding robot and a 126-foot-long automated welding line with hundreds of sensors. Although the machine replaced workers doing the welding, when the complex machine went down, it took hours to find and fix the problem. Similarly, when several imported automated-fabrication lines went down, IMT had to wait for a technician to fly in from Italy to fix them.

In Kentucky, O'Keefe and Long recognized how the tools they were learning about could put an end to such waste. Standardized work, line pacing, and kanban were just the start. Other crucial concepts included one-piece "continuous flow"—restructuring work so that people made just one item at a time, no matter the variety, with no setup time in between. This eliminated the waste of waiting time, while allowing the plant to efficiently make products to serve customers who wanted lots as small as one.

Another concept was "pull" manufacturing—with each upstream station making parts "just in time" for the next in the line. That was the point of kanban. This eliminated "buffer" inventory at the start and finish of each station. A final key tool was *jidoka*, or giving every worker the authority to hit a button to stop the entire line if he or she sensed a mistake—to avoid letting defects run out of control, like the welds in the wasted wrappers.

Returning from Kentucky, O'Keefe and Long enjoyed a flush of new energy, helping the GHSP shifter team tear down the inventory racks and revamp their inefficient line. Over five months, they helped the team vacate so much space that GHSP turned it into a volleyball court. They also enjoyed a burst of energy they would take back to make similar improvements at IMT. So exciting was the prospect that, by late 1995, the two men started sneaking into IMT after the first shift ended at 3:30 p.m.

At IMT, they started in the stamping department, where pedestal-making began. There, giant presses worked like industrial cookie cutters to stamp, shape, and cut steel parts from rolls of steel. Each time the presses chunked out a different part—the wrappers or tops or brackets of the pedestals—the press workers had to swap out one of 35 different pallet-sized metal "dies." Because swapping took three to four hours each time, they swapped dies rarely and ran parts in giant batches, an entire week's worth between changes.

Each time someone in the plant ran out of a stamped part, the downside of batch stamping became clear. People would chafe as they waited hours for die changes. In the meantime, if several parts had run out of stock at the same time, workers would fight over what part to run next. Constant shortages thus plagued the plant. The solution ran completely against the practices of batch manufacturing. "We saw the key to reducing shortages was actually reducing batch sizes," says Long, "and to reduce your setup time and run parts more frequently."

As O'Keefe and Long learned these and other lessons, the earlier plans to bolster batch manufacturing moved ahead. At the end of 1995, they learned that unit boss Ken Goodson was about to pitch a $6 million 60,000-square-foot addition to Herman Miller's board of directors. IMT needed it to pursue the stepped-up batch strategy they had earlier planned. Goodson even had architectural drawings for the addition, and he had honed his case for making the investment.

O'Keefe and Long now saw how wrongheaded the expansion plan was. They didn't need more space to improve manufacturing; they needed less. So a few days before Goodson's meeting, Long and O'Keefe met with Muscat to rethink the plan. They then stepped into Goodson's office:

Ken, said Long, we have to stop the building addition.

What are you talking about? Goodson asked.

Long showed Goodson a floor plan of the IMT plant. In red, he had highlighted all the inventory space, which came to well over the 60,000 square feet in the proposed addition. He told Goodson the addition would be a waste.

Matt, you're the one who wanted me to do this! barked Goodson. You're the guy who told me I needed the footage!

I know, said Long, but my thinking has changed.

Are you willing to bet your job on this?

We don't need the addition, Long repeated. Even if we cut the inventory space to just half what I think we can cut, we will free up all the space in the addition.

Goodson picked up the phone. Take me off the board agenda, he told his boss. I'm going to trust my guys. We don't need the addition.

O'KEEFE AND LONG FINISHED their stint at GHSP. Despite their early worries about keeping their jobs, Muscat and Goodson welcomed them back. And in February 1996, they began to make changes to the plant. They began with standardized work. In the stamping department, they further shortened setup times, using the commonsense approach they had learned at GHSP. They asked the stamping crew to work as a team, rather than having just one die changer do the whole job. Instead of racking the dies away from the presses, they staged them nearby to enable rapid swapping. They also installed new guides to center the dies quickly.

As O'Keefe and Long instigated changes throughout the plant, workers sometimes resisted. The people on the plant floor didn't completely understand the changes, and many thought they were aimed at cutting jobs, although the unit never laid anyone off. Rumors about ending batch runs and starting one-piece flow circulated among workers. Those who heard them called the one-piece idea crazy and infeasible. "A lot of the things the company was talking about sounded really far-fetched," says one worker. "We said, 'This will never work.'"

As for standardized work, many people fought the concept itself. They didn't like following the same routine as everyone else. And they didn't like documenting how they spent their time, which provided the data needed to prioritize work improvements. "Anytime they said they were going to make our jobs easier, we never believed that," says one worker. "We revolted right from the start."

O'Keefe and Long did make some progress beyond the stamping department. It came in many small steps. On the assembly line, workers installed three kinds of lock bars. They had been grabbing bunches of each kind as they needed them to match the file-cabinet batch they were working on. To improve efficiency, they placed two smaller bins of each kind beside the line, along with a kanban card to trigger refills. The kanban approach reduced assembly-line inventory and enabled people to switch to a different lock bar without a moment's delay.

As O'Keefe and Long racked up small successes, however, they knew they needed much more help. There was no "cookbook" they could turn to replicate the Toyota Production System. So Muscat, operations chief, continued to petition Mr. Ohba for help, citing IMT's early work to show the unit's earnestness. And this time,

Ohba agreed—persuaded by the president at GHSP that he should tour the IMT plant.

In late February 1996, Ohba wrote Muscat that he would visit when he was next in Michigan: "After I have had the opportunity to see your plant, I will make a determination as to whether or not we would be able to support your company."

"We were all absolutely energized," recalls Muscat, who felt he had reached perhaps the only man in America that could help them. "We were going to get Mr. Ohba here and convince him to take us on as a client."

On April 3, Ohba arrived. Muscat had prepared a presentation and plant tour. He offered a handout outlining ten stops on the factory floor. Ohba politely passed on the presentation. He wanted to see the plant operations first.

They descended the stairs onto the 200,000-square-foot shop floor. Muscat, along with Goodson and Long, realized at that point that Ohba didn't want to be led on a tour. "This is where I can't be humble enough to say," says Muscat, "he took us on tour of our own shop floor. I tried to keep him on the path I had delineated, and that was absolutely hopeless."

Muscat, serving as point man, trailed Ohba. He didn't expect to be asked so many questions—questions neither he nor Long had answers to, questions they had never thought to ask themselves, questions that might have helped them explain why their file cabinets had so many flaws, and why it took six weeks to deliver a customer order.

Ohba headed for a pedestal assembly line. "How many fasteners are there on your product?" he asked.

I don't know, Muscat said. He looked to Long, who didn't know either.

Ohba started counting.

Muscat reflected. He remembered that as an intern at General Motors he had once learned something about fasteners. A fundamental principle of assembly lines popped from his memory: The number of fasteners correlates with the requirements of assembly.

"Thirty-nine," announced Ohba. "Why such a long line for so little work?"

Muscat and Long were dumbstruck.

Again and again, Ohba asked questions.

Muscat and Long had no answers.

"It didn't take very long in the tour for me to come to the conclusion that this man is seeing things that we don't see," says Muscat. "If there was any doubt at that point whether we should do the Toyota Production System, it was gone in a nanosecond."

Once Ohba had seen enough on the plant floor, they retired to the conference room. Ohba drew the flow of the plant on the whiteboard from memory. He noted each place the plant added value to the pedestals. He then wrote on the board his goal for IMT: "1 line, 2 shifts, 16 people."

Muscat and Long couldn't believe it. The pedestal assembly department ran at that time with 2 lines (plus four work cells), 3 shifts, and 126 people.

Ohba pressed on: Why have you started your work in stamping?

Long finally felt he had a good answer: The plant is always running out of stamped parts, he said. The stamping presses are the stranglehold on production.

But Ohba corrected him: Better to start at the other end, he said, as close as you can to the customer. Ohba explained that demand at that end, in final assembly and shipping, determined the pace of work through the rest of the plant. Only when the plant learned to produce product to match customer demand would it know how many parts the presses should chunk out.

Long, despite his many initiatives, hadn't even thought about starting in final assembly.

Ohba then gave Muscat and Long three "homework" assignments. One was to review the layout of the pedestal fabrication line. Could they reduce the piles of parts building up between steps? A second was to analyze the assembly-line work elements. How would they shrink three lines to one? A third was to rethink the size of containers for parts. Why had they chosen the container sizes they had and why did they hold so many parts?

Ohba then departed. He did not say if he would return.

Muscat and Long had finally received an audience with the guru of TPS in the United States, but they didn't exactly feel exhilarated. Neither of them fully understood why they should start with the questions Ohba had given them. They couldn't piece together all of Ohba's thinking to explain why his homework assignments ranked as top priorities. They didn't know if the changes would actually help IMT survive. But they did know, as their friends at GHSP had told them, that if they ever wanted to see Ohba again they had to do the assignments—pronto.

OF THE THOUSANDS OF manufacturers in the United States, Ohba had taken on only 53 as clients. Only a few operated outside the car industry— taken on by Ohba as a gesture of the Japanese company's goodwill toward U.S. manufacturers. Although Ohba's homework assignments made no particular sense to the men, they knew that doing them was the only way to curry Ohba's favor. And they felt Ohba, though modest, quiet-spoken, and understated—spoke with unrivaled authority on how to turn around a manufacturing operation.

O'Keefe and Long lost no time in getting started. They sent Mr. Ohba an update on their analysis, proposals, and line layouts just a week after Ohba's visit. They sent another update a couple weeks after that. In their proposals, they made clear they had decided to embrace the new approach entirely. They would still run batches for a time, but the batches would shrink in size, and in final assembly shrink to lot sizes of one. They would end up with a pull system with one-piece flow.

O'Keefe and Long spent weeks at first in final assembly, per Ohba's instruction. They not only proposed a new layout but also listed 17 ideas for revamping the line—moving to snap-on glides, replacing pop rivets with fasteners, automating shrink wrapping, evaluating a straight conveyor to replace a curved one.

In July, one of Ohba's right-hand men visited IMT to check on progress. Upon leaving, he said that John Proctor, a new consultant who had accompanied him that day, would return the next week.

What does that mean? O'Keefe asked. What does it mean that Proctor will come back so soon?

That means we're going to support you.

O'Keefe was delighted. IMT had passed its first test. Ohba had decided to move IMT from outside the Toyota fold to the inside.

Proctor, an engineer from one of Toyota's U.S. plants, did return the next week, and every week for months thereafter—at no charge. Herman Miller had indeed become one of Toyota's select clients. Each Monday, Proctor created a work plan before leaving Kentucky to fly to Michigan, and each Friday he reviewed progress with Ohba after flying back home.

With Proctor as an in-factory mentor, O'Keefe and Long advanced steadily in remaking IMT into a lean operation. Workers on the floor scoffed at the goals of the new effort, but step-by-step, the changes helped the ailing business, reducing inventory, improving quality, speeding delivery. In the first year or so, IMT cut its lead time from more than a week to five days.

The early successes came from a lot of new initiatives. On the assembly line, O'Keefe and Long worked hard on line balance. They aimed to have supervisors assign every worker about the same amount of work, so every pedestal flowed off the line at about the same pace, the so-called *takt* time. A well-paced line led to a well-oiled operation. If an assembly line could be compared to a bucket brigade, everyone always had a bucket. Nobody waited for the next one or stockpiled buckets at his or her feet. Water poured forth at the end of the line at just the right rate to quench the fire of demand.

On the paint line, they worked on moving away from the same kind of batch approach as on the stamping presses. The old line, which fed the assembly line, ran hundreds of each file-cabinet part at a time. Wrappers, tops, fronts, brackets, clips—the paint team delivered them in giant batches of the same color, enough for a week of production. But the only way to run smaller batches and still keep up was to run faster and change paint colors quicker.

Thus began a series of improvements. To speed things up, they installed a "line-side store" of raw parts. The store replaced most of the work of a forklift, which ran all over the plant, and sometimes to the trailers outside, to fetch parts. Sometimes those parts, if left too long, rusted, and the plant had to scrap them and make more. With the store, they had the parts at hand, eliminating much wasted waiting, movement, and scrap.

The paint team reworked the "racks" that ferried parts through the paint booth and driers. Akin to meat hooks on an overhead rail, the racks came in dozens of configurations, depending on the part to be painted. Two people managed them, one putting the right rack on the rail and another later taking it off. In the quest to get to one-piece flow, the team developed successively better racks. First came the "Noah" rack and then finally the "Alpha" rack, on which they could hang on one hook all the parts needed for one unit. This enabled them to spray different parts of the same color at the same time. The assembly team then received everything needed all at once for each unit.

One of the biggest barriers to faster painting speeds was the time needed for color changeovers, which took three minutes between changes. Besides wasting time, they wasted paint, as the amount of paint powder in the segment of the hose between the paint gun and the paint barrel became scrap. A technician eventually came up with a quick-change manifold. Instead of a long hose running to each paint barrel, the hose ran to a giant switchboard at the paint-er's elbow, which enabled the painter to quickly detach lines, blow them clean, and reattach in seconds. The manifold won the techni-cian a patent, and the paint team got changeovers down to just one minute.

As O'Keefe and Long pressed on, workers continued to chafe. A continuous-improvement team from the plant, called a "kaizen team," would study each operation and prescribe changes. The team then rearranged people's work lives—and not everyone took it well. For one thing, the bucket-brigade pacing ran afoul of a plant-floor custom: People would gun production to build a lot of parts and then take a break to socialize.

Adding to workers' consternation, O'Keefe and Long couldn't always successfully explain the reasons for changes. Even to them, suggestions by Ohba and Proctor sometimes seemed inscrutable, only to be understood later. To the people on the plant floor, "inscru-table" could appear idiotic. The idea that reducing inventory would speed shipments to customers didn't make sense.

O'Keefe and Long, though encouraged by better plant perfor-mance, seemed to run into the law of diminishing returns. When the plant had trouble meeting takt time on the pedestal line in spring of 1997, O'Keefe met with Proctor. Not hitting takt time meant not meeting customer demand. In a memo, O'Keefe wrote, "I had told John that our supervisors don't know what to do to get the produc-tion where it should be. John stated, correctly, that we do know what to do, we're just not doing it."

The change to lean production had bogged down, and people had become the problem. They were not sticking to the standard-ized work. They were stockpiling too many work-in-process parts. They were accepting problems rather than finding root causes. They were not acting with urgency or a sense of priority. "What are all the extra people doing?" Procter asked.

WHAT THEY WERE DOING was expressing their unhappi-ness. Mike Dexter, a shift supervisor on the paint line, remembers the time well. "My team members felt done upon," he says. "We'd have these people from Zeeland or wherever come in and they'd do their kaizen and say, 'You do this,' and our direction was, 'We did that.'"

The legendary participative management at Herman Miller did not seem to be alive and well. Many workers slowed their work. A few sat down on the job. Others did their jobs the old way. Says one worker who complained of the difficulty of the work: "It's hard to tell a guy who's been working his butt off all day that, well, be happy, because you made the customers' completions."

The workers complained loudly enough that managers got wind of it. Another of Ohba's right-hand men came in with Proctor and could see the frustration: Call all your people together, he told O'Keefe and Long. You need to listen to them.

Although O'Keefe and Long had gotten excited by all the progress being made, they called everyone to the cafeteria—plant manager, department managers, supervisors, workers. With the Toyota consultants on hand, they said that they knew people were unhappy, and they asked why.

The workers boiled over with almost two years of pent-up frustration. The work is harder, they said. We can't keep up with the takt time. We can't produce good quality. We don't want to hit the jidoka button and stop the line, but we feel rushed, jerked around, and go home exhausted.

O'Keefe and Long were shaken. "I felt really lousy when I left that meeting," recalls Long, "because I knew that some of this was my fault, letting my team implement in this way, and being part of it myself, and being so focused on results that we were forgetting the people."

The episode showed they were forcing an incomplete system on their workers. They had introduced the tools of lean production, but they had not introduced new ways for people to work. If they had not solved the problems people were facing when doing the work, they had missed part of the teaching. The engineers and managers had to take care with tools *and* people.

A SIMPLE FACT WAS at the core of the frustration: People's work had become too hard to sustain day in and day out. O'Keefe and Long had to make it easier. For the time being, they set aside their goals for productivity and cost cutting. They put all their effort into two new concepts. One was "overburden," the second "workability." "Overburden" refers to working people too hard, and it signals managers to find a way to ease up. "Workability" means structuring people's work in a reasonable way.

To succeed, O'Keefe and Long had to improve both. One of their focuses became "motion kaizen," making movements natural and comfortable. They were surprised when ergonomic assessments showed that many jobs on the line scored as moderate to high risk for worker injury. There was too much awkward reaching, lifting, and bending. So they tried to bring all motion into the "strike zone," where people could work with their arms comfortably positioned.

Among the changes: elevating parts bins so people didn't have to bend over, and putting wrappers on long slides so that, via gravity, they fed worker demand on the line. Workers once had to lift ten-pound concrete file-cabinet counterweights, which keep open file cabinets from tipping over. They built tables to position the weights at the height and orientation needed for installation, although workers still had to stretch to put them in place.

At one station, workers had to drive eight self-tapping screws into a file-cabinet base. Getting each screw started and then forcing it through three layers of metal took a strong arm. It also meant absorbing a wrenching wrist torque when the drill broke through. Driving screws for eight hours with no relief put people's safety at risk and left them worn out. To remedy the problem, they bored pilot holes in the substructure and replaced the self-tapping screws with sheet-metal screws.

Over more than six months, the reconfiguring of people's jobs did lead to easier work. In a surprise, however, it also led to something else: better productivity. Measures of safety and quality also began to inch up. "That was a turning point for us," says Long. "We started asking, 'What are we doing to make the job better for the team members.'" And by making the work better, that made the business better.

AS TIME WENT ON, teams kept advancing the state of the art. They improved standardized work, line balancing, continuous flow, the pull system, and other elements of lean production. Every part of the plant changed, from the stamping stations to the assembly line to the paint shop. But Long and others then noticed another troubling signal: backsliding. Not long after they would initiate a change, parts of the old system would reappear.

Long could sense some resistance where he hadn't identified it before. Front-line supervisors would quietly thumb their noses at the new system and go back to working the old way. They seemed to be mounting a quiet rebellion. "You could see at times they were seething," says Long.

"I was somewhat of an old-school supervisor," admits Mike Dexter, the paint-line shift supervisor. "It was my line, my responsibility, my job security, my performance rating based on the production I got out. If it was my responsibility to get that production out, we were going to do it—and we were going to do it my way, because my way worked."

While Long was away, the plant manager, frustrated by the backsliding, got the supervisors together. Why aren't you guys cooperating? he asked. It looks like you're trying to work against us.

The supervisors, emotions pent up in the same way as the workers had been earlier, unloaded. This is your system not our system, they said. You've been making all these changes, coming in with all these systems, without us in mind, without us as a part of it.

Long soon heard of the uproar. He and other managers got the supervisors back together. Dexter, a big man with a cascading beard and penetrating eyes, said that he and others felt like they had been run over. The kaizen teams came in, took over an area, transformed it, and gave it back. But the supervisors, unlike the workers, hadn't taken part in the thinking that went into the change, and they didn't understand why all the changes were made. Meanwhile, they had to put up with crap from their workers.

"It was a very tough time," Dexter says. "People were feeling used and abused instead of involved and empowered."

Like the workers earlier, the supervisors were on the outside, powerlessly looking in on their own worlds. The workers and managers had gotten lots of training, but the front-line supervisors had gotten little. The whole point of the continuous-improvement system was to highlight problems. As people in the business said, "Problems are good. No problem is a big problem." But having subordinates highlight problems felt to old-school supervisors like grandstanding.

In the meeting, Long admitted he and other leaders of the lean-production campaign had made mistakes. He said they would make things right. He realized that another crucial point had escaped him and other managers: A plant needs supervisors who know how to respond to workers who bring up problems. Though changing behavior ran against the grain of human nature, the supervisors had to be excited when they saw a problem.

So Long saw they were missing a final piece—involving *all* management, every level, as they advanced the system of continuous improvement. At the time, Ohba's consultant wrote, "What must change: In the future, the kaizen activity needs to be <u>owned</u> by IMT at the project area." He suggested that IMT assign a kaizen member, supervisor, and team member—all three—to each work area.

In other words, IMT had hit a limit using tools and spreading philosophy. Those alone did not guarantee an appropriate response to problems, did not create a sustainable enterprise. Long and others, as if reprising the work of participative-management guru Carl Frost from the days of D.J. and Hugh De Pree, had to develop managers at every level. "It's the whole management structure" that makes lean production work, Long says, "not just the top management or the continuous-improvement team."

LONG NOW KNEW WHAT to do. He ramped up the intensity of training—this time with energy devoted to helping supervisors with one of the finer arts of participative management: openly accepting problems and engaging others in their solutions. Muscat and Long expanded the workshops from one to three weeks. Instead of hiring outsiders to do the training, they trained the supervisors themselves.

Dexter and other supervisors noticed the refined approach almost overnight. "I wasn't being told, 'You will do this,'" he says. Instead, managers told him where they wanted IMT to go and asked him to help them get there. He then brought his team together and did the same. "This is where we need to be," he would tell workers, "and these are the reasons why...can you help us get there?"

Old habits did die hard. "It was very difficult for me," Dexter says. He was used to telling workers that his way was right, that they were just not trying hard enough. Now he was supposed to thank people for bringing up problems and testing changes—even if the changes went awry.

Dexter noticed that his openness encouraged the flow of fresh ideas, however. On the paint line, his team had been having trouble getting paint powder to stick in file-cabinet corners. Because the guns applied charged powder particles instead of wet ones, the spray bent toward the closest grounded surface—the side of the file cabinet. His people first said, if we only had new paint guns, we could shoot those corners fine. But Dexter resisted. The new guns cost thousands of dollars. One of Dexter's people then suggested alternatives—including trying a slotted tip, which laid the powder right into the difficult-to-reach metal seams.

After a few rounds of having workers show him a better way, Dexter began to sound like a different supervisor. "My personal philosophy is my role is [to be like] support staff," he says, "I'm only as successful as the team members are who work with me every day. I need to be able to break down the barriers they are having and help with their struggles. And that's what this process is really opening my eyes to."

The lessons of more than three years coalesced for Long and the roving leaders trained in lean production. When they started, they thought the tools were the system. But they saw that, if they viewed the system like a wheel, the tools were just one spoke, and as soon as they rolled down the road a bit, the wheel broke. So they added a second spoke, the philosophy that brought the workers into focus. That helped, but the wheel needed a third spoke—a management that championed problem-solving at all levels. Long and others devised a drawing of a three-spoke wheel, and as they made the system their own, they started calling it the Herman Miller Production System.

Although they had the system figured out on paper at this point, they still had not put it entirely into practice. Ohba, in his visits, was not satisfied with what he saw at IMT. He and his team pressed managers to finish their journey. Ohba had set a goal of 18 months for them to get to "showcase" condition. It was now, in late 1999, three and a half years later. Despite the progress, Ohba kept saying the same thing: You have much work to do.

By this point, not only had Muscat and Goodson decided they had found the solution to their problems. They were enjoying the glow of turned-around financial results. Inventory had dropped from $3.8 million to $1.7 million, scrap from $960,764 to $479,249. Inventory turns, a measure of efficiency, had soared from 13 to 30. Sales had grown from $82 million to $89 million—in spite of order volumes shifting to lower-cost units for SQA. With such results, executives like CEO Mike Volkema wanted to apply the new Herman Miller Production System in every plant.

Ohba was not sure the company was ready. Everyone inside Herman Miller, however, felt they absolutely needed the guru and his team's support for spreading lean production into every corner of their operations. On December 16, 1999, Ohba agreed to meet. All the big guns were there, including CEO Volkema. Volkema then made a pitch for Ohba's help across the company.

Ohba answered flatly: No.

Despite Herman Miller's show of gratitude and earnestness, Ohba said he didn't have enough people to go to other Herman Miller plants. He urged Herman Miller to finish the work at IMT. Make IMT a model of what the Herman Miller Production System could do, he said, so that Herman Miller has its own lean-production showcase for the rest of the company.

Ohba did say he would consider helping Herman Miller with a new initiative: expanding lean production up and down IMT's value stream—to improve customer order-taking on the upstream end, for example, and file-cabinet shipping on the downstream end. But he stressed that IMT had lots of work to do to sustain day-to-day improvement on the shop floor. Top management, he said, has to question operators directly about what they see that looks like waste. Get the operators to think! he said.

After the meeting, one of Ohba's chief consultants pressed Long and others to start asking those probing questions. The guru and his disciples were not going to answer them for IMT: "What *is* showcase?" "What are the targets [for the business]? "To get to showcase, what is missing?" "What behavior changes are required from management?" "

Ohba notified Muscat a month later that he would finish the IMT coaching. And over the next six months, Long and Muscat did bring the plant to the showcase level. They moved the former batch-manufacturing operation to a one-piece-flow pull system. From then on, once every three months, Ohba's team would bring in other companies for a tour of the showcase plant, to see the tools, philosophy, and management system working together.

For their success, both Long and O'Keefe won bigger roles at Herman Miller. CEO Volkema insisted that all Herman Miller plants adopt the new production system, O'Keefe moved to the Zeeland and Holland plants. There, in just one effort, he cut the floor space for making Action Office panels to 125,000 square feet from 272,000. Long took the post of training chief for the lean-production system, eventually moving the three-spoke system from the plant to the office—and then to suppliers and dealers.

Continuous improvement didn't end at IMT. In fact, Long worried constantly that they could lose their showcase status at any time unless they kept progressing. In the end, it took five more years, until 2005, to essentially meet Ohba's original goal. By that time, IMT had long since moved the bulk of its original plant people into other jobs. And it assembled the same number of pedestals while running with one line, two shifts, and 20 people—not far off Ohba's expectations in 1996 (one line, two shifts, 16 people).

IMT had come miles in its journey from two lines, four work cells, three shifts, and 126 people. The cost savings played a big role in helping the company survive the freefall during the dot-com crash. And in spite of the smaller plant-floor workforce, IMT could now easily meet fast-turnaround requests. The stamping press operators had slashed changeover time from several hours to a matter of minutes. The elapsed time from production order to shipped file cabinet dropped from 62 to 3 hours.

Like the shift to economic profit, the new system—renamed the Herman Miller Performance System—became more than a program at Herman Miller. It became a way of life in a sustainable company. So much so that environmental chief Paul Murray would later say that the plant waste-reduction teams—teams that had worked together for 15 years since the founding of the green team—had become passé. Cutting landfill volumes, hazardous waste, and solvent-based VOCs all became natural goals in the drive for waste-free, lean production. As one company leader would say, economic profit, the Herman Miller Performance System, and environmental management—"the three create the perfect collision."

CHAPTER 8

Cradle to Cradle

Joining Herman Miller in 2001 were two young men whose knowledge of sustainability was nil. One was a chemical engineer, the other a purchasing expert. The first knew about polymers, the second about buying materials. To these men, Herman Miller's research and development team handed the job of proving that Herman Miller could put into action a rigorous method for fully sustainable design.

Gabe Wing, the engineer, had been content working in a cinder-block lab composing plastics for a nearby molding company. Scott Charon, the purchasing guy, had been buying materials for a maker of car parts, Johnson Controls. Both had heard good things about Herman Miller, and when jobs came open, they were drawn by a unique challenge: Assure that every molecule going into a new product, and every molecule coming out of a used-up product, was environmentally healthy.

Wing was used to getting a chemical problem, pondering some fundamentals, and driving straight to a chemical formula for a solution. The task at Herman Miller didn't follow a straight line. The R&D team wanted not just a solution but a program fashioned to fit within Herman Miller's way of doing things. The journey to a solution had been started by Bill Dowell a decade earlier with his DfE guidelines, kicked off by the Aeron project. Since then, the intent to design sustainably had stretched across the company. But the execution of that intent remained unfinished.

Ambitions had also grown beyond anything the early earth-friendly design team—and people like Dowell and Paul Murray—had originally imagined. The environmental leaders in the company now wanted to deliver more than product designs featuring elements of earth friendliness. They wanted products whose cycle of creation and destruction mimicked the earth's natural cycles.

The goal, in other words, was to create things that, when worn out and cast off as waste, could become new material for other products. That meant that Herman Miller would make new things from old things, new products composed of materials recycled from worn-out ones, ad infinitum, nothing lost in the cycle. This would take Bill Dowell's earlier dream of cradle-to-grave responsibility one step further. The company would figure out how not just to take back products responsibly but prepare for turning them into feedstock for new products.

Wing and Charon were named the two roving leaders to make this happen. And to them fell the ambitious goal outlined by the leaders before them: Make sure Herman Miller is the first company in the industry to come to market with a "comprehensive design protocol for sustainability."

Not everyone thought the two men could succeed. Naysayers told them: Your program is a fad. You're a passing corporate indulgence. In two years, you will be gone. Though buoyed by the chance to pioneer a new protocol, Wing and Charon found such comments disquieting.

Herman Miller's swooning business results could, alone, have disquieted anyone. After a business boom, in which dot-com companies bought Aeron chairs by the truckload, sales of the chairs had peaked. The roller coaster of the economic cycle appeared also to be peaking, and customers were starting to defer purchases of all furniture. CEO Mike Volkema, almost the day Wing and Charon started, announced layoffs of 700 people.

Amid the uncertainty, Wing and Charon set up shop in the Design Yard, the complex of offices built in 1986 to mimic a midwestern farm. Although the buildings looked on the outside like a set of low-slung steel barns abutting red silos, on the inside daylight poured onto a trade-show-like pavilion of avant-garde cubicles. From the ceiling hung life-size papier-mâché figures. One, a crouched man with the amiable, long-nosed face of D.J. De Pree, glided earthward while working butterfly wings with hand grips.

Wing and Charon were joining an organization that had attempted many untried and risky design efforts. They would carry on that tradition, in the spirit of D.J. De Pree. Once and for all, they would seek to institute a system in which Herman Miller ended the creation of harmful products—products that, during manufacture, use, or disposal, injected poisons, foreign bodies, or wastes into nature's circulatory system.

AS OUTSIDERS, WING AND Charon had one thing going for them: They had not dreamed up this challenge themselves. Research chief Gary Miller, a mechanical engineer who in 1975 similarly left a good job to take up with Herman Miller, had laid the groundwork. Manager Keith Winn, a designer in the 1990s green-building effort, led a groundbreaking team with Dowell, Murray, and others to develop an early protocol. CEO Volkema had also blessed the effort. Wing and Charon came on as the lieutenants to veteran colonels and generals who had marked this effort as the next campaign in the company's journey to sustainability.

The idea for the cradle-to-cradle system originated with Bill McDonough, the architect who had designed the Phoenix Designs building in 1994, since renamed the GreenHouse. McDonough had made three overtures trying to get Miller to consider the new system, the first in 1997. Miller was initially put off by McDonough's approach, which struck him as suggesting that companies had gone wrong with the environment and should make amends. Miller wouldn't countenance a system that came across as punishment for a reputable, profit-making company.

McDonough refined his approach, and by his third attempt, came back with an offer whose assumptions had been turned upside down. He wasn't suggesting Herman Miller act out of guilt or take blame for industry waywardness. He was suggesting a plan for continuous improvement. His program would make a good company better, rather than making a bad company good. At Miller's urging, McDonough's approach now mimicked principles in Herman Miller's new manufacturing philosophy.

Miller, won over, invited McDonough to meet with Volkema and CFO Brian Walker in May 1998. The meeting took place during Holland's annual tulip festival. McDonough arrived and gave an impassioned pitch outlining the cradle-to-cradle theory. He earned everyone's admiration, not just because he'd acted in a business-friendly way, but because he said something else: If applying a concept to design didn't make business sense, a company shouldn't do it. Companies should remake design so that green thinking made money, he said, in fact *more* money.

McDonough played on people's heartstrings, too. While laying out his plan with overhead slides and pen strokes on a whiteboard, he recounted examples of business products that ran contrary to his thinking. He pointed to black clothing—and the poisons used in making black dyes. He noted the chemicals in women's lipstick—raising alarm in a lipstick-wearing manager in the room. He decried the risk of crayons because some brands had once contained lead. Companies pay too little heed, he said, to the harm done by their products in production, use, and disposal.

McDonough described his solution: Break down the composition of all materials that go into all products. Go all the way to the molecular level. After inventorying every chemical, get rid of the bad ones. Only by dissecting the composition of all the stuff you're making, he said, can you stop using all the bad molecules. If you cut the bad molecules, you cut the bad impacts.

McDonough could convey confidence in the system because he had partnered with German chemist and green activist Michael Braungart. The two had jointly created and tested the concept. With it, Herman Miller could analyze every element in every material in every product, including the solvents in dyes, additives in plastic, and heavy metals in pigments.

McDonough did not argue for doing away with ingenious man-made plastics, alloys, and pigments. He did not say Herman Miller should make chairs only out of natural materials like wood, wool, and fur. He and Braungart, founders of McDonough Braungart Design Chemistry, or MBDC, looked at materials as having two cradle-to-cradle cycles. In the natural one, people used and recycled "biological nutrients" like wood and cotton fiber. In the man-made one, they used and recycled "technical nutrients" like plastics and metals. Either way, the nutrients flowed in closed loops, the waste from old products converted to materials for new.

In the ideal world, the use of the so-called MBDC protocol meant the end of landfilling. It also meant the death of incineration. It would nurture planetary restoration. Materials would flow as organic matter flows in a forest, from soils to treetops and back again. McDonough argued that the problem facing mankind wasn't too much stuff. It was too much stuff that couldn't be turned safely and repeatedly into materials for more stuff of the same or different kinds.

Volkema was taken by McDonough's logic. The CEO, a lawyer known for big-picture thinking, heard in the argument something new. It reconciled a nagging conflict between partisans of the environment and those of business. Green activists attacked the concept of growth for its power to despoil the planet. Businesspeople defended growth as the lifeblood of business and improved living standards. McDonough, though a green activist at heart, showed that environmentalists no longer had to cast economic growth as a villain.

"This was the first time," says Volkema, "I had somebody explain to me how a world could continue to consume—and how growth in consumption could be good—and at the same time not have the same devastating impact on the biosphere that we were currently having."

McDonough fueled the thirst of Herman Miller executives to go the next step in greening the company. Along with the cradle-to-cradle theory, which he developed with Braungart. McDonough had come with a system for putting it into practice. He had paired thinking and action. The Herman Miller executives all bought in. They decided that, in the next year, a team from Herman Miller and MBDC would construct a prototype of the "sustainability protocol."

The team, led by designer Keith Winn, initially started small. It aimed to test the concept on a single product, the Aeron. By mid-1999, though, they could see they wouldn't get far with an inventory of chemicals for a single or even several products. Isolated pilot projects, as Bill Dowell had learned during his pioneering work on the Aeron in the early 1990s, wouldn't necessarily introduce the concept to the ranks of researchers, designers, and engineers across the company. They had to take a more ambitious approach to make the protocol part of the product-development process.

They faced another problem that had also plagued Dowell—creating a program that did more than offer unbidden advice to engineers. The advisory approach left it up to engineers to decide what to do. Taking action was essentially optional. They wanted an approach that instead made green design a part of the normal work-day of engineers. That required a decision-making tool that could help engineers, when under deadline pressure, to compare options. In the same way that engineers compared options based on cost and performance data, they could compare them based on green data.

The team carried on with the pilot to test their ideas on the Aeron. They took apart the chair and laid the pieces on white paper, labeling each part and identifying its supplier. They diagrammed all the relationships on the wall, and they timed and videotaped their work. They then set out to ask every supplier by e-mail and fax for the chemical formulas of each of the materials. Getting this data was elemental for the MBDC concept to work.

The pilot bogged down in this phase. Most suppliers ignored the requests. Others mistrusted Herman Miller's intentions. One CEO called Volkema to verify the need for the data and be reassured that Herman Miller wouldn't share trade secrets with competitors. It took the team months, and multiple follow-up calls, to get just 80 percent of the data they needed, and several suppliers wouldn't cooperate.

The Aeron's armrest served as a good example of why a pilot could take so long. The armrest had a PVC skin. The skin covered polyurethane foam. The foam bonded to a rigid plastic. The plastic attached to a metal bracket. The bracket was affixed to the chair by bolts. The arm assembly alone would require an encyclo-pedic research effort. The team had to define each part's composi-tion down to 100 parts per million, identifying each chemical by its unique CAS, or Chemical Abstract Services, number, the standard chemical-industry descriptor.

The Aeron exercise also highlighted the barriers to creating a tool an engineer would actually use. No engineer could easily study reams of chemical descriptors and reconcile them with the com-pany's green strategies. And if the company wanted engineers to find a new sustainable product material, it would have to ask them to sort through a host of criteria for a material's "ecological intelli-gence." That was simply more work than engineers could or would perform.

Engineers also had to understand the two cycles. For a chemi-cal to cycle as a biological nutrient, it had to degrade completely, without persisting or accumulating in the environment. It had to prove safe for people to handle and be nontoxic and free of properties that could provoke cancer, mutations, and infertility. For a chemical to cycle as a technical nutrient, it had to come from previously used, recycled, or refurbished materials. In turn, the materials had to enter a proven recycling stream that would yield material for new products of the same kind.

If an engineer wanted to use technical nutrients, he or she had to comply with other requirements. The material first had to give years of service. It then had to appear in products in a way that allowed easy disassembly by recyclers. For recycling to actually work, the processes used to make the materials, such as steel alloys and plastics, had to run in reverse, so that if nature couldn't degrade the material, manmade processes could.

The number of new constraints posed by green design challenged the sustainability-protocol team. Part of what kept the team members going were the high aspirations of the company. In his 1999 memo appointing the team, research chief Miller wrote to team leader Winn, "It is our ambition to establish Herman Miller, Inc., as the benchmark for a Sustainable Company in the World's Industrial Community to the benefit of our end users, communities, and the planet. We believe this project can help insure our long-term vitality as a manufacturer and an employer."

A YEAR INTO THE work, in mid-2000, the team delivered its first pass on the protocol. It included a set of computer-based tools—guidelines, worksheets, spreadsheets, a database, scorecards—for integrating green decision making into the guts of the new-product development process. Because the criteria for green design were so numerous, the team simplified the job for engineers. They created a prototype to help with three tasks: how to limit material choices to those containing safe and healthy chemicals; how to choose materials with high recycled content that recycle easily; and how to design product assembly that eases disassembly. The three tasks were depicted as three points of a triangle, with material health at the top.

Miller, whose people had earlier searched hard for a workable sustainable-design system, felt the team had a winning prototype. In November, he signed McDonough—who in his trademark hyperbolic style referred to the work as the "next industrial revolution"—to a new three-year contract to help put it into action. At the core of the system would be the materials database. When finished, it would give good, bad, or indifferent readings for each material. Engineers could then easily do a good job of intelligent ecological design.

Paired with the database would be the new product-rating scorecard. The scorecard would become the most visible of the tools, detailing the chemical makeup of each material, working from a product's bill of materials. It would then rate the chemistry as green (100 percent rating) or not (0 percent rating). To make interpretation easy, materials would get a color code. Green would indicate materials as preferred; yellow, as minor risk; gray, as having too little information; and red, as risky. All red materials would be slated for phase-out.

Along with the chemistry ratings, the scorecard would include a recycling score (combining the scores for recycled content and recyclability) and an ease-of-disassembly score, each ranging from 0 percent to 100 percent. When engineers tallied all the ratings, they could get a composite score, called the DfE score. A DfE score over 50 percent was considered passably green—not perfect but darn good. Anything less was wanting (See figure 8.1.).

Though the team tried to make the database and scorecard easy to read and interpret, the thinking and machinery behind them were not. Someone would have to work out the mechanics. The team came to a consensus that the company was going to need a "Chem-E," or chemical engineer, because nobody at Herman Miller had chemical-engineering skills. And they would also need a purchasing "catalyst," because nobody at Herman Miller knew how to buy materials formulated to be green at the molecular level— and without the expertise of the buyers, the entire cradle-to-cradle machine wouldn't run.

THAT'S WHEN MILLER OPENED up jobs for Wing and Charon. Although the two men had the initial team's work to get them started, they had much more still to do. They also worried about how they would be received by company veterans. As agents of a new green order, would they come across as the environmental police? Would they find designers, engineers, and purchasing people open to their requests to comply with new problem-solving constraints?

They embarked on their efforts with essentially a blueprint and the second-hand lessons from the first team. Nobody had yet fashioned the prototypes into working tools, nor had anyone installed them within the product-development process. The MBDC protocol, often now called the "cradle-to-cradle protocol" or, at Herman Miller, simply DfE, had not yet been put into operation.

After learning what they could from old hands—Dowell, Winn, and Murray among them—Wing and Charon called the few other MBDC clients starting on this journey: Visteon, the auto-parts supplier; Interface, the carpet maker; and Nike. Nike had a year's jump on Herman Miller in this work. Although Nike's system, tailored to work for shoes and clothes, wouldn't work for furniture, it gave Wing and Charon a shot of confidence to know that the company was pursuing the same goal. Says Wing, "To find someone in a noncompetitive industry taking the same approach—and a fantastic company—that reinforced [our thinking] that 'Yes, we're on the right track.'"

Looking at how to put the blueprints into action, Wing and Charon first addressed how to weight and score products using the scorecard. They decided to give a one-third weighting each to material health, recyclability, and disassembly. They changed the colors to range from green (DfE score of 100 percent) to yellow to orange to red (DfE score 0 percent). To get the chemical database up and running, they spent $100,000 in technology costs and, as they started feeding materials to MBDC, another $300,000 on MBDC's material assessments.

Their work triggered fresh debates on the acceptability of various materials. Which were preferred? Which harmful? One material singled out as harmful was an old nemesis, PVC. Greenpeace and other green activists had long decried the material for leaching toxic additives, and during incineration, releasing carcinogens. Many people at Herman Miller—in spite of the controversy spurred five years earlier by Bill Dowell's earth-friendly design team—still doubted the gravity of the charges. They noted that, from the banding on desk edges to the jackets on wiring harnesses to the bases of Action Office panels, PVC ranked as the material of choice from the point of view of performance. So cheap, formable, durable, and versatile, it beat all competing materials hands down.

And yet MBDC ranked it as a "red" material. Braungart, McDonough's associate, and others believed PVC endangered health in every stage of its life cycle. According to MBDC, PVC was ecologically inappropriate because it contained so much organochlorine.

Figure 8.1 Herman Miller DfE Scorecard ("Product Assessment Tool"). Image courtesy of Herman Miller, Inc.

Assessment Date
00/00/00

Product Number	Description	DfE Score
CHA-1234	ECO Chair	61%

	Disassembly Score	Material Chemistry Score	Recyclability Score	Rec./Ren. Content Score
	73%	49%	76%	14%
			61%	

Bill of Material

Part Number	QTY	Description	Material - Print	Supplier	Wt (g.)	Disassembly % Weight Credit	Material Chemistry Rating	Material Chemistry % Weight Credit	Recyclability % Weight Credit	Rec./Ren. Content % Weight Credit
123456-BK	1.00	FRAME, SEAT	16 Ga. 1008-1010 Steel	Frame Inc.	2,500	100	Yellow	50	100	28
123457	1.00	PAN - SEAT	20% GF Polypropylene	Molders Plus	600	0	Yellow	50	50	0
123458	4.00	FASTENER - PU	Sintered Metal	Fastener Land	42	100	Green	100	100	20
123459	4.00	FASTENER - ST	Spring Steel	Fastener Land	1	100	Yellow	50	100	20
123460	4.00	BUMPER	Super Rubber	Importers RUs	26	100	Orange	25	0	0
123461	4.00	CONNECTOR CLIP	Nylon 6/6	Molders Plus	26	0	Yellow	50	100	0
123462	1.00	BACK	20% GF Polypropylene	Molders Plus	1,000	100	Yellow	50	50	0
123464	2.00	ARM ASSY,RH & LH	380 Aluminum	Importers RUs	404	0	Orange	25	50	0
123467	2.00	ARM LH / RL	Polyrazz 1234	Molders Plus	188	0	Yellow	50	50	0
123468	2.00	O-RING	Silicone Rubber Fill	Importers RUs	1	0	Red	0	0	0
123469	2.00	SPRING	Steel	Importers RUs	10	0	Yellow	50	50	0
123470	4.00	CHAIR FEET	Sintered Metal	Importers RUs	100	0	Green	100	50	0
					4,898					

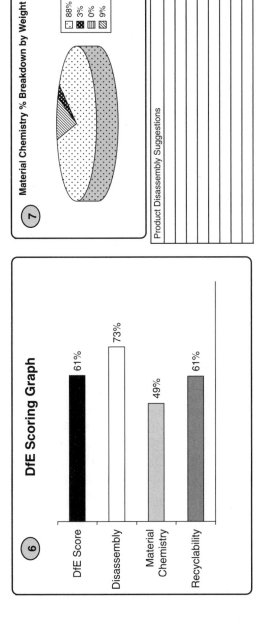

6 DfE Scoring Graph

- DfE Score — 61%
- Disassembly — 73%
- Material Chemistry — 49%
- Recyclability — 61%

7 Material Chemistry % Breakdown by Weight

- 88%
- 3%
- 0%
- 9%

Product Disassembly Suggestions

This chart represents a simplified version of the assessment tool Herman Miller's Design for the Environment (DfE) team uses to rate a product's overall sustainability.

The tool assigns each product a series of credits related to factors including its ease of disassembly, material chemistry, and recyclability. Added together, the credits give the product a score that rates its overall sustainability, per internal Herman Miller standards.

The example shown is fictitious and designed only to illustrate how the assessment tool works, as of 2011.

Key to Sections

1. This section provides a breakdown of all components of the product, including material composition and weight.
2. This section assesses the degree of disassembly possible for each product component. A component that can be disassembled (such as the seat frame) earns a "credit" of 100%; a component that cannot be disassembled (such as a glued assembly), receives a 0% credit.
3. The "Material Chemistry" section rates the human health and environmental factors of each product component on a color scale that extends from green (preferred, 100% credit) to red (problematic, 0% credit).
4. This section represents the recyclability of the material after the product's useful life, along with the recycled and/or renewable content of the material.
5. This is the product's overall DfE score, determined by averaging the Disassembly Score, Material Chemistry Score, and Recyclability Score.
6. This color-coded bar graph summarizes the product's key scoring.
7. This pie chart breaks down the product's material chemistry rating by total weight. In the example, the product is 88% yellow, 9% orange, 3% green, and 0% red.

It generated chronic toxicants in manufacture—notably carcinogens vinyl chloride monomer and dioxins. And it generated dioxins and furans when incinerated. Even the recycling industry had concerns about PVC, since it could contaminate reclaimed PET (soda bottles), making the recycled PET brittle and yellow.

The debates led to an investigation to determine how hard getting rid of PVC would be. The results showed that the plastic turned up in most Herman Miller products. The most prominent one was the Aeron chair, which had PVC-covered arm pads. Another prominent one was the new Resolve system, which Bill Dowell had vetted a few years earlier. Resolve was an otherwise green product, a vastly dematerialized office-panel product made mostly of steel.

While the debates over materials like PVC raged, Wing and Charon had other work to do. The most critical was to start feeding data into the cradle-to-cradle assessment machinery. The entire DfE protocol depended on data, but they had not yet collected any. To rectify that, they had to reach out to suppliers in a big way. They would have to research material chemistries, go to suppliers asking for secret chemical formulas, and press suppliers to reformulate chemicals to deliver clean and green materials.

Having learned from the Aeron pilot that phone, fax, and e-mail requests didn't work, they took to the road, touring supplier factories making leather, plastic parts, steel, laminates, fabrics, and glass. In their first six months, they visited 200 companies. The two men figured the face-to-face approach would build the trust needed to get proprietary chemical information. It would succeed where phone calls had failed. They knew they were traveling into sensitive territory, though, and they wondered: What if nobody gives us their formulas?

They decided to take a straightforward approach. During supplier visits, they introduced the new DfE program and guided suppliers through its philosophy and workings. They then directly asked for the chemical formulas, promising to work with suppliers to find alternatives if questionable chemicals turned up. They also promised—often signing nondisclosure agreements—to keep the data confidential.

Few suppliers simply handed over the information. They had never been asked for it before, and few even had it at hand, since the composition and processes used to produce most industrial substances are trade secrets. As one supplier said, it was like asking for the recipe to Coca-Cola Classic. Some said they would play along, but others flatly said no. Some of the suppliers who wouldn't cooperate simply felt, given the plunge in Herman Miller sales during the dot-com crash, that the request was not worth bothering with—and they told Wing and Charon so.

Wing and Charon had no choice but to persist. They couldn't do their jobs without the data. Although the two men tried not to get pushy, they did exercise the leverage they had. For one thing, with time and money, they could use chemical analysis to determine the material compositions themselves. The secrets would yield to chemical investigation. But more important, they could use the cooperation of one supplier to encourage the cooperation of the next.

The first supplier they went to, BASF, gave them the formulas without hesitating. BASF, also an MBDC client, supplied Herman Miller with multiple plastics, the most notable being the Petra-brand PET, or polyethylene terephthalate. This was the same PET used in the Aeron seat and back frames. With a giant like BASF in their camp, Wing and Charon could gently pressure the suppliers: If you don't give us your chemical data, we can buy our materials from another big company. Often, everyone in the room could guess the name of the big competitor.

Some companies still declined. But with BASF in line, resistance by suppliers of similar materials started to wane. One even reversed course when faced with losing business in the downturn.

The most virulent resistance to their work came as a result of a philosophical debate. Wing found that most chemical companies assessed material safety based on risk. In the science of risk assessment, a chemical at a low enough concentration, bound tightly enough in a composite, poses no danger to users. One company that refused to offer data brought in its PhD toxicologist to push risk reasoning. He argued that the legally required health and safety information was readily available on Material Safety Data Sheets, or MSDSs, a standard chemical-industry form. Company scientists had done their homework, he said, and their material was free of risk.

But Wing explained that Herman Miller assessed materials based on hazard. Wing and Charon aimed not at minimizing risk but at assessing and eliminating hazard across a material's life cycle. Some people called this the "precautionary" approach. If a chemical could cause harm at any time—in manufacture, use, disposal, incineration—Herman Miller wanted to stay clear of it.

"We're fully convinced our products are safe as used," Wing says he told the man, "but the question is, Are they the best choices we can make?"

The toxicologist, and later other suppliers, reacted angrily to the precautionary approach. One expert, galled by the position, denounced both Herman Miller's effort and MBDC's cradle-to-cradle system, attacking people personally in the process.

Wing and Charon didn't try to win this or similar debates. They simply tried to position their work as a business decision: If you don't play, that's okay; we'll turn elsewhere. Says Wing: "It's a fundamental shift, for sure, and they saw it as a threat... [but] there's less risk to us as a manufacturing company if we move on the precautionary path."

By late 2001, Wing and Charon had constructed a working system of the new DfE protocol. They had not only filled in their database with the supplier data, they had refined the other parts of the DfE system, namely, the scorecard and guidelines for disassembly. Their work was a milestone. With the new system, an engineer could make materials choices, and with each selection, check how his or her DfE score rose or fell. The system went well beyond an advisory service. Product managers, who might once have simply asked for a greener product, could now specify what they meant: Make sure we use no red materials, and work on this until we hit a DfE score of 50 percent.

DESPITE ALL THE WORK, many people in the design and engineering groups had not traveled as far in their thinking as Wing, Charon, and the leaders of the environmental team. Ironically, the steering committee for the DfE effort, which included Murray and others, had mixed feelings about letting the DfE tool drive all decisions. Wing and Charon saw this clearly when they heard that, behind the scenes one of the members, the company's purchasing chief Drew Schramm, planned to replace the steel runners capping the Ethospace line of office panels with PVC.

In light of having advanced the DfE work to such an extent, Wing and Charon thought the move preposterous. It raised the question: Are the leaders' hearts really in this?

Wing and Charon asked the steering committee to address the subject, and when the day of the meeting arrived, they found that

Schramm came unrepentant. Hired in 1998 to shape up Herman Miller's purchasing operation, he thought the changeover to PVC a no-brainer. The high-tech sector of the U.S. economy was going bust. Herman Miller sales, down a gut-wrenching 31 percent in the last half of the year, had nosedived along with the Nasdaq stock index, now 60 percent off its 2000 high. Under the circumstances, Schramm felt he had responded perfectly to the company's drive to save money. This was an emergency.

Schramm's response put Wing and Charon at a crossroads. They understood the economic imperatives, but they were charged with responding to the environmental ones. They presented lots of data to remind the committee of the cloud over PVC. It created toxins in the making. It gave off potentially unhealthy gases during use. It released toxins during incineration. As for business concerns, they said, more and more customers were asking for PVC-free products.

Hard-charging and headstrong, Schramm, who majored in business and later earned an MBA, nonetheless made a strong case. In his world, people were driven by dollar signs. The simple fact was this: Using PVC would save the company $2.5 million. That $2.5 million would flow straight to the company's bottom line.

Wing and Charon persisted. Others in the room joined their cause. They wanted Schramm to reverse the PVC changeover.

Schramm thought the DfE duo and their supporters weren't thinking clearly. Prove to me, he said, how we're going to get that $2.5 million back.

One person on the committee suggested that using PVC-free products would burnish the Herman Miller brand image. A greener image would spur interest in the company's products.

Schramm wouldn't have any of it: So I am to believe, he said, that I'm not going to save this $2.5 million because it's going to damage our brand image? Show me how the brand image is going to get us $2.5 million in profit!

No one had much of an answer.

Look, Schramm persisted, if you can't prove that to me, why are we doing it?

Schramm had worked before at Praxair Industrial Gases, Abbott Laboratories, and Avon. At all of these companies, if a buyer didn't cut costs, company bosses found someone else who did. In Schramm's world, people defined a winner as a buyer who cut costs by acquiring materials more cheaply. A winner met his or her goals—and got rewarded for it. A winner took steps to stop the bleeding during an economic disaster. In his view, anyone in favor of PVC in the worst downturn in the furniture business since the Great Depression was in favor of hurting the company.

The meeting ended without a final decision. As for Schramm, he left feeling he was the corporate soldier riding to the company's economic rescue. As for Wing and Charon, they left on edge. Just having the PVC question up for grabs was unnerving. With so many people in the company losing jobs, what did it mean if the DfE committee's commitment to sustainability faltered? Would the jobs of the DfE duo be the next to go?

The decision was escalated to CEO Volkema. At the time, Volkema was deep into a task that would define his tenure, the company's restructuring. He was merging operations, laying people off, closing plants, cutting programs. Still, Volkema's message came back: We're going to keep pursuing the route to sustainability.

"It was an easy question to answer," says Volkema. "We all knew we had to get rid of PVC. It was a small component of a much larger commitment that we had made around the environment, so it would be incongruent to go, well...we don't have to pursue it any more because this is hard. Hey, all this stuff is hard at the beginning."

Schramm was stunned. He would have to find other ways to save money. He would have to go back to his people and explain the danger of PVC. And hardest of all, he would have to rethink his role as a Herman Miller executive. The decision shook his certainty about approaching decisions as a numbers-driven, right-brain businessman.

Wing and Charon saw the power of the company's dedication to sustainability. They felt reaffirmed that they were leading the company down the right path. "That really sold us," says Charon, "That was kind of our epiphany...upper management was committed to our program."

WITH VOLKEMA'S LANDMARK SUPPORT for putting the long-term green of environment above the short-term green of finance, two things appeared certain. One, top-level support wasn't going to go away, even amid scarce profits. Two, business-minded people elsewhere in the organization, as if by reflex, would continue to favor cost and performance in preference to everything else. That was just the way they were wired.

That brought front and center the challenge that would define Wing's and Charon's tenures: winning the hearts and minds not just of an adversary or two, but of everyone in the ranks of Herman Miller's design, engineering, and purchasing operations. However convincing their argument, most people they worked with had been trained to deliver reasonably priced products that looked, worked, and lasted exceedingly well. To succeed with furniture, as the saying went, "You have to win the beauty contest." Engineers would default to that task every time.

Wing and Charon attacked this challenge first by launching a series of sessions to train all designers, engineers, and purchasing people in the new protocol. They spent six months showing 300 people the scorecard and explaining materials chemistry, design for disassembly, and recyclability. To give people a hands-on understanding of how these characteristics affected recyclability, they gave teams a chair and handed them a screwdriver, wrench, pry bar, and hammer. Disassemble the chair, they said, weigh the parts, time yourself.

They gave most teams a Caper chair, a light, plastic, four-legged, nonswiveling utility chair with a caster on each leg. Taking the chair apart and spreading out the parts opened people's eyes to disassembly, and in turn, to the chemistry and recyclability of each part. Most parts had no label, for example, so for starters, they learned how difficult recycling would be if they didn't ask suppliers to mark the composition of each part.

"A lot of people thought this would just be another program that would come and go," says Charon. "It was our job to tell people, 'No, this is the way we're going to do business.'"

By early 2002, Wing and Charon had taken the program far enough that Herman Miller publicly announced its "measurable progress" in developing "a protocol for sustainability that creates economic value while also valuing the environment." The two men had taken a major step in integrating DfE into the standard process for bringing Herman Miller products to market. Every product manager already worked from a checklist—defining market channels, verifying quality and durability, testing performance. Now DfE also appeared on that list.

Wing and Charon started to influence key products still in development. One, code-named Liz, was a new task chair, a mid-priced complement to the high-end Aeron. Sales of the Equa and Ergon chairs had flattened, and the company wanted to offer a chair that gave better value for the money. Designers and engineers aimed to set a new reference point for sustainable comfort, ergonomic innovation, intuitive operation, refreshing aesthetics, and earth-friendly design. They also wanted to hit a more economical price range.

Although Liz design meetings began in 1999, the Liz design team ramped up in mid-2001. In May, with Bill Dowell, the erstwhile DfE evangelist working on chair ergonomics, the team evaluated a prototype, testing the tilt, mat-like back, lumbar support, and controls. Though they hadn't yet shared their work with Wing or Charon, they felt the chair was reasonably earth friendly. They did tell their engineers to keep away from one design element—a hunk of steel embedded in plastic to create a sturdy spine. It would be impossible to recycle.

In October 2001, Wing and Charon got started with their review. They agreed that the spine was what McDonough would call a "monstrous hybrid"—no recycler could take it apart. The engineers came back with a spine made of two pieces of recyclable nylon. This spine contained no steel at all, cost less, and was clever enough to win a patent. It showed that complying with the green-design constraint could also save money.

The company decided the chair would be a full-fledged test of using the DfE program as part of the new-product development process. Wing and Charon collected data on 180 components made from 40 materials. They determined that steel accounted for 56 percent of the chair, plastics 29 percent, aluminum 12 percent, foam 2 percent, and other materials like powder coatings and colorants, 1 percent. The chair as a whole contained 200 chemicals. In partnership with MBDC, they assessed every one.

They singled out the use of an MBDC red material in the process—PVC once again. The chair had PVC in both the arm-pad skins and the cable jacketing. The PVC accounted for only a tiny amount of material, but the red rating made the chair fail the basic DfE test. The PVC's cost was peanuts, only a few dollars of the chair's overall cost, and this would become a sticking point. The low cost helped the team in its struggle to meet cost goals.

WING AND CHARON SOON found they had another PVC clash on their hands. The chemical seemed to have become the litmus test for their program's success. They could not dictate the decisions of the Liz design team, and the product team insisted on sticking with PVC for the arm-pad skins. They saw no alternative. The two men, objecting to the engineering team's choice of PVC, asked for a hearing with the DfE steering committee.

The committee gathered in August, 2002. Given the company's dire financial straits, committee members still weren't weighing decisions by giving green concerns automatic, overriding priority. This was in spite of Volkema's earlier support. Since the previous year, Herman Miller sales had collapsed from $2.2 billion to $1.5 billion. Bonuses had evaporated. Nearly 4,000 people had lost their jobs. Volkema had vacated one million square feet of space. The company had put aside $82 million to cover the costs of closures and layoffs.

Schramm again weighed heavily the dollars-and-cents aspects of the decision. If Herman Miller came to market with a PVC-free product, what would that cost? And what new costs would it trigger if customers demanded other PVC-free products—in fact, demanded PVC-free versions of all of the items on the company's backlist? The precedent could start a landslide of new-material and engineering expenses.

The engineers and materials buyers had already made up their minds based on economics and performance. They were invested in PVC as the answer. As for the chair's cables, in a bow to green concerns, they had replaced PVC with nylon at no extra cost. As for the arm-pad skins, so far as they knew, no other material cost so little—by a long shot—nor would it form as well, resist scratches, or hold up as well over time. Changing from what was essentially the perfect material was too risky.

Many felt eliminating PVC in this case didn't really offer much of an advantage. For one thing, every company in the industry used PVC to cover foam padding. What would Herman Miller gain for being different? For another, the small amount in the arm-pad skin didn't change the DfE score much. A change at this point would delay introduction, slated for the industry's biggest trade show, NeoCon, in June. Besides, to meet the launch schedule, the supply group had already spent thousands of dollars on PVC tooling.

Although the right thing to do from an economic standpoint was obvious, the right thing to do as a company was another matter, especially during an economic crisis. To Wing and Charon, sticking with PVC was a nonstarter. By the time of the meeting, Liz had become a flagship test of the new protocol. It was destined to emerge as a showcase, an unprecedented effort by a manufacturer to produce a product designed from scratch using the MBDC protocol.

Both sides in the debate made strong points. As in the earlier decision, however, upper management stepped in. Breaking the logjam this time was the vice president in charge of product launches. Inspired by talking with Bill McDonough, he issued an edict: We're not launching the chair with any PVC. We've committed to sustainability, and we're going to make a green chair.

Wing and Charon saw that an appeal to values continued to guide key decisions at Herman Miller. "That made everything fall in place again," says Wing. "Had we not...had that support, I'm sure that because we were so close to launch we would have gone with PVC. Somebody drew a hard line in the sand and said, 'We're not going to do this.'"

WING COULDN'T QUITE RELAX, however. There was another part to the edict. The vice president told Wing, who had the most experience in plastic formulation and molding, to find a PVC substitute. To the winner of the feud over holding the line on DfE went the responsibility for finding a way forward.

Wing spent two intense weeks on the project. While few people gave a second thought to chair arm pads, they demanded rigorous engineering. They had to be comfortable while resisting abrasion, tears, and breakdown from UV light. PVC remained the benchmark for an ideal plastic, and Wing had little hope of replacing the performance and low cost of a material developed 75 years earlier by an industry making millions of tons of the stuff every year.

Along with a materials supplier and local molding company, Wing did investigate alternatives. Some of them didn't offer enough abrasion resistance. One was too tacky. All were more expensive. But he did find one plastic—thermoplastic urethane (TPU)—that appeared to be more scratch-resistant than PVC. It cost twice as much, and it increased the cost of the arm-pad assembly by a third. But TPU offered an option everyone could live with. Since the extra expense came after the discovery of the cost savings on the new nylon spine, it was easier to stomach.

In April 2003, Herman Miller introduced its PVC-free chair to the market. From the start to the end, engineers used the tools refined by Wing and Charon, and raised the material chemistry score from 48 percent to 75 percent. They increased the recyclability to 96 percent. They cut disassembly time to less than 15 minutes, which was 45 minutes less than the similarly outfitted Ergon. The chair's composite DfE score hit 80 percent, two-thirds more than the initial 63 percent.

The new chair, named the Mirra, was indeed a flagship product. It was Herman Miller's first chair designed with the cradle-to-cradle protocol, proving that the company could succeed with molecule-by-molecule analysis to guide green design. Inside the company, Mirra catalyzed more progress. By early 2003, Wing had evaluated over 250 chemicals that made up the thousands of materials Herman Miller used. The new green database contained over 850 materials. Along with the simple spreadsheet program for scoring DfE progress, the data gave engineers a tool that fit right into the way they worked, serving as a real-time gauge of green design.

By the mid-2000s, the company's top executives threw all their weight behind the new DfE approach. That put Wing and Charon in the limelight. It put their naysayers in retreat. Schramm, once the chief skeptic, completed his turnabout from antagonist to advocate. He even spearheaded an effort to get suppliers to help, piggybacking DfE on his program to extend the Herman Miller Performance System to suppliers' factory floors. And he readily admitted he had changed forever. "It probably took me a good half a year to the point where I went from fighting to listening," he says. It took "another year to agree and another year to start to become an advocate."

In time, Schramm even started to qualify suppliers based on their support for DfE. Only suppliers who handed over chemical data, reported on recyclability, and ran green factories got top grades. Schramm then revamped his and his team's performance goals to include targets for bettering DfE scores. So passionate did he become that industry peers sought him out to speak on greening the supply chain. Schramm had become one of the roving leaders of corporate environmentalism. He even took a post on the Institute for Supply Management's Committee on Sustainability and Social Responsibility.

Wing and Charon continued to integrate DfE into the business. They had come a long way from where they started in 2001, when they were utterly ignorant of DfE. Charon, who had an MBA in finance, had never even taken a course on sustainable business practices before he joined the company. Wing, though an MS in chemical engineering, had no knowledge of green chemistry. But they now took to heart the job of looking out for future generations, especially since they now had kids of their own.

In 2005, as the company introduced another green chair, the Celle, they saw their role expand again: They were charged with applying the new protocol to all products, not just new ones. Now they had to worry not just about twenty-first-century products designed from scratch, but also about products like the Eames chair and the Action Office panels designed in the 1950s, 1960s, and 1970s.

The future once predicted by many environmental leaders was coming to pass. Ninety-five percent of customer requests for Herman Miller proposals in 2010 asked questions about the environmental sustainability of the company's products. Many asked specifically about PVC. Cost and performance aside, sustainability became customers' keenest concern. Despite a backlash against stronger environmental protections during the 2008–2010 recession, 60 percent of Americans still called themselves environmentalists.

That put Herman Miller in a strong position. It also put more pressure on the roving leaders across Herman Miller, as they recognized the ever-stricter definition of "green" emerging. Even on the Mirra, only half the materials fit a hard-core environmentalist's notion of sustainability. The leaf spring, foam arm pads, and woven "AirWeav" seat were nonrecyclable. Mirra's DfE score came in short of the 100 percent that would signify that its materials would actually cycle, cradle to cradle, as biological or technical nutrients.

That's partly why chairman Volkema, despite all the progress, remained modest about the company's leap toward the cradle-to-cradle ideal. "It's still an idea in germination a decade later," he says, referring specifically to the recycling system for technical nutrients, which remains poorly developed. The take-back requirements that captured the attention of Dowell and other environmental leaders in the early 1990s had still not come to pass—at least not in the United States.

Yet the idea in germination was driving Herman Miller design on a new and promising track. The Mirra, though not yet a perfect green product, appealed to the market. In 2010, its unit sales broke the one million mark.

Meanwhile, the cradle-to-cradle ideal continued to inspire. In 2010, the governor of California, Arnold Schwarzenegger, committed his state to underwriting MBDC's now trademarked Cradle to Cradle protocol. In a region that sets precedents for green lawmaking, the governor's support marked the arrival of cradle-to-cradle chemical assessment as a new standard for manufactured products. On stage at Google headquarters, Schwarzenegger introduced two CEOs as role models in the movement. One was Shaw Industries CEO Vance Bell. The other was Herman Miller chairman Mike Volkema.

CHAPTER 9

Whiz Bang

In 2001, Gary Miller stepped down from his post as Herman Miller's research and development chief. He set out instead to take on the challenge of a lifetime: Apply Herman Miller's problem-solving design approach to bigger problems, break into bigger markets. Miller, 51, a bearded, reflective man, had made his name in bringing furniture to market. He had joined the company in 1975, just as sales of Action Office had exploded. He headed the research department in the 1990s and fended off attacks by insiders on the Aeron chair project. He now dared to guide the company beyond the comfortable realm of office furniture.

Miller took on the challenge at the urging of his boss. CEO Mike Volkema was worried that the glory days of office-furniture sales were ending. Sales growth had run at a healthy clip of 6 to 15 percent per year through the 1990s. But as the millennium was closing in 1999, that growth rate sputtered at just over 1 percent. Volkema believed big employers had downshifted their white-collar hiring machines. That deceleration, if it kept up, would sap Herman Miller's momentum.

Volkema and Miller cut a deal: Miller would relinquish his post as chief of research and development. In turn, he would find a way to double or triple the size of the company's business playing field in three to five years.

A bigger playing field. Double or triple the size. That kind of challenge came along only every 20 years at Herman Miller. It reprised the one given to Bob Propst by Hugh De Pree in the 1960s. At that time, Propst, who invented Action Office, took the company into the new world of office systems. As a result, Herman Miller turned from a desk and chair company into a firm leading a revolution in modern offices.

Miller wanted to plant the seeds of a similar revolution. If Herman Miller flexed its design muscle, what fresh changes could it bring about? Propst had seen a new way of working and living emerging in the 1960s, and so did research maven Miller in the 2000s. Society was being upended by shifts in technology, aesthetics, building engineering, and management of people. As he put together an internal venturing unit, Miller wondered: Can we come up with successful new products to serve the new society?

Miller knew that companies often failed at radical innovation. Bob Propst had remarked that embryonic innovation was like a toddler, fragile, faced with ruthless antagonists. Miller, a man whose eyes sparkled at the thought of a new design adventure, knew he could similarly face ruthless antagonists. But he felt he had not just his own 25 years of experience on his side, but Propst's and Herman Miller's breakthrough design legacy to guide him.

MILLER CHOSE AN ELITE team. He tapped people who could figure out into what markets Herman Miller could naturally move, and to which problems Herman Miller could find novel solutions. With Volkema's blessing, he set up a unit with its own budget. He handpicked seven people to work with him—a new set of roving leaders. And he located his group in the back of the Design Yard, where they could operate independently of the rest of the company.

Miller, who in his spare time sailed on Lake Michigan and played the guitar, practiced a management style that stimulated the blue-sky research he sought. Many bosses keep their own counsel and impose their will on the people who work for them. Miller thought through ideas aloud, with others. He came to meetings not with answers but with questions. When people disagreed, he didn't allow one to cut the other down to size. He challenged them to make each other better.

Early on, he asked his team to coin a code name for its work. At the time, during the implosion of the dot-com euphoria, people at the company were feeling bruised by the body blows of Volkema's restructuring. When Miller posed his question, a woman on his team suggested calling the effort "Purple," in reference to the tumult. Yes, Purple, others echoed. The name stuck.

Over a number of weeks, the Purple team singled out five fields of business that cried out for problem solving: how to design and build structures; how to use materials and technologies to define interior spaces; how to use new design and technologies to enrich interiors; how to deploy new lighting; and how to use digital technologies to tie everything together. Miller told each team member to choose a topic, book plane tickets, and go out and learn all he or she could about products in these fields—security-control systems, ceiling structures, wireless switches, building sensors, sound-masking machines.

One team member went to look at microtechnology embedded in fabric. An MIT professor demonstrated a jacket with a keyboard inside. Another went to Philips, Apple, and Microsoft to study the convergence of technologies. A third visited the big light makers, Osram Sylvania, GE, and Philips, to look at LED, or solid state, lighting.

The construction industry stood out as a big opportunity. Just in New York City, building renovations created nearly 3 million tons of waste a year. The amount of that waste sent to landfills exceeded that of the city's other trash and garbage. When tenants refurbished their offices, they didn't save anything. They pulled out all the wiring, the conduit, the drywall. They sent trucks loaded with waste from renovation sites like coal mines sent train cars out of the mines.

Herman Miller had not applied its sustainability expertise to the construction industry. But the industry consumed so much material and burned so much energy that the company could surely apply problem-solving design to make big improvements. Could it develop products that lowered customer energy bills? Products that reduced the amount of "stuff" customers bought and disposed of? Products that allowed customers to re-use materials rather than pitching them into dumpsters?

Miller's team pressed him hard on the sustainability theme. The company had already made sustainability a part of company operations and design. Now, an intriguing next step beckoned: Figure out how to move Herman Miller's advances in sustainability into customers' offices—that is, make products that helped customers help themselves become more sustainable.

BY SUMMER 2001, THE team had investigated many markets and had an inkling of where the company could find market openings. As best the team could tell, the big companies worked within the black-and-white constraints of their existing product lines. They were not looking at products emerging in between the narrow confines of their work, and they were not trying to integrate technologies that crossed boundaries between product lines.

Miller went to visit CEO Volkema. We have our first "big idea," he said. He described the market openings left by the dominant firms. "That's our opportunity," he said. "It's in the gray space."

In the world of lighting, he said, the big companies rule when it comes to developing LED replacements for current lights. But the replacements take their form and function from the constraints of the current lights' high-voltage AC current. Since the LED lights run on low-voltage DC current, they can safely occupy many new locations—in many shapes, colors, embedded in new materials, programmed to change, movable at the whim of untrained office workers. There was an untapped opportunity.

Miller argued that Herman Miller could create a panoply of products to outfit entire office interiors in new ways, products that could have environmental advantages of all kinds. They would cut waste during construction, cut the consumption of energy, and cut material consumed. Miller wrote in his notes: "Environmental sustainability has moved from crazies and tree huggers to emergent, profitable business propositions."

Miller described for Volkema a new world of products beyond furniture. And he described the new mission in simple words: To help customers create "great places" to work, study, heal, and play. He stressed that the new direction played to a demand for a new aesthetic, lower costs, more productive settings, and healthier interiors.

Volkema gave his blessing, and by late 2001, Miller took the next step, hiring designers. He resolved to hire fresh thinkers for design. By fiat, he said: We're not going to go to any of our current designers—or constrain ourselves to the world of furniture and commercial interiors. He also departed from Herman Miller practice by asking his team to produce purposely sketchy design "briefs"—on lighting, ceilings, "place making," flexible panels, sound design, and so on. The team members outlined product ideas for the designers rather than prescribing details.

Miller hired three people in late 2001: Danny Hillis, Bran Ferren, and Sheila Kennedy. Hillis and Ferren ran Applied Minds, a Glendale, California, contract R&D firm, whose clients included General Motors, the Defense Department, and NASA. Hillis, whose inventions ranged from amusement park attractions to advances in artificial intelligence, had pioneered parallel computing. Ferren, a movie-industry veteran, made his name in digital-effects technology, acoustics, theater, and auditorium design. Kennedy, who taught at Harvard, founded Kennedy and Violich Architecture in Boston. She also launched a firm to develop photovoltaics and solid-state lighting.

Miller gave the threesome three high-end constraints: Invent product concepts that come at no added cost to customers. Advance sustainability. And give users the power, without an electrician or builder, to change their surroundings—to move walls and lights, vary colors and acoustics, relocate displays and ceiling elements.

In their first meeting, the three took to the challenge immediately, relishing the chance to operate with so much freedom. Soon thereafter, Miller received a call from Hillis. In typical fashion, Hillis had stepped back from the detail in the design briefs. It seems to me, he said, that the investment by companies in interiors—in capability, technology, and creativity—is inversely proportional to the distance from the floor.

Hillis had realized that to make a sturdy office panel, Herman Miller had to use a lot of material, or mass, so that partitions and cubicles stayed put. The more mass used, the more supporting material needed. Herman Miller was caught in a negative feedback loop. One bad thing (mass) led to another (more mass). In the process, sustainability suffered. Hillis argued that the way to escape the loop came from the ceiling.

Miller realized instantly that Hillis was right. All kinds of things were happening from belt height down, but many of the technologies in the office were stale, old, and uninnovative.

Hillis asked for Miller's thoughts.

Keep going! he said. The notion was tantalizing: Building from the top down, not the bottom up.

Hillis's idea was to hang partitions instead of erecting them. Replace the function of mass—which exacts a heavy environmental toll in consumption of materials, energy, and waste—with gravity. With that in mind, he masterminded a new office infrastructure, a set of steel rails that hung from the ceiling. The resulting grid served triple duty. It distributed electricity, supported office-interior components, and carried the communications network. It was so simple that lay people could plug in lights, motors, computers, fans, or any other device— and they could move them from one place to another at their whim.

Hillis designed a control device to go along with the grid: a two-button wand. To "wire" a new light, he pointed at the light, clicked the wand, pointed at a wall switch, and clicked again. Voila, the clicked-on switch controlled the clicked-on light.

Hillis, Ferren, and Kennedy then built a model of a new building interior, based on the grid, in a 5,000-square-foot warehouse space. Over six months, in the latter part of 2002, they prototyped and installed a life-size model in Glendale. Ferren created the lighting plan. He used light as décor and to create color and motion. He also used it to channel people in the right direction, delineate spaces, and, along with sensors, to control energy use.

Kennedy masterminded the architectural pieces that held the rooms together. The pieces included lightweight walls made of textiles that hung from the grid. Integrated with LED lights or displays, the walls could delineate or illuminate space, give information, create an ambience, or enrich the interior look. She also created moveable ceiling shields, textiles that would allow architects to carve, sculpt, and create ceiling-scapes.

The pieces created by the threesome departed radically from the fittings of conventional interiors. Gone were fixed walls that need a demolition crew to take down. Gone were fixed lights and devices tethered to fixed outlets. Gone was the 1950s design of flat, acoustic, hung ceilings. With gravity providing structural integrity for pieces hung from the grid, Kennedy slashed the amount of material and energy consumed in manufacturing.

The new Purple vision more than met the goals for sustainable interiors. It also gave power to the people who worked in these interiors to change their environment at will—transform a lobby to a meeting room to a corridor. No construction skills or special equipment required. In the same way that PCs had earlier shifted control of computers from backroom specialists to regular working people, Purple moved control of interiors from backroom specialists to people on the office floor.

THE IDEAS IN GLENDALE had a whiz-bang feel, to say the least. They ranged from unfamiliar to extraordinary. They illustrated a future far from what customers were used to. Miller and his team then had to face a practical question: Would the novel and unconventional pieces fly with people outside the Purple team's creative bubble? How would customers feel about lighted walls? Would they accept textile partitions instead of heavy, particle-board-based panels?

The first moment of truth came in December 2002, when the board of directors flew to California to visit Glendale. Although the team had no salable products yet, and although involving a board in early-stage development was risky, Volkema felt the project was too big to not get a reading by the company's overseers. He and Miller wanted the board to do a walk-through—and they sought approval for moving forward with such a big-budget effort.

Hillis, Ferren, and Kennedy had turned Glendale into an office of the future, with spaces for reception, meetings, work, a think tank, and library. Overhead stretched the grid. Hanging from it were lights, articulating ceiling planes, mobile walls. Fabric-thin partitions illuminated by LED lights replaced particle-board panels. Instead of spot lighting, the lab featured illuminated LED planes and quilted, baffled, or accordion-like fabric. Only the products on the floor looked familiar—lightweight Herman Miller furniture.

The board got to see all the whiz-bang inventions. The products shown were so innovative that Herman Miller had 16 patents in the works. One invention, a movable curtain embedded with microphones, actually masked office conversation. When the curtain sensed human speech, a computer algorithm triggered sounds, turning voices into the burbling background of a busy office. The curtain's digital technology, instead of a panel's mass, provided privacy.

Volkema held a board meeting at the end of the walk-though. Miller pitched the Purple vision, which by this time, the board had seen for itself. Miller also had a new way of describing his R&D approach. It came from the work of Clayton Christensen, the Harvard Business School professor celebrated for the concept of "disruptive innovation." Christensen had long sought to explain how new, more convenient, and cheaper technologies could drive established companies out of a market, seemingly overnight.

When a company introduces a "disruptive" innovation, Christensen argued, it produces something that allows unskilled people to do what could once only be done by skilled people, and easier, faster, and for less money. Alternatively, it brings to market a change in how companies do business—what they do, when, how, and by whom. As examples, mini-mills represented disruptive innovation in the steel industry, as small recycled-steel plants undercut large integrated factories. Digital music players (think iPod) represented disruptive innovation in music. Christensen had done a seminal study of how disk-drive makers had successively driven each other to the brink as they introduced technologies that leapfrogged one another.

And that's just what the Purple system would do, said Miller. It would change the interiors game for building owners, developers, architects, consultants, and building managers. It would let people revamp their offices much more cheaply, much faster, more frequently, and in a much more sustainable way. They would no longer have to call in the architects, facilities managers, furniture dealers, installers, and electricians every time they wanted to remake interiors to meet the new needs of their work.

To the board, Miller painted a picture of vast potential. Linking things in one gray space to another produced a flurry of product ideas. And an unprecedented number of elements would work together—electricity, communications, wall support, ceilings, lighting. The company could invade existing markets and steal market share from established companies. The grid and its software had a promising future.

In a cover memo to the board, he wrote, "The . . . team continues to wrestle with the question, 'Does Purple constitute a potential home run for Herman Miller?' We believe the answer is, 'It's at least the start of a rally.'" It could take off like Action Office did in the 1970s, catapulted by new business drivers, a new customer audience, and its stealth advantage as a disruptive innovation.

The board members liked what they saw. In a debriefing, several pointed Miller to the grid: Don't fool around with the rest of it, they told him, get going on that. They liked Hillis's earlier emphasis on how Purple formed a new "platform" for interiors. A platform had awesome power. In the same way that thousands of software companies built on Microsoft's Windows operating system, thousands of building-industry companies could create products on the Purple grid.

The board then looked at the business risks. Miller recalls: "Some board members felt it was too far afield from what we do and therefore an inordinate risk. At the other end of the spectrum were venturesome board members who said, 'This is exactly what Herman Miller needs to do ... taking these sorts of leaps of faith, risk.'" In between, board members simply expressed impatience. Let's get going, they said.

Miller had seen this all before. The board members had acted the same way with the Aeron chair in the early 1990s. They had kept asking, When are we going to have it done and how big is the market opportunity? This put Miller in an awkward spot. He had told the board back then that, frankly, he had no idea. At the time, no defined market existed for a high-end office chair that lacked cushions and upholstery.

This time Miller said the same thing. And then, without offering any guarantees, he made his request: I need 24 months and a multimillion-dollar budget to go the next step. The time has come to prove out the concept with a few customers.

The board, though of two minds, approved.

MILLER FACED A TICKLISH phase in development. Though the products in Glendale looked real, they were prototypes. They gave lay people the impression Herman Miller had everything figured out. In fact, they were only mock-ups. If Herman Miller was to sell products, work remained on electrical engineering, the power supply, software, assemblies, sensors, and a thousand other details.

The Purple team hired experts for concept studies—to draw sketches of Purple installed in actual retail, office, classroom, library, and other settings. An architecture firm did one study. Its sketches showed that office renovations with Purple could save 15 percent on space. The cost would be about the same ("a wash") as for conventional office systems. Still, the team had to work out problems of electrical safety, ease of connection, safety of egress, and people's willingness to change their work habits and perceptions of privacy.

Miller didn't have a polished product to sell, but he still had to find buyers. He had promised the board he would produce "zealot" customers. Zealots, in his mind, suffered such pain from an unsolved business problem they willingly put up with the first, error-prone draft of a product. Only the buy-in by such "early adopters" would confirm the validity of Purple. And these people would have to *pay* for the privilege of trying the untested.

Finding zealot customers took the expertise of a specialist. The job description would go something like this: Entrepreneurial sales person needed to find the visionaries—using any tips, contacts, and connections available. Must get people so enthralled with new product concept they will fly to California to take a look. Talent for finding buyers who dare adopt bleeding-edge technology is essential.

Miller knew just the person. He phoned Deanne Beckwith, who had earned her chops with him on an earlier product-development project. Beckwith, a design graduate of North Carolina State University, had shown her mettle in the face of a remarkable sales challenge: selling a promise without a product.

Beckwith played an unusual role on the Purple project. She was something akin to a mystery entrepreneur. She showed up solo. She carried no business card with the Herman Miller logo. She didn't have any products to demonstrate, any photographs or brochures to show, any PowerPoint presentation to flash on the wall. All she had were a few sketches and some choice words about a dazzling new idea. With her kindly and gentle manner, she made her pitch face to face—to building managers and other customers who thirsted for the future.

Would you take a chance and fly to Glendale? she asked. And if you won't, I can't tell you more.

"They all wanted to know who was behind the project," she says, "And I said, 'I can't tell you.' But I asked, 'Does this seem compelling to you, something you would want to do?' "

She couldn't tell people she worked for Herman Miller because a measure of her success was simply whether she could get people on a plane to make the trip. If she couldn't do that, she couldn't go further with her sales cycle. "That would be a big coup if I could get them to do that," she says.

Beckwith intrigued people with two principal messages: "radical flexibility" and "sustainability." Flexibility meant that customers could remake office interiors whenever and however they liked. Sustainability meant they could save energy and materials, and they could get more life out of a building, because they didn't have to throw out interior components when they renovated.

Of course, she also appealed to other advantages of Purple. One of the main ones: Owners and developers could earn more money over the life of a building, by saving time and foregone rent during renovations. Another was that they would save energy by putting sensors in offices that would automatically turn off lights and thus save power when nobody was around. A third was the concept introduced with the Aeron and advanced during Herman Miller's cradle-to-cradle work: They could dematerialize. Developers especially liked the suggestion of buying and tearing out a lot less drywall during renovations.

When Beckwith succeeded, she didn't give herself all the credit. She simply believed she had found zealots to whom the ideas sold themselves. Purple should sound so compelling that a genuine zealot couldn't resist seeing how it played out in California. If people could resist a trip to the laboratory, Beckwith simply didn't have a real zealot.

Once at Glendale with those who couldn't resist, she revealed the secrets of Purple and of the Purple product effort. Her first zealot flew in from a research campus in Oklahoma. He was planning four high-rise buildings. Purple appealed to his hunger for flexibility, as his world-class research center had to serve a revolving door of researchers. Beckwith even had plans drawn up for him. Alas, he had to start building before the Purple product line was ready.

Other zealots were equally smitten—even as Beckwith stressed that the lab was a model, representing no actual products, essentially make believe. She encouraged people to buy into the dream, to feel the magic. And to many zealots the magic was there. "It's like being on the starship," said one.

The time came to get past courtship, however. By late 2003, the investment in Purple had grown large. Miller had approved the building of a second prototype Purple installation, this time a 7,500-square-foot space in the Design Yard in Holland. Each time the board met, Miller would get the same questions: When are we going to market? How much is this worth?

Miller frustrated his overseers: He couldn't give an answer on the size of the market when the market still didn't exist. The pressure was on, though. He needed someone who would write a check. He had to show customer backing for Purple and its vision of flexibility and sustainability. "I [would] wake up in the middle of the night thinking, wow, how much money have we spent. . . . It just makes your gut churn," he says. "It does take patience with ambiguity to the nth degree to do this."

THE BREAKTHROUGH CAME AT Harvard University. Miller had suggested to the board in September 2002 that the Purple team would finish the first zealot project in twelve months. In early 2004, no installation was in process. Beckwith was starting to wonder if she could come up with a paying customer. She turned from the zealots she had been courting to people she had worked with before.

The timing was good when she spoke with a professor she knew at Harvard School of Design. The professor had a classroom ready to outfit in a new way. He wanted to create an atmosphere where students could comfortably give presentations to each other and to other professors. He felt each student should have control of the class interior, be able to set it up, break it down, and arrange as needed the lights, displays, sound, walls, and furniture. The radical flexibility of Purple won him over, and he signed the first Purple deal in March 2004.

Beckwith hit a series of snags. Of most concern, she didn't have approval of the grid from Underwriter Laboratories (UL), the arbiter of global product safety standards. UL had denied Purple approval in August 2003, and the Purple team had to reapply in early 2004. The professor ordered the system with UL approval pending. But as the back-to-school August 2004 installation deadline neared, approval still hadn't come through. Without it, Beckwith couldn't power up the system—and risked failing on her first Purple delivery.

The Herman Miller engineering team jumped into action. Citing the press of time, it was able to get UL to agree to send a field inspector to Harvard on the day before the room was to go live. With the first class of the fall scheduled for the next day, he did approve the system, applying the UL stickers by hand. The room lit up. Herman Miller, for the first time, had exposed its Purple concept in an installation visible to the public.

Though a modest 1,000 square feet in size, classroom 109 put Purple on the product map. All the main features appeared in the room: the grid, switches, ceiling cover, lighting, mobile walls. Students and faculty could configure the walls according to their tastes in boundaries, lighting, display walls, and projection screens. They could rearrange the pieces and reprogram the switches. The room would go on to become a student and faculty favorite, with students, dubbed "wandmasters," helping with room changeovers.

FOLLOWING THE HARVARD SALE, other zealots came through. Urban Outfitters became Beckwith's biggest win. The clothing retailer wanted a makeover of its Third Avenue store in New York. At 17,000 square feet on three floors, the store took Purple into a much bigger space. It also drew the team into an unfamiliar way of selling. Whereas Beckwith had made her case to one professor at Harvard, this time she had to persuade facility managers, store engineers, and even the electrical-code board in New York City.

Beckwith had the most trouble with the code board. She won approval, but not before she and a Herman Miller engineer put a model of the grid in a wooden crate and rolled it down the sidewalk and into a hearing. And not before Herman Miller hired a New York consultant—essentially a fixer—to help them run the board's gauntlet.

Urban Outfitters saw in Purple a way to solve a design problem specific to the retail business. They had to revamp stores at least three times a year, for the back-to-school, Christmas, and spring seasons. They also wanted to experiment with new concepts and change their windows with new setups frequently. During seasonal sales spikes, a store could also run short of changing rooms—and lose sales. Herman Miller created a knock-down changing room, allowing the retailer to add capacity seasonally to keep customers in the store.

The experience showed that Purple did apply to markets outside Herman Miller's mainstay office business. It also showed something else. Those markets called for new capabilities by Herman Miller.

Urban Outfitters may have liked the knock-down changing rooms, but nobody outside the retail market cared. Similarly, Harvard may have liked the way Purple's movable displays and partitions made students comfortable in front of their peers, but who else cared about that?

Miller realized in a fresh way that customers in every market would value something different. The Urban Outfitters installation tipped him off that the scope of the challenge was bigger than he first thought. He realized this even more clearly when his team put before him an analysis of the opportunity for Purple in all the sectors they targeted: offices ($5 billion), retail ($3.3 billion), education ($9.6 billion), group care facilities ($4.8 billion), hospitality ($7.25 billon), and homes ($3.6 billion).

All along, Miller had sought to develop Purple to address as many markets as possible. As his team tailored actual solutions for customers, though, he saw just how steep the learning curve was going to be. The Purple team would have to learn so many new things, sell in so many new ways, and design so many new products for every market. The scale of the challenge startled him.

To be sure, it was exactly what Miller had aimed for—to take the company onto new territory—to double or triple its playing field. But now he was facing the prospect of supplying an awful lot more of a good thing, to a much bigger field, than he had planned. The unknowns seemed overwhelming.

Something had to give. In spring 2005, he met with his venture board of directors, including Volkema, now chairman, and Brian Walker, CEO since the previous year. He compared Purple with the development of Aeron, launched in 1994. With Aeron, he said, Herman Miller had faced far fewer unknowns. "We knew the general seating market, we knew who the competitors were, we knew the pricing position, we knew who the suppliers would be, we knew how to distribute it, we knew what kind of margins we needed to sustain the business," he says. "What we didn't know was whether or not the new design could be built—it was replete with never-tried technologies and processes—and second, if it could be built, how many customers would embrace its radical design."

With Purple, on the other hand, they had very little figured out. "We didn't know anything," he says, not the market, not the distribution, not the pricing, not the selling, not the dealer network, not the marketing messages, not anything central to running such a business. Aeron was a "cakewalk," says Miller, compared to what they faced with Purple.

Miller knew they had hit another decision point. For months he had debated with Volkema about the right time to ramp Purple up into a full-blown business, to hire a seasoned entrepreneur and launch a start-up. Purple was not just another line of furniture they could merge into an existing business unit. The list of unknowns with Purple compelled them to hire someone to answer all these new questions—and specifically to answer the question of how to commercialize Purple.

Volkema and Walker agreed. So in June 2005, they tapped a veteran of the high-tech industry, a serial entrepreneur by the name of Randy Storch, to launch Purple on its own. Storch was to take a radically new product, nurtured in the test-tube atmosphere of a secret R&D operation, and "scale it up" into a big business.

Storch had earned a reputation for taking technologies and building real businesses out of them. He had started a company whose software became the granddaddy to online airline reservation systems. He founded two other high-tech startups later, including one in internet security. In 1997, the accounting firm Ernst & Young named him an Entrepreneur of the Year.

Storch liked what he saw in Glendale, and he signed on with confidence in the Herman Miller brand and portfolio of Purple technology. His initial challenge was to decide which technologies to carry forward—and what "value proposition," or message about value for the money, to sell to customers. When he had visited Glendale, he had reveled in the magic of the place, just like the zealot customers before him. What he found jaw-dropping was the wand. One click here, one click there, and he could "rewire" lights instantly.

With the wand as the emblematic product, Storch set out to sound out the market. Where was the opportunity for a growing business? Whereas Beckwith went largely after small zealot customers to prove out the technology, Storch aimed for big ones to start making money. At first, he peddled the entire Purple vision. In league with Beckwith, he got solid interest, but he didn't get enough interest to suggest he could build a robust business.

Storch learned quickly from big customers that the product set had limitations. One that concerned him: It worked only in open-ceiling buildings. It didn't work with drop-ceiling finished interiors, where products require a UL plenum rating. A plenum, a wiring and ductwork cavity in the ceiling, requires compliance with building codes related to fireproofing and toxic fumes.

He also found the grid had marketing limitations. Among his early observations: People invariably asked, Is it worth paying $8 per square foot for Purple when we can pay $3 to $5 per square foot for traditional setups? Purple would pay off over time, but many tenants couldn't justify the "first cost." Another was that the grid ran at 120 volts, while most big office buildings run on 277 volts. Though this didn't pose a limitation for many of the sites the Purple team had targeted, Storch found it a barrier to making large sales.

The target market for Purple appeared smaller than Storch expected, in fact, a "needle in a haystack." Purple did offer big benefits for developers, tenants, architects, and construction people. Developers could charge higher rents, offer more modern infrastructure, build interiors faster and change them faster, avoid demolition costs between tenants, depreciate their work quicker, and even win points for the sought-after certification by the U.S. Green Building Council LEED program, Leadership in Energy and Environmental Design.

Storch and Beckwith approached "beachhead" developers with these sales points. At one juncture, they proposed getting five to seven developers across the country that each had one to three million square feet of space. They were already working with a couple of them. One prospect was affiliated with Beckwith's alma mater, North Carolina State University. A memo at the time noted the potential sales opportunity in the United States as $11 billion a year.

DESPITE THE PROMISE OF Purple, though, Storch gradually learned some tough news: The walls and grid differed too much to sell together through the electrical sales channel, that is, through the people who specify, engineer, and build electrical infrastructure. The walls involved architectural expertise, foreign to the people dealing in electricity. Maybe, thought Storch, the sales of walls and ceilings should be sold through the Herman Miller sales force.

Miller didn't like splitting the Purple vision, but in league with Volkema and Walker, he agreed to do so. The three of them figured that Storch, a denizen of software engineering, was not playing to his forte with interior architecture. And so they took back responsibility for selling the walls and ceilings.

Storch, a man of forceful opinions, gradually learned something else. The technical limitations of the product posed an insurmountable barrier to scaling up sales. During the summer of 2006, he invited over 50 electrical contractors from all over the country to the Purple floor space in Holland. The contractors liked the wand, but they didn't like the constraints posed by the grid's electrical properties. Storch told Miller: Purple is such a cool product, and we have a bunch of cool pilot projects all over the country, but we can't win sales in spaces bigger than a few thousand square feet. We can't because we don't have a plenum rating. We can't because we're unable sell to all those people who like finished drop ceilings. We can't because we only have a 120-volt system.

Storch said, To heck with the grid. We can't rely on it to sell more product to bigger customers to make enough money to grow. So we have to offer something that fits better into the market for electrical infrastructure.

He also felt he had to strip the grander Purple idea to the core magic. He was still enamored with the wand, which still made jaws drop when he went on sales calls. He felt he had to take that most valuable part of Purple, the two-click programmability, and make money from that in priority to everything else. The grid wasn't a prerequisite. It had become a hindrance and cost burden.

Miller, Walker, and Volkema agreed to this as well. Miller was full of wonder at how much they were departing from the original vision. They were losing so much of the Purple ambition. Ever the manager to put confidence in his people, he reminded himself—as D.J. De Pree would have done decades before—the only thing you can guarantee from a venture this ambitious is that, wherever you end up, it won't be where you thought.

Some members of the Purple team, passionate about the ideas at Glendale, took this decision hard. When Storch swooped into a meeting, it sounded to many veterans like he was telling them they were wrong. Miller, however, stayed convinced that Storch fought the same battle they did, the battle to win the war of commercialization. Miller also felt Storch's experience with Purple had grown to a point where he knew more about commercial prospects than the team.

Storch jettisoned the grid as the foundation of the system. He retained all the electronics that made the Purple vision cool, but he recognized he had to come up with packaging that more closely resembled other electrical-control products. Without that alternative packaging at hand, he did keep trying to sell the grid. He and Beckwith called on managers of government buildings in Washington, D.C., to drum up interest. But he also hired an engineer and told him: The new packaging can't be based on the grid. It has to be plenum-rated. It has to run on 277 volts, the standard for big office buildings.

So with Miller's blessing, Storch redirected the business and revamped the flagship product. Miller listened to his team, as they complained about the authority being given to the entrepreneur. "That was a source of real lingering frustrations," Miller recalls, "that at some point we didn't just force him to execute the plan as we saw it. And that was tough."

But he also listened to his conscience as a company officer. Herman Miller had to make a dollar on this vision. If the company couldn't commercialize the original vision, it had to commercialize another. Whatever the team's ambitions at the start to address problems of flexibility, of waste, of the emergence of a new aesthetic, of the demand for greater sustainability, the market had the final word on what worked.

IN NOVEMBER 2006, AT Greenbuild, the United States' premier green-building trade show, Herman Miller announced the new business: Convia. It offered two options for the products that had originated under the code name Purple: modular and grid. The modular packaging hadn't gone on sale. It would take a year to get UL approval. But Storch now sold a story to appeal to many more customers: The Convia "infrastructure," rail or modular, would work with open and suspended ceilings, in big buildings and small, enabled by the magic of a two-click wand.

Storch still stressed flexibility as a sales message. He invited architects, interior designers, electrical contractors, building owners and tenants to install Convia and "go reconfigure." The "plug and play" capability, he said, let anyone install, upgrade, and move lights, security cameras, video displays, thermostats, speakers, sensors, and more.

He also stressed sustainability. Convia could cut landfill waste because 100 percent of its components came out for reuse. Renovation of a conventional 20,000-square-foot space would yield on average waste of approximately 10,000 feet of branch conduit, 600 back-boxes for branch wiring, 40,000 feet of branch circuit wire, and 62,000 feet of telephone and data wires. None of that waste would result if a company used Convia.

Storch got good reviews of the modular prototypes, and he pressed ahead, winning over many facilities managers with his sales pitches. A few audiences gave him standing ovations. He even built up a $30 million pipeline of sales prospects.

But the momentum didn't last. In just one month, every one of the people on his $30 million list trickled off. He then realized he had to make more changes in his sales and distribution approach. One problem was that even after he sold facilities managers on Convia, he often failed to sell their engineers, and later, their electrical contractors. Another was that Herman Miller didn't have credibility with electricians, so he had to hire electrical sales reps to sell Convia for him.

Storch did rack up sales for a 200,000-square-foot office in Ohio, and an 80,000-square-foot office in Washington, D.C., none other than the U.S. Green Building Council headquarters. But Miller's earlier concerns about not knowing anything about the business continued to haunt the Convia team. Every time they thought they were about to get market traction, they started spinning their wheels. The Purple team had built the Glendale lab mockup five years earlier, but Convia still wasn't making money. Storch and Miller grappled endlessly with the problem: What is preventing our success in closing deals?

Only in the late 2000s, as the price of oil soared to a high of $145 a barrel, Did Storch see the aspect of Convia that people wanted most. It wasn't flexibility. It was energy savings. He started on a new sales pitch: Facilities managers can meter energy use from every Convia box. They can control energy use from a central spot. Network sensors can turn on the lights just as people come to work and adjust them as people move, automatically. Convia, he stressed, can cut energy use 30 percent compared to traditional setups. It can pay for itself in three years.

Storch and Miller meanwhile saw a better way to go to market with Convia. In May 2009, Herman Miller partnered with Legrand, a global specialist in electrical installations and information networks. Convia integrated its technology into products under Legrand's Wiremold brand. Convia thus rode the coattails of a company respected by electricians to produce a leading product in the market for energy control in buildings. A product that had started as the grand Purple vision, found its footing in another company's product line.

The original vision of Purple seemed to have disappeared. Or did it? Miller kept the magic of Glendale alive. He asked Beckwith and others to keep on the trail of zealot customers. As Herman Miller placed its commercial bet on Convia, Miller continued to make a side bet on the Purple dream. In other words, he didn't let the commercialized vision turn out the lights on Purple's initial potential. After all, for the right customers, no product offered a solution as complete as the original.

Meanwhile, under the wings of Legrand, Convia made sparks that suggested the future still lay in the theme of sustainability. In 2010, Storch announced that Convia's components and energy-metering and control software would let a 150,000-square-foot school in Irving, Texas, reach "net zero" in energy consumption. The Ladybird Johnson Middle School would consume no more energy than its onsite windmills and solar cells produced. Convia would dim lights, control thermostats, and alter plug loads automatically to keep the building within its power-producing capacity. The school, to open in 2011, would use 50 percent less electricity than schools of similar size.

The outsized ambitions of Volkema and Miller in 2001 never came to pass. "We never met the aspiration of a robust portfolio of multiple initiatives," says Volkema. "We began to start to queue them up, but we just found we couldn't invest enough to keep them going." The effort of doubling or tripling the playing field had become just too much in a company battered by two recessions in less than ten years.

Some of the Purple pioneers felt the company bosses had chosen the wrong way to develop the idea. Some felt they didn't insist on enough of Purple going into commercialization. One person close to the group says, "They were onto something, but they didn't quite have the balls to say, guess what, we're taking this kind of step [to produce the entire Purple vision], in the same way, right after World War II....they were able to launch a very major lifestyle concept" in coming out with the work of George Nelson and Bob Propst.

Miller admits he questioned his decisions in hindsight. "I do it nightly," he says. "It's intriguing. . . . And I waver probably twice a day over whether we made the right choices or not."

The question would have to remain unsettled. The judgment of the market under different circumstances, or using a different timeline, was impossible to know. It took 15 years after Gilbert Rohde introduced his "utterly plain" designs in 1932 before there was widespread commercialization of modern furniture. That came only after World War II. It took more than ten years, after the introduction of Action Office in 1965, for the winds of the market to blow in favor of office systems. It even took several years for a new chair, the Aeron, to soar in the 1990s.

What would it take to entice the market into buying installations of the original Purple vision by the hundreds or thousands? What would it take to win purchase orders for a new platform that helped customers radically improve their own sustainability? While that question remained in the air, Miller would have to settle for Convia's remarkable energy-management features.

Miller nursed the belief that what they pursued in Glendale would inevitably play out in his side bets with Beckwith. Trends pointed more clearly all the time to people demanding both the flexibility and sustainability of the initial vision. Come 2017, ten years after the launch of Convia, would Herman Miller, the pioneer of Purple, reap success? Miller believed it remained positioned to do so.

"The only issue is an issue of timing, of commercial relevance, of scale, not of applicability," Miller says. "That knowledge sustains me . . . because the idea itself and the ultimate product . . . are pretty damn compelling, and compelling in era where more of this kind of thinking has to happen, and customers are reaching out for anyone who can help them come to terms with these questions" about how to install flexible, sustainable interiors.

CHAPTER 10

A Better World

W hen members of the Herman Miller board of directors met in late 2003, one of their topics was the future
CEO. Mike Volkema, who had held the post for nine
years, was ready to relinquish it. At his urging, the directors had
decided that Brian Walker, already named chief operating officer,
would take over. With that decided, the board had another concern.
Walker's start date was July 2004, and the board instructed him:
The time has come for you to develop your own vision for Herman
Miller.

Volkema and Walker, lawyer and accountant, had worked as
closely as two executives can for almost a decade. When Volkema
was named CEO in 1995, he named Walker CFO soon thereafter.
The two men's strategy and vision for the organization were much
the same. Still, Volkema said to Walker, I think it would be helpful
for you to step back and ask, What's important to me?

Keeping a clear fix on what was important had challenged
Volkema. At first, he seemed to have everything under tight control. He had presided over a tremendous surge in growth, seeing a
doubling of sales from the start of this tenure in 1995 to 2001. He

was also at the helm when they fell precipitously in the wake of the dot–com crash, a crisis that sent him to the board for approval of shutdowns and layoffs not once but an agonizing four times. "One night I went to bed a genius and woke up the town idiot," he later told a reporter.

Forced to administer triage, Volkema and Walker had developed a plan to remake the company as more focused and efficient—a job they felt was probably overdue. But as they put this vision in place, Volkema realized a lot of employees thought the boss and his CFO had their values sideways.

Now Walker, a partner in the 30-month-long restructuring, was being asked by his overseers to clarify where he thought the company should go. Like many CEOs, he felt his job was to build on the legacy left to him, to leave the company healthy for future generations. With recovery finally on the horizon, he felt the key question went deeper than just one of vision. It was instead, What do I believe in? And how will I show that to the rest of the company?

Walker, the numbers man who had championed the pursuit of economic profits, had the reputation of being a technician. He had a casual, open air, and was affable and worldly. He had touched many employees with his humanity, but they all wondered: What will an accountant do in the top job? How will he act? The environmental people wondered: How will he make the company more sustainable?

WALKER HAD TRADITION TO guide him as he sorted out these questions. The De Prees had always stressed values, as had their successor, Dick Ruch. And Volkema, when he took over, had spent months honing his words before publishing, in 1998, "Blueprint for Community," an essay about values. The entire roster of CEOs, in fact, had made a tradition of restating to employees what they and the company stood for.

In "Blueprint," Volkema called Herman Miller "a high-performance, values-driven community of people tied together by a common purpose." He reiterated or enshrined values like problem-solving design, participatory management, developing people's potential, making a contribution, cultivating community, creating economic value, living with integrity, respecting the environment—and in doing so, characterized the "Herman Miller way."

The Blueprint emerged in boom times. Herman Miller was reporting record sales, earnings, new orders, cash flow, and economic profit. American business was enjoying one of the longest-ever periods of prosperity—a period marked by such excess that General Motors started selling the over-the-top civilian version of the military's Humvee, the Hummer. Herman Miller, as confident as any Michigan business, published an annual report in keeping with the sunny atmosphere. The report came with a spring-loaded, pop-up smiley face and a cutout megaphone—for "more than the usual number of things to cheer about."

So much money was afoot in the late 1990s that cash alone could have papered over cracks in many businesses. But the money then started to run out. At Herman Miller, the sunshine vanished into a dark reality. Volkema and Walker began the restructuring. Over three years, they laid off 4,500 of their 12,500 employees. They shuttered 1.4 million square feet of space—in Georgia, California, and Michigan.

The question of how to keep faith with the company's values was becoming ever tougher. To help find his way, Volkema drew three concentric circles. In the outer ring, he put the words "strategy, structure, and priorities." In the middle, he put "cultural practices." In the core, he put "values." He believed CEOs had to manage and change things in the outer ring. That was their main job. When times demanded it, they had to change and abandon things in the middle ring—but only a few. That's what leadership was all about. In no case could they meddle with the core, the values.

"True values . . . have become so indoctrinated" in a company, says Volkema, "that a CEO can't change them because the organization will chew up and spit out the CEO before he or she has a chance to change them."

In the dark days of the early 2000s, Volkema did have to make changes to the middle ring. He was forced to deal with employees' expectations of lifetime employment, one of the cultural practices he felt had been mistaken as a value. Though Max De Pree had told people in the 1980s that he couldn't guarantee employment unless employees guaranteed customers, a lot of people had nevertheless continued to take lifetime jobs for granted. Volkema had to stand in front of his people and say, No, lifetime employment is not a value. It is a cultural practice.

Volkema told employees: So long as you work at the company, Herman Miller will invest in you. And we expect you to invest in Herman Miller. But we may, at times, have to go our separate ways. Saving the company—and saving most of the people on payroll—takes precedence. "The social contract has changed," he said. "No leader who is truthful suggests in a rapidly changing world that you can guarantee employment for life."

At the time, saving the company was not assured. Herman Miller was stumbling badly in creating economic profit, and as sales fell off a cliff, so did EVA. EVA went so far negative that Volkema and Walker stopped reporting it in the annual report in 2003.

The question of honoring values wracked Volkema and every other manager who had a hand in the painful task of laying off valued, hardworking people. How, Volkema kept asking, do I do this and preserve that values-driven community?

Volkema had no satisfying answer. The company did give a good severance package to "bridge" people to a new job. The package included two weeks of pay for every year of employment. It came with helpful job-hunting counseling and services. But once he and other managers provided this bridge, they could offer little more than conducting the layoffs with the human touch preached since the time of D.J. De Pree.

Volkema personally told hundreds of people the company no longer had work for them. He received many letters in response. Most of them, he maintains, recounted stories of jobless people using the bridge to make better lives for themselves. But he received "heartbreakers" as well—letters from people asking him for their jobs back, letters describing formerly bright lives gone dark, letters of families become desperate.

Volkema would lie in bed at night, often sleepless. "You're thinking, 'How can I wake up and be smart enough not to have to let that next 500 people go?'" he says. "And yet when an industry contracts almost 40 percent over two years, and you almost don't know where the bottom is, you start to ask, 'Do I put at risk everyone's employment if I don't make the appropriate commitment?'"

Volkema and Walker tried to keep people informed. As the fortunes of the company sank, they updated employees regularly. They met personally with the people losing their jobs. They put themselves in a seat facing the people who would reel from the decision.

VOLKEMA HAD TALKED ABOUT one value in particular: preserving community. He and his team had decided that, not only was the company a community, so was each plant. People at each plant worked together, ate together, did volunteer work together. If Volkema had to shut down a plant—a panel plant, a chair plant—how could he treat both the plant and company communities in a way consistent with company values?

He and his team decided that when they shut down a plant, they would confine the damage to just one community, the plant, laying off everyone. In a departure from typical practices in unionized Michigan, they would not cut by seniority, laying off new hires at closing plants and moving senior people to surviving ones. That would require laying off new hires at the surviving plants to make openings for relocated veterans.

During the shutdown of one Michigan plant, their policy was put to the test. One of the workers appealed to Volkema: My spouse and I both work at the plant. If you fire both of us, you'll wipe out our entire family income.

Volkema and his team hadn't thought through all the intricacies. And they backpedaled: Okay, they said, we should make an exception. If a shutdown will destroy an entire family's livelihood, we'll keep one spouse.

But then someone came to Volkema: Hey, said the person, my wife doesn't work, and you're taking away my entire family income, too. I should be kept on also.

Volkema and his team realized they couldn't justify the difference between the two kinds of layoffs. The family with two people at the plant had chosen to take that risk. The family with a sole breadwinner had chosen a risk as well. Should one get special consideration? The sole breadwinner, after all, may have had no choice, since some spouses couldn't work.

"To take away a family's income is taking away an income, whether it's two people working or one," Volkema says. They decided to stick to their original policy no matter what the family situation. "We decided, we're just not going to make that distinction, as hard as that sounds." They laid off both spouses and gave them the bridge package like everyone else.

Struggling with such conflicts, and convulsed by alternating impulses of compassion, common sense, and corporate welfare, Volkema and his team worked uneasily through the downturn. In a couple of years, they shut down three of five major business initiatives, merging even the high-flying unit built by Bix Norman at the GreenHouse into the rest of company.

Through much of 2001 through 2003, Volkema and his team never could spot the bottom of the slump. Business had plunged in 2002, dropped again in 2003, and showed no recovery in 2004. In the late 1990s, the company had hit the high peaks, which had lofted company executives' personal wealth with soaring bonuses and stock-price appreciation—the stock had gone up 600 percent since Volkema took over. It had seemed as though the boom period would be Volkema's legacy to the company. But then came the descent, and in the descent they had gone just as far down, to the lip of the unknown.

"It was a radical rethinking of a lot of the dimensions of business, and it wasn't fun for anybody," Volkema says. Though the restructuring aimed to put the company on a new, more sustainable path, Volkema never knew how things would turn out. And he couldn't exactly feel gratified by the work. During one stretch, he didn't sleep through the night for more than a year.

The best evidence he could offer that they had succeeded in shrinking the company with dignity was that virtually no one sued the company. This was grim reassurance. As for surviving employees, survey results of "overall satisfaction," though down in 2002 and 2003, rose in 2004.

Volkema, humbled by the experience, would speak uncomfortably about it years later. Still, he would find a way to make sense of his being personally socked by the company's most bruising business reversal ever. Says Volkema, "I now have personally come to grips with the notion that I was there for precisely the opportunity to live our values in the midst of a crisis."

WHEN WALKER BECAME CEO, the crisis had just begun to ebb. The experience, however, had changed him and everyone else in the executive ranks. "When you go through one of those periods," he says, "people [in the company] are looking around and saying, geez, I'm a survivor. I got to the other side. Now there's got to be something more to this than surviving."

The time had come for Walker to paint a more complete picture of that something. As best he and Volkema could tell, they had saved the company from a debilitating erosion of values. They had remained faithful to "doing what's right" when it came to the treatment of customers, employees, shareholders, the community, and the environment. In fact, they had committed to those values repeatedly.

Throughout what some people viewed as the most unlikely of times, Volkema and Walker kept funding Paul Murray's, Gabe Wing's, and Scott Charon's environmental work. They kept the money spigot open for Gary Miller's work on the Purple project. Despite the downturn, they voted with the corporate purse for venerable values like design, innovation, the environment, and community giving.

By having stuck to those values, they could show benefits they would have otherwise lost—benefits that indeed gave the company a future. The cradle-to-cradle effort was about to yield Mirra, the sustainable chair with PVC-free armrests. Work in the plants was reducing waste every day. At Spring Lake, people in the paint shop replaced the company's last liquid-paint metal-coating line in September 2003. They installed an emission-free powder-coating process that emitted 110 fewer tons of solvents annually, largely ending all of Herman Miller's VOC emissions from metal coating.

Even before he became CEO, Walker chose the environment as a way to make his first clear statement of what he believed in. In 2003, he attended a meeting of the green team, an annual ritual for Volkema. Though it was just April, everyone knew Walker was on track to get the CEO post, and Murray and everyone else wanted to know: What do you think about our work? Are we giving customers value? Where do you think we should go from here?

Walker told the group he was happy with its mission of making Herman Miller a sustainable company. He had gotten first-hand reassurance of the worthiness of this goal as he fielded questions from customers. People often asked him about Herman Miller's LEED buildings, DfE protocol, and other green efforts.

Walker had long believed deeply in two principles of management. First, people can only remember a limited number of things. Second, they respond only to goals that are measured and made part of an overall objective of the company. With these in mind, he asked Murray and his group to clarify their goals. To the group, he said, Remember, what gets measured gets done.

The group wanted to know what kind of goals Walker specifically wanted from them.

Walker recalled the green group's zero-landfill goal. That is so easy to understand, he said. Can you devise a way to measure and report progress toward sustainability as a single number, so we can work toward one sustainability goal?

The group was unsure.

Walker said that the company had so many environmental projects in the works that he had trouble telling whether its performance was getting better overall. How can I quickly explain our environmental performance to the rest of the company? he asked. Can you word the goals so all 6,000-plus employees can understand them?

When Walker left, the environmental leaders started formulating answers. When Murray got together with the leaders later, they felt buoyed by the soon-to-be-CEO's support. Murray let his ambitions run. He floated the idea of coming up with a goal for 2020. He liked how the date played on the metaphor of 20/20 vision, and he wanted to move beyond the three-year goals they had used for some time.

What if we did something radical, Murray said to the group, something ambitious like our zero landfill goal?

What about zero for everything? someone else said.

Everything? came the reply. What's "everything" mean?

"Everything," they eventually decided, included five items they already had worked so hard on: hazardous waste, air emissions, landfill waste, process-water consumption, and energy consumption from "brown" (nonrenewable) sources. Although "everything" didn't include *everything,* it came close.

Could we shoot for zero for all five? came the next question.

A new magic zero to rally around. Just like the landfill goal announced by Kerm Campbell in 1995.

They toyed with this idea.

That led to the next question. Can we, as Walker asked, come up with a single sustainability measure—one number, one goal, akin to economic profit as a financial measure? Can we somehow put all five measures together?

Indeed they could. In the end, they devised a measure called the "environmental footprint." The footprint put all five "everythings" in one calculation. It was computed by averaging the percentage progress toward zero for all five environmental measures.

They also set a new goal: By 2020 they would completely eliminate the footprint—achieve 100 percent cuts in all impacts.

One-hundred percent cuts. Zero "everything." Nothing short of having no net impact at all.

That was an outlandish goal for a big company. To be sure, the footprint didn't cover the company's buildings, but they were already covered by the board's decision in the late 1990s to bring all buildings up to silver-level LEED certification. The LEED objective would remain the goal for 2020.

The footprint didn't cover green product development, either. That's when they came up with the measure Gabe Wing and Scott Charon would embrace: Assure that every product gained DfE approval. Zero misses. By 2020, every one of Herman Miller's products would comply with constraints on recycled content, recyclability, design for disassembly, and avoiding "red" materials.

With all these measures together, the green team formed a picture of the future they all wanted to embrace. They called it Operation Clear Vision 20/20. Under Clear Vision, they had 16 years to reach their zero-impact-by-2020 goal. That meant doing 6.25 percent of the job each year (100 percent reduction/16 years = 6.25 percent/year.). Murray noted that they had already eliminated 57 percent of the impact from the base year, 1994. Now they just had to do the rest.

MURRAY TOOK THESE IDEAS to Walker a few months before Walker became CEO. The boss of North American operations was pleased with the concept. He liked the long-term approach. He liked the yearly increments. He liked how the green leaders had replaced an open-ended goal—to become a sustainable company—with a close-ended one—to become sustainable by 2020. He liked how the goals lined up with Herman Miller's values.

Walker wasn't at all sure how the company would get there. "At the time, it seemed almost like lunacy," he says. But the goal fit his philosophy of setting goals higher than people think they can reach, setting them well in the future, and trusting people to figure out along the way how to get there. They also fit his personal belief, not widely known at the time, that zeroing out the company's impact was the right thing to do.

Walker did have one concern. Along the way to doing the right thing, they had to figure out how to add economic profit. That, of course, was another company value. He worried, in particular, that one of the proposed goals might be hard to accept while at the same time adding that profit—and that goal was zeroing out brown energy.

We can't break the bank on this, he told Murray. How are we going to pay for buying so much green power?

Murray had a suggestion: How about we fund it with energy-efficiency savings? Whatever we save, we put that money in a pot. Every time someone makes a suggestion for savings, we put those savings in the pot, too. Whatever we end up with, we get to use to pay for green power.

Walker was intrigued.

Murray reminded Walker that energy-savings projects had been yielding a 33 percent return on investment. With that kind of payback, they could spend a lot of dollars on green energy without adding net energy costs.

After seeing the economic profit figures for the plan later on, Walker bought in. Herman Miller's electricity bills wouldn't rise, and economic value added wouldn't take a hit. The more the people could figure out how to save, the more green energy the company could buy.

By the time the company announced Walker's promotion to CEO in April 2004, Walker backed the zero brown energy goal along with the remaining slate of measures. He also backed a new name: Perfect Vision. Walker was now the new environmental champion. He backed zero brown energy—and zero percent everything else.

When people inside the company saw Walker's environmental goals, Murray started getting phone calls: Aren't you worried about these numbers? Well, yes, Murray replied, he was worried about all the work that was needed to fulfill the new ambitions. But no, the numbers didn't surprise him at all—he and the other environmental leaders had suggested them.

JUST AS HE TOOK over as company leader, Walker was making one thing that he believed in clear. He would take the company's historical commitment to the environment and go one better. The environmental leaders had helped him give the company a new green bottom line. He now faced the larger question: What do I put on the full schedule of items that I call important?

Walker had never doubted that he would stand on the platform built by leaders before him. The De Prees had put down plank after plank of values years before. Volkema had reframed and reinforced them. Walker didn't propose changes exactly. But he did want to outline the values in a bolder way. During the downturn, some planks had shaken loose from the strain. Other things had slipped through the cracks. How would he secure the proper set of values for the future?

Walker believed the company could get too hung up on history. If the dot-com nightmare had taught anything, it was that even if core values stay the same, the company can't stay in the same place. Although he planned to use company history as an asset, he had to continue to separate values from outmoded cultural practices. Eventually he would capture his view of historical values this way: The company would use history not as an anchor but as a sail.

One value that Walker prized as a sail was "inclusiveness." For years, D.J. De Pree had told the story from 1927 of visiting the home of a factory widow. Her husband, a millwright, had died at the Herman Miller plant that morning. In that era, De Pree referred to his factory workers in a haughty way, calling them those "birds." But at the widow's home, he discovered that the millwright was a craftsman, a poet, and a trusted counselor to a man wracked by guilt from killings in World War I.

With the widow watching, De Pree read a few of the millwright's poems with amazement. He had never thought of his workers as so talented. De Pree recalled repeatedly, until his own death at 99, his walk home after the funeral. "I was deeply moved," he said in 1982. "By the time I got home, I decided we were all extraordinary. These men were my peers... They were the ones that were adding value to a natural resource, and that's the only way we get real wealth.... So all of this came into focus in a rather sharp and quick way. My whole attitude toward the work force changed."

That was one piece of lore Walker particularly liked. The story of the millwright captured what he meant by inclusiveness: to embrace the unique qualities of all employees. In 2004, people in other companies often referred to this as a commitment to "diversity." But Herman Miller had hired diversity trainers in the 1990s, and the trainers had unwittingly pitted one ethnicity against another and men against women. The training alienated many employees. Walker no longer made "diversity" part of his corporate vocabulary.

Another piece of history Walker embraced was the De Prees' habit of sharing information with workers. In a company of roving leaders,

Walker was convinced he needed people to come clean with each other at every level—even more than they had in the past. They had to routinely engage their bosses in candid conversation. And their bosses had to do the same. Walker called this "transparency."

Walker feared what had long been called "Herman Miller nice." People faced each other in a meeting, talked over an issue, nodded their heads, and then outside the room said: That's a dumb idea. I'm not going to do that. Walker joked that Herman Miller people, bred to embrace participative management, operated with a measure of "civil disobedience." He might be CEO, but he couldn't get people to do anything they didn't believe in, even if they nodded their heads at a meeting. To get people to align their views, he had to get them to embrace transparency.

With such notions as a start, Walker took the next step in his effort to clarify what mattered, and he assembled his top team to help him. Among the team were Gary Miller, human-resources chief Andy Lock, and Walker's CFO successor, Beth Nickels. Together, they would restate the company's values—update them for the new millennium.

The team held wide-ranging talks, sometimes even doing soul-searching exercises to reveal, state, and defend their own values. When they came to the subject of the environment, they all agreed it held a central spot in what mattered to Herman Miller. On the other hand, they felt the company's environmental work stemmed from a larger concern.

Aren't we just exploring another value that relates to social responsibility? they asked. Doesn't the environment fall in a category of all the good things the company does, things like giving away money and volunteering in the community?

The group agreed that was so. They didn't like the catchphrase "corporate social responsibility," though. However popular, the phrase didn't seem to fit Herman Miller.

Why does Herman Miller do so many socially responsible things, they asked, if not to act socially responsible? Why does it buy computers for local schools, build Habitat for Humanity houses, and support an annual bicycle fund-raising event for juvenile diabetes?

There was another reason, they agreed. Herman Miller did these things not out of responsibility, or a reaction to conscience, but out of a desire to give. Aren't all these things important because we want to make a better world? someone asked.

A better world. People liked the phrase.

And it stuck, as simple as it was. The team adopted "a better world" as a value.

Walker and his team then met with 120 managers to share their thinking and ask for edits. Afterwards, they issued "Things That Matter," a statement that spelled out nine values, a set of principles that characterized the beliefs held dear by the Herman Miller community. The new list included both the explicit values of the past but also the implicit ones that had often remained unspoken: curiosity and exploration, performance, engagement, design, people relationships, inclusiveness, a better world, transparency, and foundations (history).

In some ways, the list was new. It described the company values with fresh words, in sharper outline, expressing touchstones from the crucible of the dot-com crisis. In other ways, it was not at all new: It put into words things that the De Pree family had emphasized since 1923 and that Mike Volkema had relied on during his time on the job. This, then, was Walker's statement of what was important to him in 2004.

HERMAN MILLER PRINTED "THINGS That Matter" and distributed it to people in the company. The board and everyone else would now know where Walker stood. In many organizations, that's as far as values statements issued by the CEO go. But Walker had in mind more than posting values on a bulletin board for people to (hopefully) absorb. He had in mind putting them into action. He believed they held the key to making the company realize the potential the De Prees had so often talked about.

Putting something into action, to Walker, meant one thing above all: Expressing the goals numerically, just as the environmental leaders had done with Perfect Vision. It also meant something else: Setting interim goals to compel progress. The interim milestones, steps on the journey, would firm people's resolve and fire up their imaginations on how to reach the ultimate vision.

In the process, Walker phoned Murray. I'm putting together a scorecard for 2010, he said. I need a bunch of five-year goals. What do you suggest for sustainability?

Murray lit up. Never before had the CEO of Herman Miller made sustainability a corporate goal—or in effect the goal for which the

CEO would become accountable to the board of directors. But that was what Walker was saying he was going to do.

Murray, seeing his passion taken up by the CEO, thought: Why not offer a couple of goals? Why not see what the chief goes for? So he reminded Walker of Perfect Vision's footprint, the average of five environmental efforts.

What's our footprint number today? asked Walker.

Fifty-seven percent, said Murray.

Round that to 60, said Walker. What about shooting for 80 percent by 2010?

Eighty percent! We've got 15 years to get to zero, Murray said. Eighty is halfway there in just the first five years.

Yeah, well, the first half is always easier, said Walker. Let's do 80 percent.

And what other goals do you have? asked Walker.

What about getting 100 percent of our product sales DfE-approved? Murray answered.

And where are we on that?

About 1 percent.

Okay, let's get to 50 percent by 2010.

Fifty percent! Murray protested again about Walker asking for so much progress in so little time. Pretty much all the company had done so far was introduce the Mirra chair.

Walker insisted on going for outsized gains, however. To nurture growth in a company in any way at all, he figured, he had to give people those big goals, ask them to devise measures to gauge progress toward those goals, grade people's performance candidly, and invent ways to move performance up.

Walker had similar conversations with other company leaders. He talked to Andy Lock about making Herman Miller a great place to work. He spoke to his philanthropy chief about more good works for communities. Everyone expected aggressive sales goals from the former CFO and head of North American operations. And they expected tough money-making goals, too. What they didn't expect was Walker calling for goals casting Herman Miller as an advocate on so many socially conscious fronts at once.

Walker had assembled in his head a new map of the Herman Miller business system. To him, one element of "Things That Matter" played with the all the others. The once-isolated continents of corporate financial, social, and operational action locked neatly into one unified world.

In the fall of 2004, Walker made his new map clear to everyone, as he announced his Powers of Ten goals—a set of ten goals that captured his aspirations for Herman Miller by 2010. Just as Walker had earlier surprised Murray, he surprised the rest of the organization. The goals included five business goals (for sales, innovation, mergers, emerging-market growth, and wealth creation), two environmental ones (on the environmental footprint and DfE), one on volunteerism, one on philanthropy, and one on becoming a great place to work.

Not only had Walker adopted goals to advance the cause of corporate environmentalism. He had adopted goals across the board for advancing all Herman Miller values.

The goals were ambitious. When Walker initially told people the goal for volunteering was 10,000 hours, everyone groaned, thinking he meant 10,000 hours over five years. Uh, no, he said. I mean 10,000 hours every year. Although he didn't have goals for inclusiveness (he assigned a task force to help him come up with them), he made a statement that raised eyebrows. In the conservative, mostly white, region of West Michigan, he and his team said every person—white, black, Hispanic, young, old, heterosexual, gay, lesbian, bisexual, transgender—would get a chance to realize his or her potential at Herman Miller.

The announcement of the goals stirred pride in many people—especially those who felt close to social issues. Murray could see that Walker was taking Herman Miller across a threshold. The CEO was moving sustainability from just a company value to a company strategy. Creating a sustainable company wasn't only the right thing to do. Walker was suggesting it was the smartest way to win.

The announcement stirred anxieties. The people running programs related to the environment, inclusiveness, philanthropy, and the work place knew they would get more money and attention. But they also knew they had to deliver a level of progress they had never before contemplated. Vice President Lock was taken aback when Walker returned with the final numbers. Lock was a booster of reaching for the stars, but he marveled that one of the goals was to win a slot in the top ten of *Fortune* magazine's "100 Best Places to Work For" list.

"That was a stretch goal," Lock says. "We weren't even on the list at the time." Indeed, the company had fallen off the list in 2000.

Some observers wondered if Walker had gone too far. He was essentially redefining the sustainable business. True, customers and architects were asking for better social performance. They had specifically said they wanted Herman Miller to make strong environmental commitments. But was this much broader approach the formula for winning in the 2000s?

Few investors had asked questions about social performance. Certainly none of them would bid up the stock price based on this move. But Walker felt that every component in the Powers of Ten, though weighted to favor the "soft stuff," would boost economic profit, which in turn would boost stock price. He couldn't give anyone proof for his conviction. He just felt that the evidence was piling up.

WALKER THEN DID WHAT Herman Miller CEOs always had done: He gave the job of making this happen to the roving leaders around the company. With the Powers of Ten, the leaders had the numerical expression—Walker's equation—to guide them in the new, more sustainable approach to business. And the equation, built on hard numbers, left no room for slacking off.

When Walker's inclusiveness committee members reported in 2005, he made it even clearer. He adopted a footprint-like goal from them that was as stringent as the environmental one. Like Murray's team, the group suggested five areas for improvement and a composite score for grading progress. The footprint measure, moreover, would gauge not only diversity at Herman Miller but at suppliers and dealers.

Purchasing chief Drew Schramm found himself once again facing goals he felt impossible to reach. He was charged with pumping up Herman Miller's buying from minority-owned suppliers from roughly 9 percent to 20 percent. In a replay of the PVC debate of a few years earlier, he at first declared the goal mad. Herman Miller had 30 big suppliers who accounted for four-fifths of the company's buying. To get to the minority-spending goal, he would have to replace every one of his existing 175 smaller suppliers with a minority-owned business.

Schramm was dumbfounded. Did Walker want him to ditch all the small guys?

But Schramm and his team soon came up with a solution. And they would never have dreamt it up had they faced a more modest goal. If Herman Miller couldn't replace all its small suppliers, Schramm would ask his 30 biggest suppliers to take up the slack. He told the big guys that *they* had to invest in minority-owned suppliers, and in that way add minority-owned business to the supply chain. And what if they didn't get with the program? They would gradually lose Herman Miller's business.

A few suppliers took offense—Schramm was forcing them to hand over to other companies business they had fought hard for. Why should we give up our hard-earned revenues? some business owners asked. But faced with no alternative, they started to comply, and some even admitted later to Schramm that the move earned them kudos from their other customers. Schramm's numbers rose to near 16 percent, boosting Herman Miller buying from minority-owned companies to $120 million.

Says Schramm: "It took that stupid, bodacious goal to make us completely change."

Walker didn't favor rapping knuckles, but he kept score, and he graded people like a schoolmarm. Murray had to report in mid-2006 that the green team had missed two of its five footprint measures—landfill and air emissions. Walker gave the green leaders a C grade. Murray reported that results for DfE also fell short of Walker's expectations. Again, Walker handed out a C. By the standards of U.S. industry, Murray told his team, they would have gotten an A. But by their own yardstick—a yardstick the team had produced itself in Perfect Vision—they had fallen behind.

Walker believed deeply in his equation to spur action, but as the effort took across the company, the amount of action surprised even him. People tracked their progress as if they were tracking horses in a race, and they liked seeing results flash across the company's intranet. They even requested that Walker update them during plant visits or his monthly business video. Volunteer hours reflected the new energy. In 2006, after just two years, people had put in almost four years' worth of time—37,872 hours.

When it came to charity, Walker had always thought Herman Miller got too little mileage out of its spending. D.J. De Pree, ever devoted to biblical teaching, preached against showy good deeds. The company had never, in fact, revealed its donations to charity. New hires were referred to Matthew 6:1-4: "When you give alms, sound no trumpet before you, as the hypocrites do in the synagogues and in the streets, that they be praised by men. . . . your alms may be in secret; and your Father who sees in secret will reward you."

But in the 2000s, Walker felt that the values of the founder were constraining potential. Walker saw beyond the risk of hypocrisy to the risk of detachment. If the left hand of workers didn't know what the right hand of the company's charitable arm was doing, the employees could never derive satisfaction from gift-giving. He could energize people, he felt, by helping them see their company's role in good works. He could perhaps even give them a greater sense of meaning.

Vice President Lock, who at 51 referred to himself as "an old guy," often led the conversation about giving. "I want to be able to look back on my life and say I actually did something that I think mattered, and I feel contributed in some sense to it," he says. "I can manage the value in my life when I'm not at work, but I'm going to spend more of my life at work than I will spend anywhere else. So if I can't be involved with an organization that reflects my values . . . then I would be working for the wrong company."

Lock suggested that the charity arm release small grants for projects Herman Miller could publicize, at least inside the company. Walker and the board agreed.

Lock set an example. He schemed up a trip for employees to build desks and chairs for a school in Tharangambadi, India, a village wiped out by the Asian tsunami of 2004. A deluge of applications poured in from around Herman Miller. Lock took a dozen people. Those not chosen could help by giving advice, donating vacation hours to those who went, or even by donating money. Lock wanted to give back to a community he had visited during business travel a few years before.

In the end, he did much more, helping people at Herman Miller realize their potential in a new way. Said one woman after Lock's second visit to help school kids: "We took away far more than what we ever felt like we contributed. . . . And everyone has a different way of describing it: It filled a hole in their life."

That's just what Walker wanted. The trip, though a potent esprit de corps–building exercise, also gave a sense to people that their everyday work at Herman Miller had a purpose beyond earning a paycheck. Whether they went to India or not, they were contributors. They were fulfilling a meaningful company mission: To build a better world at work, at home, in the community, and in the world.

CFO Beth Nickels got the same reaction in March 2007. She got in touch with Women for Women, a group that ministers to women survivors of war, helping them rebuild their lives. Nickels, soon named president of Herman Miller's healthcare unit, arranged for the company to sponsor 90 victims in Kosovo. The U.S. women committed to spending a year as pen pals and donors to "sisters" who were trying to put their world back together. Nickels had Herman Miller women gather to write letters and read replies, opening a fresh avenue for the privileged to aid the dispossessed.

"People...want to feel like their work matters," says Nickels, "and this is all a part of helping to do that.... We're not looking for publicity for publicity's sake. We're looking for whether it can energize a cause among employees."

As the recession took hold at the end of the decade, layoffs again threatened to fray the new threads of sustainability. Walker faced a 40-percent plunge in sales, rivaling the dot-com freefall. Once again, he and his team had to cut the company to the bone, laying off 1,900 people, more than a quarter of the workforce.

Although the bloodletting wounded morale, Walker maintained his focus on the new purpose-driven organization. As orders started to dive in 2008, Lock suggested a more modest community project. Instead of going to India, he and 120 Herman Miller employees and family members helped build a playground in nearby Muskegon, Michigan. The work day came in July 2009, and Herman Miller employees labored alongside people from the neighborhood, creating new friendships in the community. Walker believed the sense of purpose from such encounters gave a return ordinary spending couldn't buy.

In spite of the values-driven behavior, the fall in sales and job cutting took its toll. Once again, sacrifices abounded. Walker worried that more layoffs would hurt the company's future, but he had to cut workforce costs by 10 percent more. He and Lock came up with an alternate plan. Walker furloughed all employees every other Friday. He also halted matching funding for 401(k) retirement plans. The cuts applied not just to workers but to executives as well.

Walker and Lock felt they had to ease the pain of salary cuts somehow. They invented a "wage-recovery plan." Herman Miller would pay people back for at least some of money lost in the furlough so long as the company hit predefined targets needed for financial sustainability. After hitting the target, the company would split every dollar 50/50 between employees and shareholders. The finance group would calculate the necessary financial return so people had a preset threshold to meet.

Some of the members of the board of directors balked when Walker told them about the plan. They complained: You're going to pay people for a day when they don't even work?

Yes, that's it, Walker replied. In the feeble economy, the only way to sustain the business is to sustain the current ranks of the employed—and give people some hope for earning a full wage if they help close the financial gap.

Walker was again deploying his strategy of giving people big goals. It was entirely up to employees to redouble their efforts to cut costs and improve productivity to bring the company back from the abyss. Although sales remained moribund, in several quarters starting in 2009, people did break the threshold. In one quarter, employees won a wage-recovery bonus worth more than half their foregone pay.

So Walker did actually pay people for time not worked. But he told outsiders he had no regrets. The program gave credibility to top management for the effort to stick with company values. And it reinforced a tradition that had served Herman Miller so well for so long—in this case, paying people extra for improving company fortunes, just the way D.J. De Pree had done nearly 60 years before.

By year end 2010, Walker's Powers of Ten approach proved he had calculated correctly with his new equation for sustainable management. To be sure, the company missed its financial goals owing to the recession. But it hit or surpassed most goals related to sustainability. The environmental leaders around the company cut the footprint by 91 percent. The product teams, embracing DfE, delivered 55 percent of sales from products approved according to DfE criteria. The workforce amassed 13,600 volunteer hours in 2010 alone. And the company still ranked on *Fortune's* 100 Best Places to Work list, even though at number 97 it didn't hit the top ten.

Walker then set new goals for 2013. He added another component to his equation, aimed at reducing greenhouse gases. In league with Murray, he agreed to measure progress in eliminating the company's carbon footprint by 2020. Ever the accountant, Walker would continue driving toward the target that defined the new bottom line for sustainability: the magic zero. Meantime, he insisted on completing half of the remaining progress to zero in just the first three of the final ten years.

Walker showed that he stood apart with his view of sustainability. He also showed that his broader view in no way conflicted with the hallowed word in business: "growth." "The only way you can sustain yourself is if you are growing," he says. "And that means you have to be both growing financially and growing in your capabilities and achievements."

Growth as a business. Growth as an organization. Growth for and by the people. Walker's philosophy in executing this vision echoed that of Hugh De Pree, who 25 years earlier wrote: "The escort of vision is values, for a business is not defined by the assets it shows on the balance sheet, nor by the profit it makes, nor only by the products it makes. Rather, it is defined by the beliefs and values held by its people."

Epilogue

Paul Murray started work at Herman Miller in 1988 facing a number of questions. One was how to run his wood-finishing line without scrapping tens of thousands of dollars of blistered product. Another was how to rid the line of solvent-based paints—the coatings, thinned with toxic chemicals, that once sent his son into fits of choking. Banishing the solvents had the tightest grip on his psyche, and remained the question always in the back of his mind.

Twenty years later, Murray had answered those questions. He had also, along with an ever-growing band of roving leaders, answered another one: Can we make our company—the entire company—sustainable? In the early 1990s, that question had risen to the top of many people's minds. In 1992, it was on the minds of leaders around the world, as they gathered in Rio de Janeiro, Brazil, for the first United Nations environmental confab, attended by the most powerful people on earth.

Nobody at that time had any idea of how to do it. Nearly all thought it largely impossible. The story of Murray and other leaders at Herman Miller proved otherwise. The leaders at Herman Miller showed how to find a way to succeed in the goal a U.N. committee had earlier defined as "meeting the needs of the present without compromising the ability of future generations to meet their own needs."

To be sure, Herman Miller has not arrived at the utopia of sustainability. But it has worked through many variables in the sustainability equation over 20 years. And its story points a way to future success for other organizations and industries.

The force behind the march to sustainability at Herman Miller turns out to be values. On the surface, solutions often depend on hard, technical fixes. They also depend on tactics and technology and strategy—as well as programs and policy and people who champion the work. But underneath, as Brian Walker reaffirmed in the 2000s, the force that carries the work forward, as surely as the waters of a river carry sustenance and life to a continent, is management that relies on values as their wellspring of inspiration.

Imbued with the values exemplified by the De Pree family, the roving leaders of Herman Miller fashioned a workable approach to sustainable management. One of the values that helped the most is worth special attention: a commitment to problem-solving design. Problem-solving design means design guided by the values of a changing society. Design underpinned by honesty and integrity in concept, materials, and workmanship. Design directed to fulfill not a style but a real need. Design aimed at *serving* customers, employees, the community, and others.

With this commitment to problem-solving design, the roving leaders understood they were not to compromise easily—no more than Charles Eames compromised on the function, performance, or aesthetics of the Eames lounge chair. Nor were they to simply throw money at a solution, or farm out a problem, or stick their heads in the sand and ignore what ailed them. They were to apply themselves to continuously reworking products, processes, jobs, and the organization until they found an ingenious—even elegant—solution that satisfied all constraints.

Sometimes the solutions weren't straightforward. Over 20 years, the roving leaders often ended up on circuitous journeys of discovery, sometimes sidetracked for months or years, as they tried to reconcile cost, performance, and sustainability. But they pioneered routes to success—relating to solvents, tropical woods, landfill wastes, product design, building construction, lean manufacturing—in a way that leaves an inspiring tale for others.

The Herman Miller story beckons all of us. Why should we care about men like Murray? Or about Foley and Johnston? Or Nagelkirk, Dowell, Wing, Charon, and their bosses Walker and Volkema? We care because they traveled a path in which they wrestled with the daily forces in business that defeat so many kinds of improvements. Yet they prevailed. We care about their stories out of a concern for how they rethink work, life, and management—and for what their insights can teach us.

Murray, for his part, first answered the solvents question with a detour. He didn't ride to success overnight like so many managers glorified in the pages of the business press. Over two decades, he and his successors found a water-based paint that worked, and in 2008, they installed a $3.2 million water-based, UV-curable coating line. The changeover, including dismantling and recycling the old thermal oxidizers, finally zeroed out the solvents' emissions.

Bill Foley and Bob Johnston, the proponents of banning the use of unsustainably logged tropical wood, answered their problem temporarily as well. Cherry and walnut replaced the revered rosewood specified by Charles Eames in his famous lounge chair. Herman Miller's willpower to do the right thing was put to the test after the decision. In 1993, the company had to figure out how to dispose of the remaining 277,287 square feet of unused rosewood veneer—and some people argued for making a final run of Eames chairs.

Johnston's boss stepped in. He argued that re-introducing rosewood would damage the company's reputation. He showed how doing the right thing could ring the cash register of financial value. Referring to the *Business Week* article about the decision that had pictured Foley, he wrote: "Typically, the believability and influence of an article is three times that of an ad. The cost of a comparable ad...is $110,000. Therefore, one can calculate that we gained $330,000 worth of positive image influence by this one article."

Foley and Johnston's successors finally found a substitute for rosewood, santos palisander, a wood from sustainable forests in Brazil and Bolivia. Herman Miller used up rosewood it had in stock doing a special run of the Eames-designed molded-plywood screens and molded-plywood chairs, donating part of the profits to environmental groups. But it waited until 2006, when it had a bona fide substitute for rosewood, to restore the original Eames look, which cherry and walnut could not imitate.

Murray took even longer to hit the zero-landfill goal. Some landfill wastes had defied easy elimination—especially the ash from the cogeneration plant. But in December 2010, a local municipality agreed to take that ash, the remains of Herman Miller sawdust, and mix it with other materials for composting. Murray finally hit magic zero—at least for Herman Miller's West Michigan plants.

Ed Nagelkirk, project manager for the first green building, continued to make the company's buildings more sustainable. In 1995, the U.S. Green Building Council chose the 300,000-square-foot Phoenix Designs building—by then called the GreenHouse—as a pilot for the development of its green building standards, dubbed LEED, Leadership in Energy and Environmental Design. The council later awarded the building "pioneer" status for setting a precedent for LEED certification.

Following Mike Volkema's 1998 goal of making all buildings meet the silver LEED certification, Nagelkirk and other leaders oversaw so much upgrading that the company had won by 2010 a total of 15 LEED awards – including 10 gold and one platinum – for company buildings and interiors. In the same way that architect Bill McDonough had inspired Herman Miller to do great things, the upgrading overseen by Nagelkirk showed how a company on the sustainability trail can inspire others.

Ray Muscat and Matt Long, company pioneers in spreading lean manufacturing expertise, kept on their campaign to turn the entire company into a lean operation. Guided by the principles of the Toyota Production System, they taught the Herman Miller Performance System to people across the company. The stunning result: By 2010 Herman Miller ran its factories with less than half the people required in 2000. So much waste had lean principles cut from manufacturing that the company made roughly 50 percent more product in 50 percent less space.

The Aeron chair was a standout, an example of the enduring value of lean manufacturing. Herman Miller had once run three lines in 27,000 square feet, in three shifts, with 77 people. By 2010, it made three times the number of chairs on one line in 2,500 square feet with 24 people.

Ironically, Ken Goodson, operations chief, ordered the IMT file-cabinet plant at Spring Lake closed in 2009. Goodson had calculated that, given the company's growing lean expertise, all production could fit on a merged line at another nearby plant. That new line then made twice the variety of file cabinets as before—and Herman Miller cut 200,000 square feet from its manufacturing footprint.

Goodson understood well the closure's symbolic impact. He was head of the unit in 1995, and the plant had served for nine years as a showcase for the Toyota Production System. No other honor in the world of manufacturing could match that imprimatur. Mr. Ohba's successors came to inspect the new, more complex line—and they reaffirmed the company's showcase status. Fifteen years after the lean kickoff, Herman Miller showed the journey to lean continues unabated.

Gabe Wing and Scott Charon, the leaders of the cradle-to-cradle design effort, moved steadily to make 100 percent of products DfE-approved. By 2010, they had not succeeded in every way they had hoped. When they vetted a chair named Setu, introduced in 2009, they noted that it took much less material than many previous products. But they couldn't figure out how to make one piece entirely of olefinic plastic (polypropylene, polyethylene). They had to build the chair with a two-part plastic component, nylon bonded to polyurethane. Lest the arms fail prematurely, they actually created a "monstrous hybrid," fit only for incineration at the end of its life.

But the two men showed how a company with the will can march steadily, if unevenly, with its DfE efforts. As they stepped up to the goal of reengineering old products to improve their sustainability, they sought a replacement for the PVC on the arm pads of the Aeron. The change, owing to more expensive material, cost roughly $1 million. But in 2009, fifteen years after the chair's debut, with the blessing of CEO Walker, the company introduced the new version of its bestseller to the market.

Gary Miller, the leader of the Purple team, retired in 2010. As a part-time consultant, he worked on a license agreement to transfer primary development and commercialization responsibility of Convia to Herman Miller electrical-distribution partner Legrand. Although Miller and his roving leaders did not scale up their vision as they once hoped, the route they pioneered for advancing sustainability remained alive. Miller retained some of his team to nurture aspects of the original Purple vision. In 2010, Microsoft outfitted its Envisioning Lab in Redmond, Washington, with the Purple grid. The lab, a 2,000-square-foot software gallery and amphitheatre, gave Microsoft engineers a place to escort executive customers through a vision of the future the engineers could change at will.

Brian Walker, as CEO, continued to insist on financial literacy as an element of sustainability. His latest test came during the recession of 2008–2009. Once again, although the company lost money, he limited the loss to just a single quarter in 2009. The discipline of economic profit allowed him to move on many agenda items even as financial results faltered. And when the company updated its mission in 2010, he didn't back off his values-based campaign. He agreed to stress values even more, showing that his values-based approach continued to thrive in good times and bad.

Whereas "a better world" once played just a part in the mission, Walker agreed to elevate it to the organization's purpose. "Our ultimate mission," says Walker, "is to 'create a better world around you,' whether you're a customer, an employee, a dealer, a neighbor, or a partner."

Mike Volkema, chairman since Walker took over, lauded his successor for enduring the barbs of other CEOs while preaching that growth would come from values. "It's not easy when you have to go out and talk to [Wall Street] analysts and explain why it costs 1 cent a share more," he says, to do "the right thing" versus the "economic" thing.

"There is a world out there that's about money and math," Volkema adds. "Their view is you don't spend money on anything that doesn't give you a [good return]. I have to tell them, " 'I don't do everything for the short term. I'm here to do something that's viable and purposeful and sometimes goes back to the reason for a corporation in the beginning as a legal entity...to provide some benefit to society.' "

In that way, Volkema, Walker, and the roving leaders who started the upwelling of support for sustainability kept echoing De Pree values, the same kind of values that guide organizations of all kinds on the road to sustainability. As Max De Pree said in a 1997 interview, "We saw ourselves as not being separated from society. We saw ourselves as being a legitimate member of the community, wherever we were.... We also always worked on the assumption that you had to make a profit to survive. We saw profit as the normal consequence of doing the right thing and doing it well."

NOTES

Merchants of Virtue stems from two years of research and interviews. Starting in early 2009, I spoke with over 100 people and reviewed thousands of documents, mainly from the Herman Miller archives in Holland, Michigan. People who agreed to speak with me came from both within the company and from the outside, including many who left during two difficult layoff periods. The most important people I interviewed are listed by chapter below.

The stories of many companies contain legend as well as fact. To assure that *Merchants of Virtue* remained a work of nonfiction, wherever possible I interviewed a second or third person about each important event covered in the book. I corroborated the dates and the gist of decisions and conversations with letters, meeting minutes, reports, speech transcripts, emails, video recordings and any other document available. No events were created. No names were changed.

Because my experience suggests that people rarely remember conversations verbatim, I almost never used direct quotes of past conversations. I instead usually used indirect quotes, without quotation marks. An example of trustworthy verbatim quotes would be remarks taken from a video of an event. I also quoted people directly when they commented during my interviews about the past.

To finish the book, I double checked quotes against my audio recordings, and then spent a month fact-checking the text with all critical sources to weed out remaining errors. Despite the care taken with the text, errors surely remain. I would appreciate the help of any readers who take the time to send me corrections. I am always available via billbirchard.com.

1 Rosewood

The story of the rosewood controversy comes mainly from interviews with Bill Foley and Bob Johnston in 2009 and 2010. Other important sources include John Berry, Keister Evans, Dick Ruch, Marsha Skidmore, and Bob Vandenbosch, all of whom spoke with me during the same period. In an interesting epilogue to the story, on July 1, 2010, Bob Johnston succeeded Keister Evans as executive director of the Tropical Forest Foundation.

For those interested in a view of leadership thinking at this time, see then-CEO Dick Ruch's *Leaders and Followers: Lessons From 45 Years at Herman Miller, Inc.* (Holland, Michigan: Star Publishers, 2002).

2 Honest Design

The early years of Herman Miller are well documented in the speeches of D.J. De Pree. De Pree left several fascinating in-depth interviews done in the 1980s, available both in the Herman Miller archives and in the Joint Archive of Holland at Hope College. These show clearly how his thinking ran ahead of its time. De Pree's sons, Hugh and Max, wrote much about the early years. I relied often on Hugh's memoir, *Business as Unusual,* (Zeeland, Michigan: Herman Miller, Inc., 1986) for an account of working with early designers and the history of Action Office. I relied on Max's bestselling *Leadership is an Art* (New York: Doubleday, 1989), as well as an interview in 2010 with Max, to portray the De Prees' management values.

For those interested in the design thinking in the early 1900s that influenced D.J. De Pree, an incomparable source is Phyllis Ross's *Gilbert Rohde: Modern Design for Modern Living.* Those interested in design thinking at the birth of panel systems (office cubicles) should see Robert Propst's *The Office: A Facility Based on Change,* still published by Herman Miller. Those curious about design thinking in the 1970s should see *The Design of Herman Miller* by Ralph Caplan. For an excellent, up-to-date, and wonderfully illustrated story of design at Herman Miller, see John Berry's *Herman Miller: The Purpose of Design.* I relied on all these sources for background and historical facts to complete this chapter. Following are specific citations:

Page 24: "I wrote him that I thought they were manual..." D.J. De Pree, untitled speech to employees, Zeeland, Michigan, August 7, 1978. Interview transcript in Herman Miller archives, Holland, Michigan.

Page 25: "You're not making furniture anymore..." D.J. De Pree, interview with Abby Jewett, Holland, Michigan, June 11, 1982. Interview transcript in Joint Archives of Holland at Hope College, Holland, Michigan, page 7. Online: http://www.hope.edu /jointarchives/Oral%20Interviews/1982/DePree,DJ.pdf

Page 26: "If any designers think you are..." George Nelson, as quoted in Hugh De Pree, *Business as Unusual: The People and Principles of Herman Miller.* (Zeeland, Michigan: Herman Miller Inc., 1986), 28.

Page 27: "When Eames heard someone utter..." Charles Eames as quoted in Hugh De Pree, *Business as Unusual: The People and Principles of Herman Miller.* (Zeeland, Michigan: Herman Miller Inc., 1986), 34.

Page 31: "For management, he [Frost] was often..." Hugh De Pree, *Business as Unusual: The People and Principles of Herman Miller.* (Zeeland, Michigan: Herman Miller Inc., 1986), 125.

Page 31: "This is my place of work..." D.J. De Pree, interview with Abby Jewett, Holland, Michigan, June 11, 1982. Interview transcript in Joint Archives of Holland at Hope College, Holland, Michigan, page 9. Online: http://www.hope.edu/jointarchives /Oral%20Interviews/1982/DePree,DJ.pdf

Page 31: "This was fun, it was simple..." Hugh De Pree, *Business as Unusual: The People and Principles of Herman Miller.* (Zeeland, Michigan: Herman Miller Inc., 1986), 80.

Page 37: "If you want a corporation to be truly..." Max De Pree, *Leadership is an Art.* (New York: Doubleday, 1989), 79.

3   Magic Zero

A host of people helped launch Herman Miller on its long campaign to reduce waste, many of whose names could not, unfortunately, appear in the chapter. The most important sources for this chapter were Tom Ankney, Joe Azzarello, Willie Beattie, Kerm Campbell, Marty Dugan, Jim Gillespie, Bob Johnston, Pat Laurie, Paul Murray, and Ted Venti. All of them told their stories to me in 2009 and 2010.

Early on, the roving environmental leaders at Herman Miller were influenced by a few seminal books of the era. As relevant as ever is Paul Hawken's *The Ecology of Commerce.* Though fiction, Daniel Quinn's *Ishmael* (New York: Bantam, 1992) inspired a number of people to take environmental action.

4   The Teacher

Key sources for this chapter included Max De Pree, Marty Dugan, Bob Enders, Del Ensing, Clark Malcolm, Bill McDonough, Ed Nagelkirk, Bix Norman, Keith Winn, Dyan Van Fossen, Gary Van Spronsen, Chris Hays, formerly a McDonough associate and now at Hays + Ewing Design Studio, and Roger Schickedantz, a current McDonough associate. I spoke with all of them in 2009 and 2010.

Another key source, and an excellent book on architectural design principles at Herman Miller, is Jeffrey Cruikshank and Clark Malcolm's *Herman Miller, Inc.: Buildings and Beliefs*. Today's standards in green building design, which were influenced by Herman Miller, are set by the U.S. Green Building Council using its Leadership in Energy and Environmental Design, or LEED, system. See http://www .usgbc.org.

Page 60: "Once a building is up, it's publicly..." Jeffrey L. Cruikshank and Clark Malcolm, *Herman Miller Inc.: Buildings and Beliefs*. (Washington, D.C.: The American Institute of Architects Press, 1994), 8.

5   Thirty Questions

My major sources on Herman Miller's early Design for the Environment, or DfE, effort were interviews in 2009 and 2010 with Tom Ankney, Catherine Bragdon, Bill Dowell, Tracy Hazzard, Pat Laurie, Amory Lovins, Carolyn Maalouf, Gary Miller, Paul Murray, Tom Newhouse, and Ted Venti. Once again, a seminal work for people in this era was Paul Hawken's *Ecology of Commerce*.

Page 81: "Lovins didn't know which car company..." In an interesting epilogue to this story, Lovins helped start a firm, Fiberforge, which commercialized a thermoplastic-and-carbon-fiber manufacturing process. By 2010, the process was adopted by the aerospace and other sectors. Major automakers showed rapidly growing interest. BMW announced a mass-produced carbon-fiber car for 2013.

6   Dollar Sense

The two people most responsible for advances in business literacy in the mid-1990s were Brian Walker and Dave Guy. The material from this period comes from interviews with Guy and Walker in 1998 and Walker in 2009 and 2010. A good number of the facts in this chapter stem from documents left in the archives, both those left by the business-literacy team in the 1980s and from the papers of Dave Guy upon his departure from the company. Also important to this chapter were interviews in 2009 and 2010 with Ray Bennett, Matt Campbell, Justin Pettit, Joel Stern, and Mike Volkema.

The seminal book on economic profit during the 1990s was Bennett Stewarts's *A Quest for Value*. The notion of economic profit was not unique to the Stern Stewart consultancy, and other firms have their own ways of calculating true economic returns.

Page 96: "Hugh De Pree, who admitted that financial acumen was wanting..." Hugh De Pree, *Business as Unusual: The People and Principles of Herman Miller* (Zeeland, Michigan: Herman Miller Inc., 1986), 125.

Page 102: "in his 800-page book, *Quest for Value*..." G. Bennett Stewart, *The Quest for Value* (New York: HarperBusiness, 1991).

7   Mister Ohba

The main sources for this chapter were interviews in 2009 and 2010 with Ken Goodson, Matt Long, Ray Muscat, and Larry O'Keefe. Owing to many requests by outsiders, these men have documented their journey to lean manufacturing in detail, and they willingly shared their notes. Also important to this chapter were comments from plant-floor workers who took part in the transformation at IMT, also known as the Spring Lake plant. In 2010, I interviewed Mike Dexter, Lori Twining, and Tim Wilde.

The former Toyota Supplier Support Center, now called the Toyota Production System Support Center, still provides support for companies wishing to learn lean manufacturing. See http://www.tssc.com.

8   Cradle to Cradle

The bulk of the story in Chapter 8 comes from Gabe Wing and Scott Charon, whom I interviewed in 2009 and 2010. Other people I interviewed were Chris Ewell, an associate of Bill McDonough's, Dyan Van Fossen, Bill McDonough, Gary Miller, Fred Pettinga, and Drew Schramm. Keith Winn, who led the team laying the groundwork for the sustainability protocol, was especially generous in describing the early years of the project.

Bill McDonough and Michael Braungart published a book about their Design for Environment ideas. The book still captures the philosophy well, although not the technical protocol. See *Cradle to Cradle: Remaking the Way We Make Things* (New York: North Point Press, 2002). Another book that provides inspiration for green design is Janine Benyus's *Biomimicry: Innovation Inspired by Nature* (New York: HarperCollins, 1997).

9   Whiz Bang

Many people spoke with me in 2009 and 2010 about the Purple project, which later became the Convia business. Chief among them were Deanne Beckwith, Danny Hillis, Sheila Kennedy, Jim Long, Jennifer Magnolfi, Gary Miller, Ken Munsch, Randy Storch, Mike Volkema, and Brian Walker. Gary Miller generously shared documents from the project, revealing a fascinating paper trail of the exciting work of bleeding-edge product development.

The book on "disruptive" product innovation that became a touchstone for Gary Miller and his Purple team is Clayton Christensen's now-classic *The Innovator's Dilemma: When New Technologies Cause Great Firms to Fail* (Boston: Harvard Business School Press, 1997).

10   A Better World

Many people contributed their recollections to this final chapter. The most important were Abe Carillo, Andy Lock, Paul Murray, Beth Nickels, Mike Ramirez, Drew Schramm, Mike Volkema, and Brian Walker. I also interviewed several people who lost their jobs during the two downturns in the 2000s.

Herman Miller in recent years has reported its work to meet its "better world" goals in detail in company reports, available online at hermanmiller.com. The reports offer a template of the work of a company that has broadened its sustainability mission far beyond just taking care of the environment. See http://www.hermanmiller.com.

Page 178: "One night I went to bed a genius..." Linda Tischler, "Herman Miller's Leap of Faith," *Fortune,* June 2006, 52-57.

Epilogue

Page 199: "...meeting the needs of the present without compromising..." World Commission on Environment and Development, *Our Common Future* (Oxford: Oxford University Press, 1987), 43. Online see http://www.un-documents.net/wced-ocf.htm.

Page 200: "Typically, the believability and influence of an article..." John Berry, "Rosewood Disposition" memorandum to Bill Bundy and Andy McGregor, January 21, 1993, in Herman Miller Archives, Holland, Michigan.

SELECTED READING

A number of books have influenced Herman Miller's progress toward corporate sustainability in the last 20 years. Most of them are as relevant as ever.

Anderson, Ray. *Mid-Course Correction: Toward a Sustainable Enterprise: The Interface Model.* Atlanta: Peregrinzilla Press, 1999.

Benyus, Janine M. *Biomimicry: Innovation Inspired by Nature.* New York: HarperCollins, 1997.

De Pree, Max. *Leadership is an Art.* New York: Currency Doubleday (Random House), 1989. (Originally published in 1987 by Michigan State University Press.)

Hawken, Paul. *The Ecology of Commerce: A Declaration of Sustainability.* New York: HarperCollins Publishers, 1993.

Hawken, Paul, Amory Lovins, and L. Hunter Lovins. *Natural Capitalism: Creating the Next Industrial Revolution.* New York: Little Brown and Company, 1999.

Makower, Joel. *Strategies for the Green Economy: Opportunities and Challenges in the New World of Business.* New York: McGraw-Hill, 2009.

McDonough, William, and Michael Braungart. *Cradle to Cradle: Remaking the Way We Make Things.* New York: North Point Press (Farrar, Strauss, Giroux), 2002.

Nattrass, Brian, and Mary Altomare. *The Natural Step for Business: Wealth, Ecology, and the Evolutionary Corporation.* Gabriola Island, British Columbia: New Society Publishers, 1999.

Quinn, Daniel. *Ishmael: An Adventure of the Mind and Spirit.* New York: Bantam Books (Random House), 1992.

Several other books stand out as guides to building the sustainable business today.

Epstein, Marc J., *Making Sustainability Work: Best Practices in Managing and Measuring Corporate Social, Environmental, and Economic Impacts.* San Francisco: Berrett-Koehler Publishers, 2008.

Esty, Daniel C., and Andrew S. Winston. *Green to Gold: How Smart Companies Use Environmental Strategy to Innovate, Create Value, and Build Competitive Advantage.* Hoboken, NJ: John Wiley & Sons, 2009.

Hart, Stuart L. *Capitalism at the Crossroads: The Unlimited Business Opportunities in Solving the World's Most Difficult Problems.* Upper Saddle River, NJ: Wharton School Publishing (Pearson Education), 2005.

INDEX